THE SACRIFICE OF DARKNESS ™

Based on the short story *We Are The Sacrifice of Darkness* by
ROXANE GAY

Published by
ARCHAIA ™

THE SACR

OF DAR

RIFICE
RKNESS ™

Written by
ROXANE GAY and **TRACY LYNNE OLIVER**

Illustrated by
REBECCA KIRBY

Colored by
JAMES FENNER

Lettered by
ANDWORLD DESIGN

THE SACRIFICE OF DARKNESS, October 2020. Published by Archaia, a division of
Boom Entertainment, Inc. The Sacrifice of Darkness is ™ & © 2020 One N Productions .
All rights reserved. Archaia™ and the Archaia logo are trademarks of Boom Entertainment,
Inc., registered in various countries and categories. All characters, events, and institutions
depicted herein are fictional. Any similarity between any of the names, characters, persons,
events, and/or institutions in this publication to actual names, characters, and persons.
whether living or dead, events, and/or institutions is unintended and purely coincidental.

BOOM! Studios, 5670 Wilshire Boulevard, Suite 400, Los Angeles, CA 90036-5679.
Printed in China. First Printing.

ISBN: 978-1-68415-624-5, eISBN: 978-1-64668-036-8

ARCHAIA™

Cover by **Rebecca Kirby**
With colors by **James Fenner**

Designers **Scott Newman** with **Jillian Crab**

Associate Editor **Amanda LaFranco**
Editor **Dafna Pleban**

Special thanks to **Allyson Gronowitz**

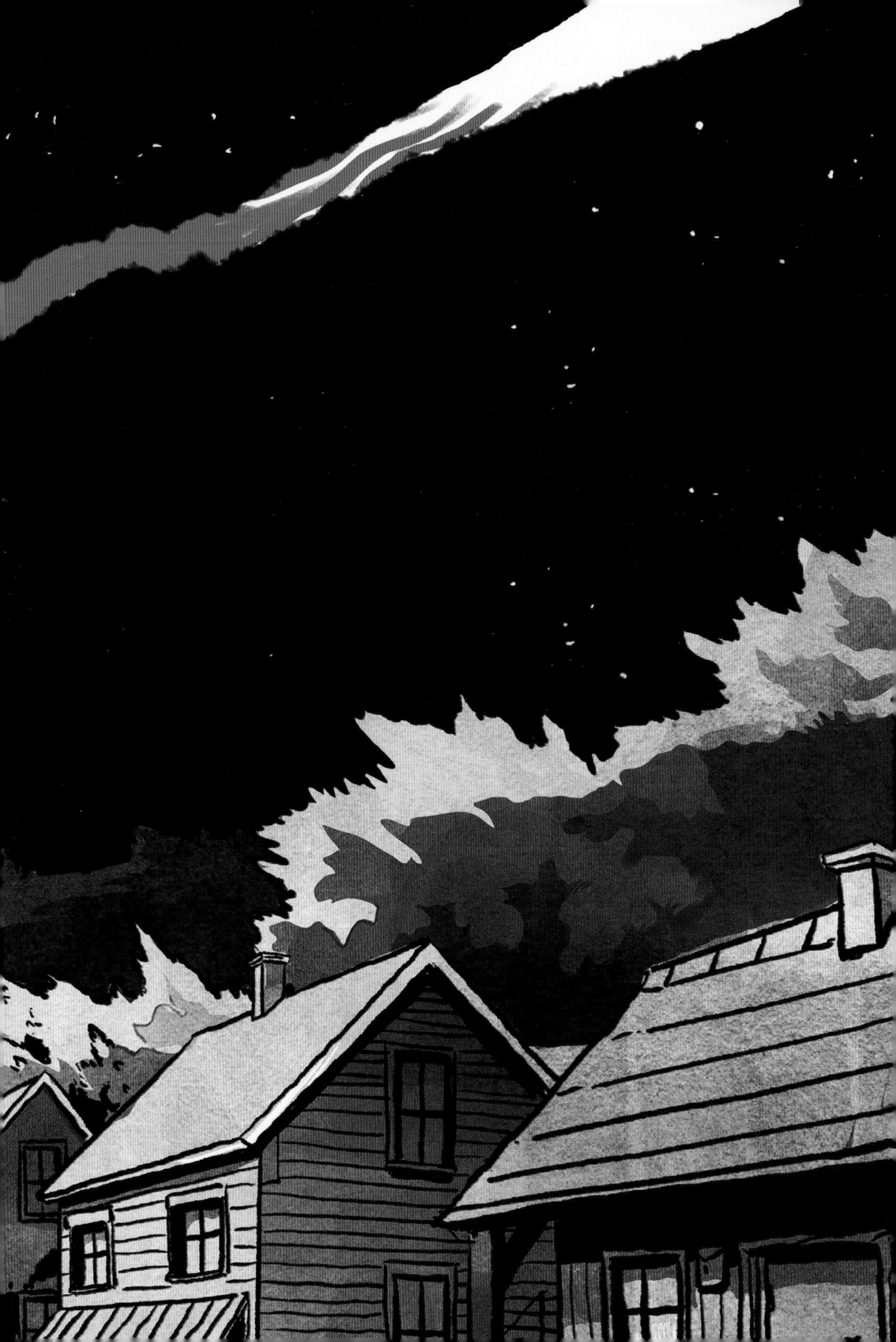

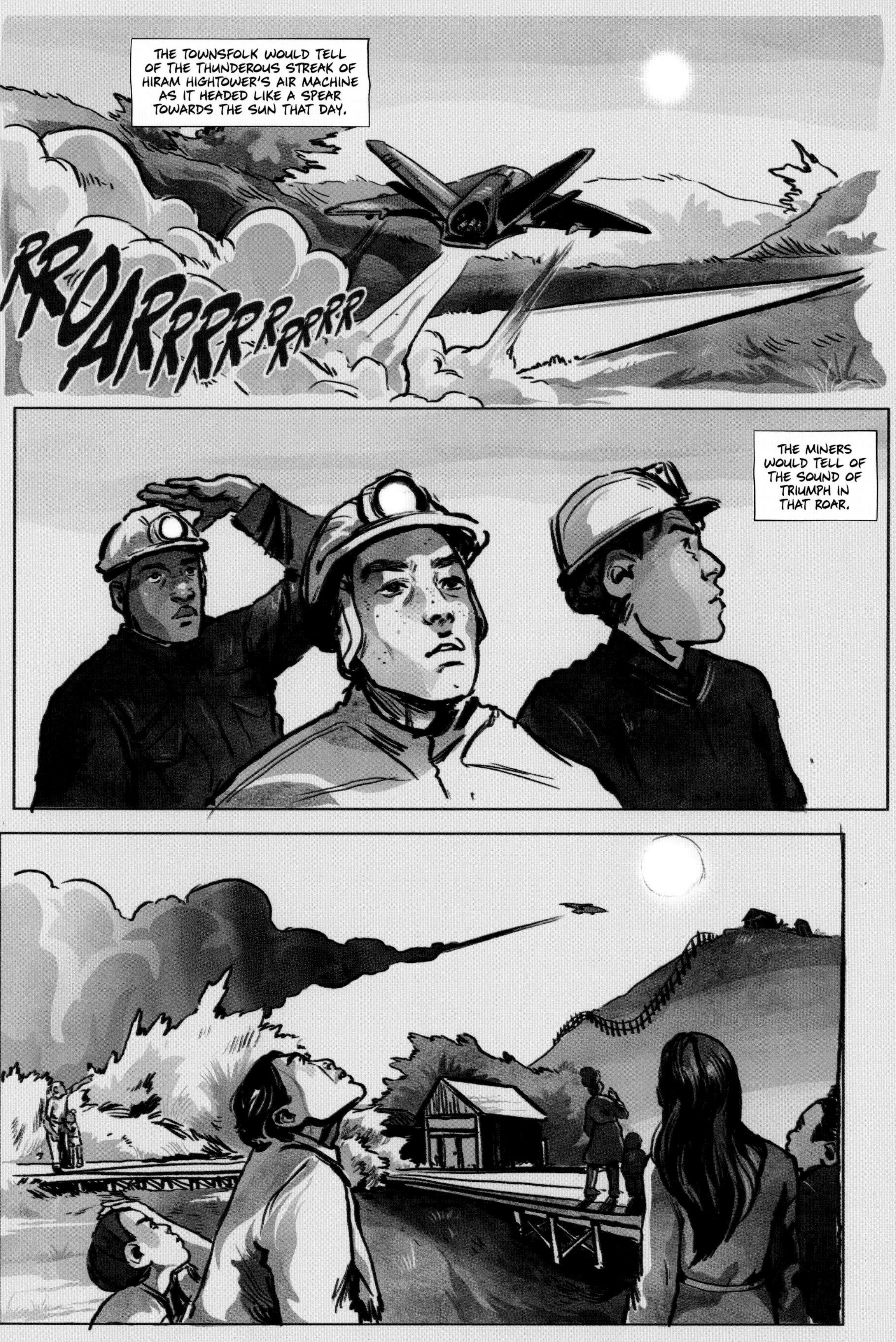
THE TOWNSFOLK WOULD TELL OF THE THUNDEROUS STREAK OF HIRAM HIGHTOWER'S AIR MACHINE AS IT HEADED LIKE A SPEAR TOWARDS THE SUN THAT DAY.
RROARRRRRRRRRR
THE MINERS WOULD TELL OF THE SOUND OF TRIUMPH IN THAT ROAR.

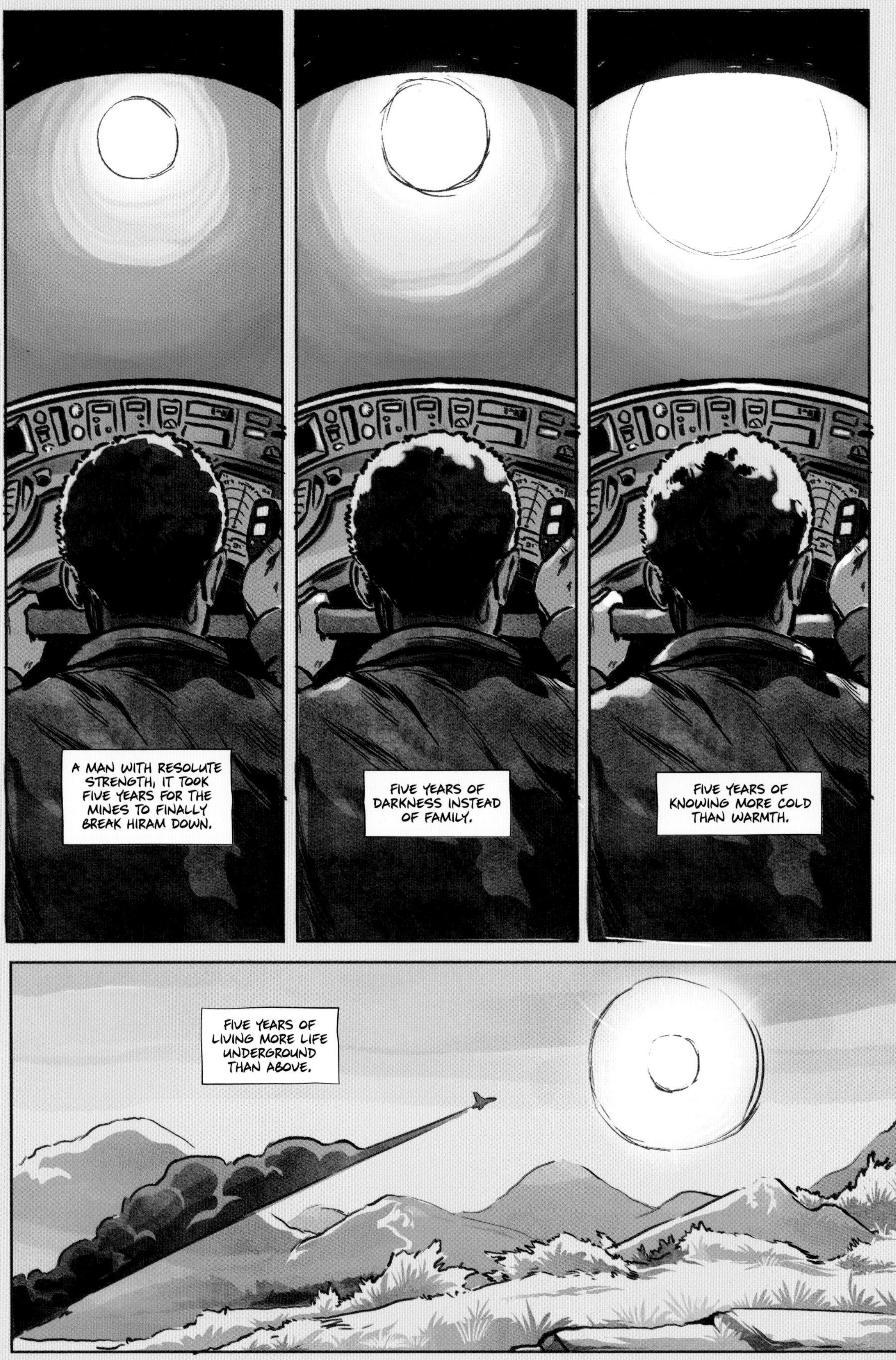
A MAN WITH RESOLUTE STRENGTH, IT TOOK FIVE YEARS FOR THE MINES TO FINALLY BREAK HIRAM DOWN.
FIVE YEARS OF DARKNESS INSTEAD OF FAMILY.
FIVE YEARS OF KNOWING MORE COLD THAN WARMTH.
FIVE YEARS OF LIVING MORE LIFE UNDERGROUND THAN ABOVE.

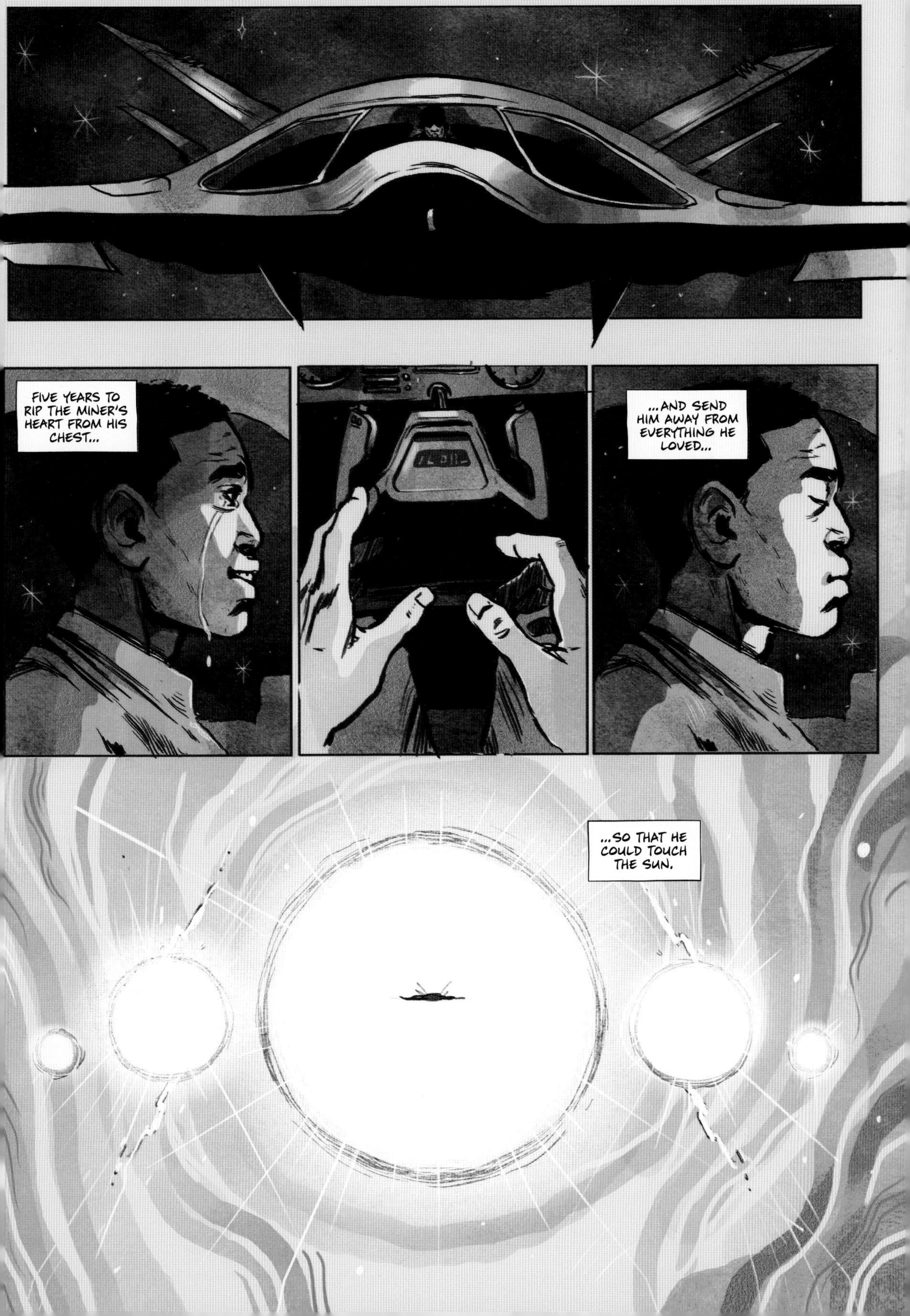
FIVE YEARS TO RIP THE MINER'S HEART FROM HIS CHEST...
...AND SEND HIM AWAY FROM EVERYTHING HE LOVED...
...SO THAT HE COULD TOUCH THE SUN.

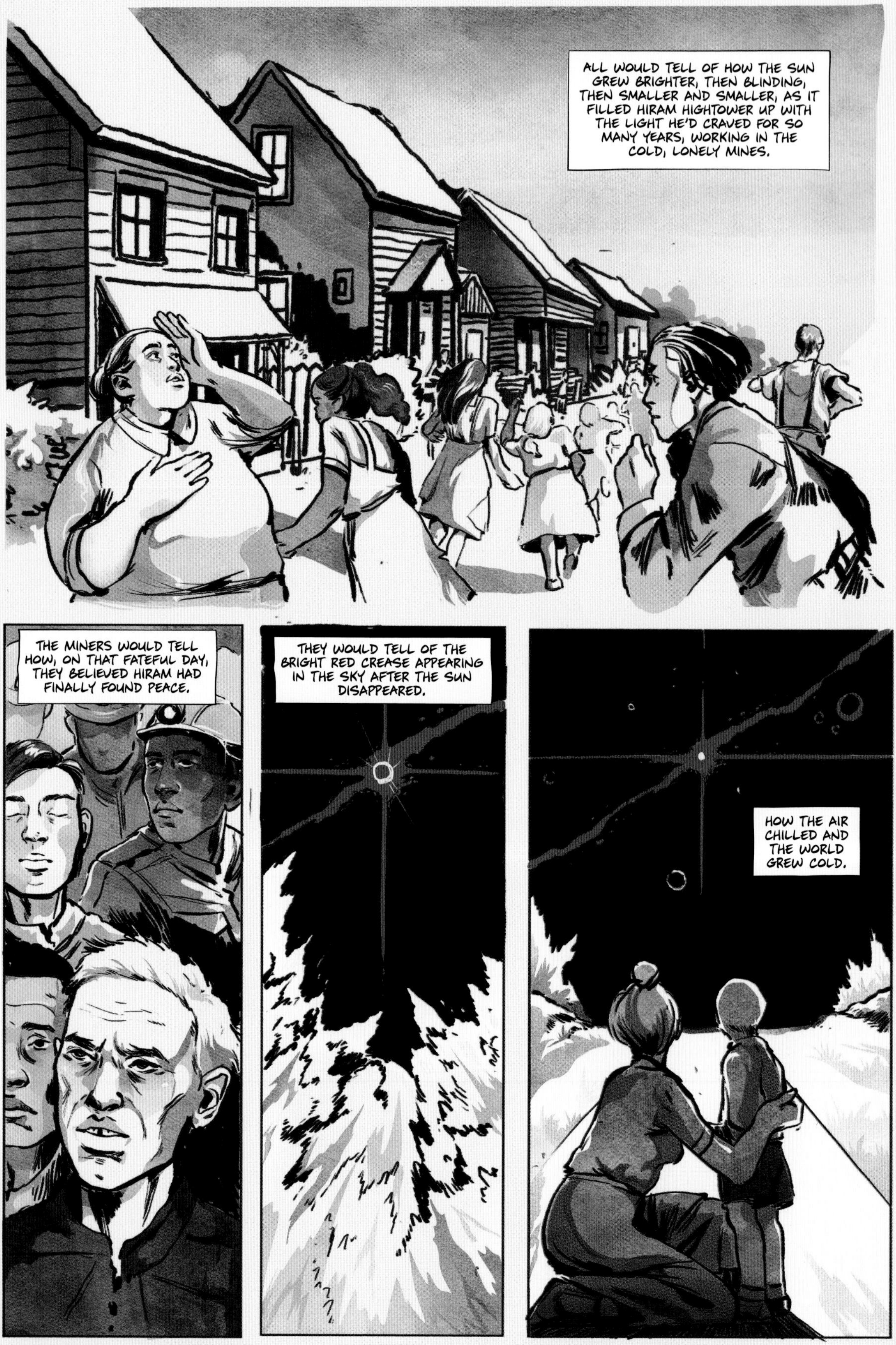
ALL WOULD TELL OF HOW THE SUN GREW BRIGHTER, THEN BLINDING, THEN SMALLER AND SMALLER, AS IT FILLED HIRAM HIGHTOWER UP WITH THE LIGHT HE'D CRAVED FOR SO MANY YEARS, WORKING IN THE COLD, LONELY MINES.
THE MINERS WOULD TELL HOW, ON THAT FATEFUL DAY, THEY BELIEVED HIRAM HAD FINALLY FOUND PEACE.
THEY WOULD TELL OF THE BRIGHT RED CREASE APPEARING IN THE SKY AFTER THE SUN DISAPPEARED.
HOW THE AIR CHILLED AND THE WORLD GREW COLD.

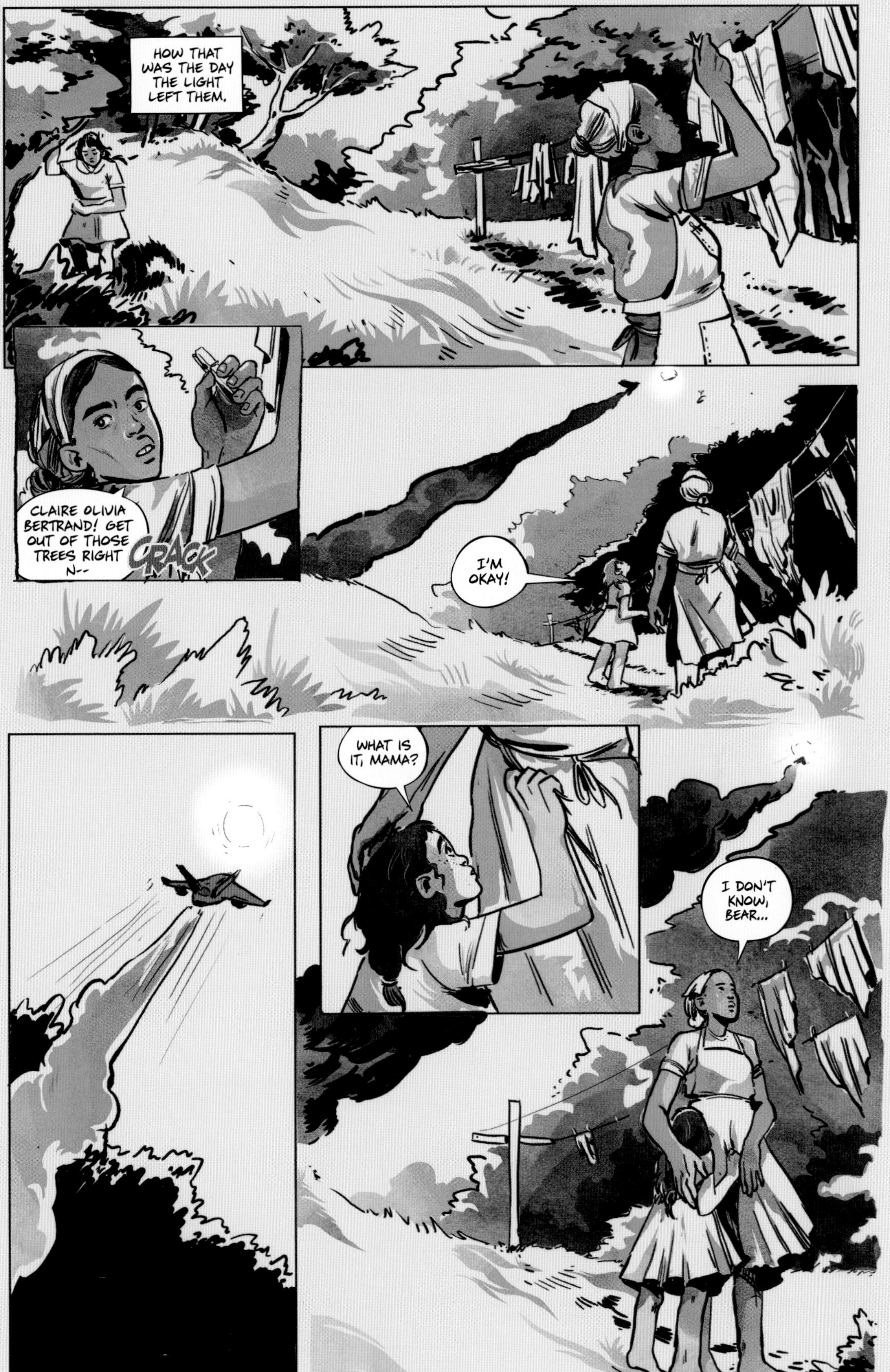
HOW THAT WAS THE DAY THE LIGHT LEFT THEM.
CLAIRE OLIVIA BERTRAND! GET OUT OF THOSE TREES RIGHT N--
CRACK
I'M OKAY!
WHAT IS IT, MAMA?
I DON'T KNOW, BEAR...

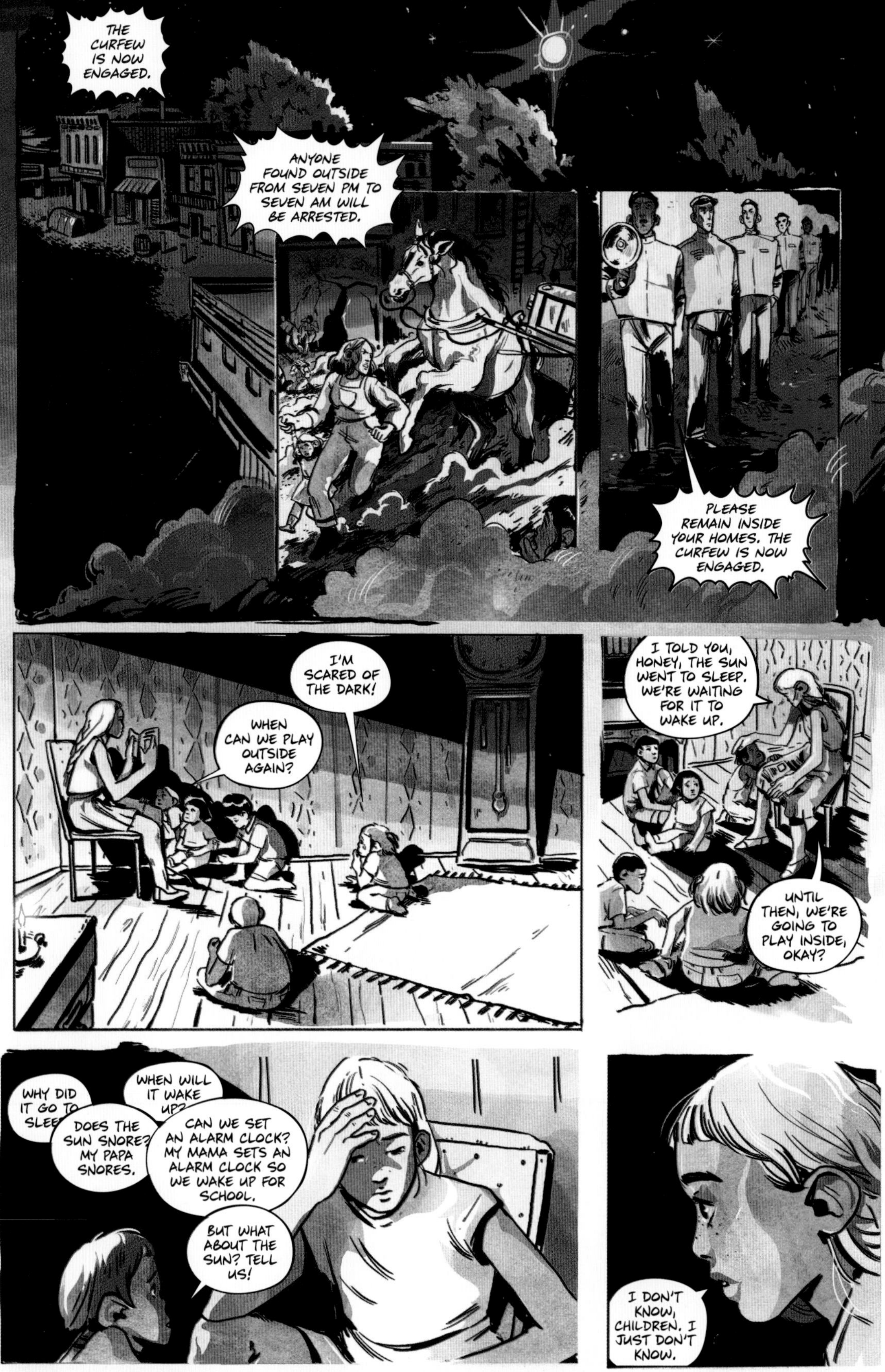
THE CURFEW IS NOW ENGAGED.
ANYONE FOUND OUTSIDE FROM SEVEN PM TO SEVEN AM WILL BE ARRESTED.
PLEASE REMAIN INSIDE YOUR HOMES. THE CURFEW IS NOW ENGAGED.
WHEN CAN WE PLAY OUTSIDE AGAIN?
I'M SCARED OF THE DARK!
I TOLD YOU, HONEY, THE SUN WENT TO SLEEP. WE'RE WAITING FOR IT TO WAKE UP.
UNTIL THEN, WE'RE GOING TO PLAY INSIDE, OKAY?
WHY DID IT GO TO
WHEN WILL IT WAKE
DOES THE SUN SNORE? MY PAPA SNORES.
CAN WE SET AN ALARM CLOCK? MY MAMA SETS AN ALARM CLOCK SO WE WAKE UP FOR SCHOOL.
BUT WHAT ABOUT THE SUN? TELL US!
I DON'T KNOW, CHILDREN. I JUST DON'T KNOW.

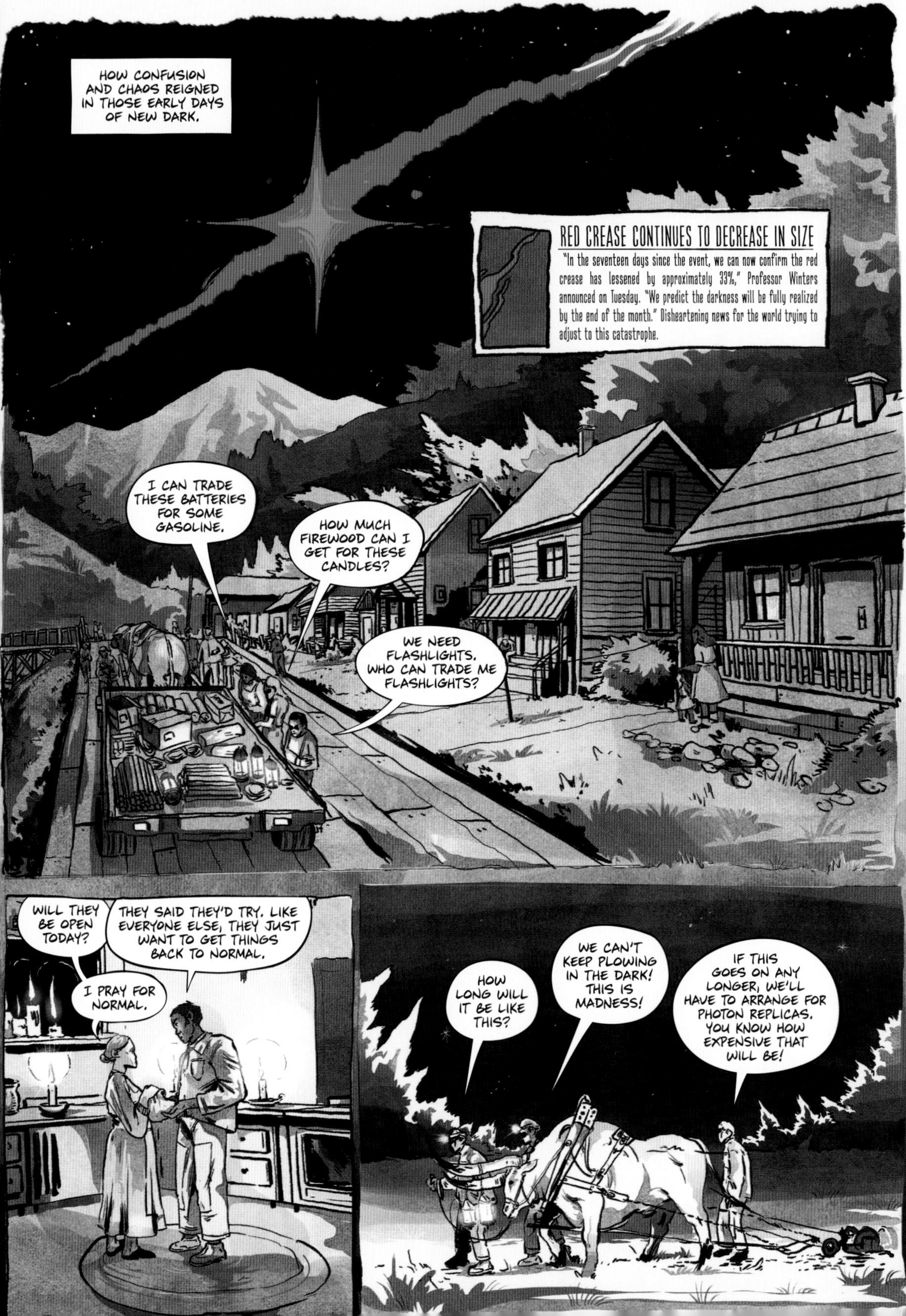

HOW CONFUSION AND CHAOS REIGNED IN THOSE EARLY DAYS OF NEW DARK.
RED CREASE CONTINUES TO DECREASE IN SIZE
"In the seventeen days since the event, we can now confirm the red crease has lessened by approximately 33%," Professor Winters announced on Tuesday. "We predict the darkness will be fully realized by the end of the month." Disheartening news for the world trying to adjust to this catastrophe.
I CAN TRADE THESE BATTERIES FOR SOME GASOLINE.
HOW MUCH FIREWOOD CAN I GET FOR THESE CANDLES?
WE NEED FLASHLIGHTS. WHO CAN TRADE ME FLASHLIGHTS?
WILL THEY BE OPEN TODAY?
THEY SAID THEY'D TRY. LIKE EVERYONE ELSE, THEY JUST WANT TO GET THINGS BACK TO NORMAL.
I PRAY FOR NORMAL.
HOW LONG WILL IT BE LIKE THIS?
WE CAN'T KEEP PLOWING IN THE DARK! THIS IS MADNESS!
IF THIS GOES ON ANY LONGER, WE'LL HAVE TO ARRANGE FOR PHOTON REPLICAS. YOU KNOW HOW EXPENSIVE THAT WILL BE!

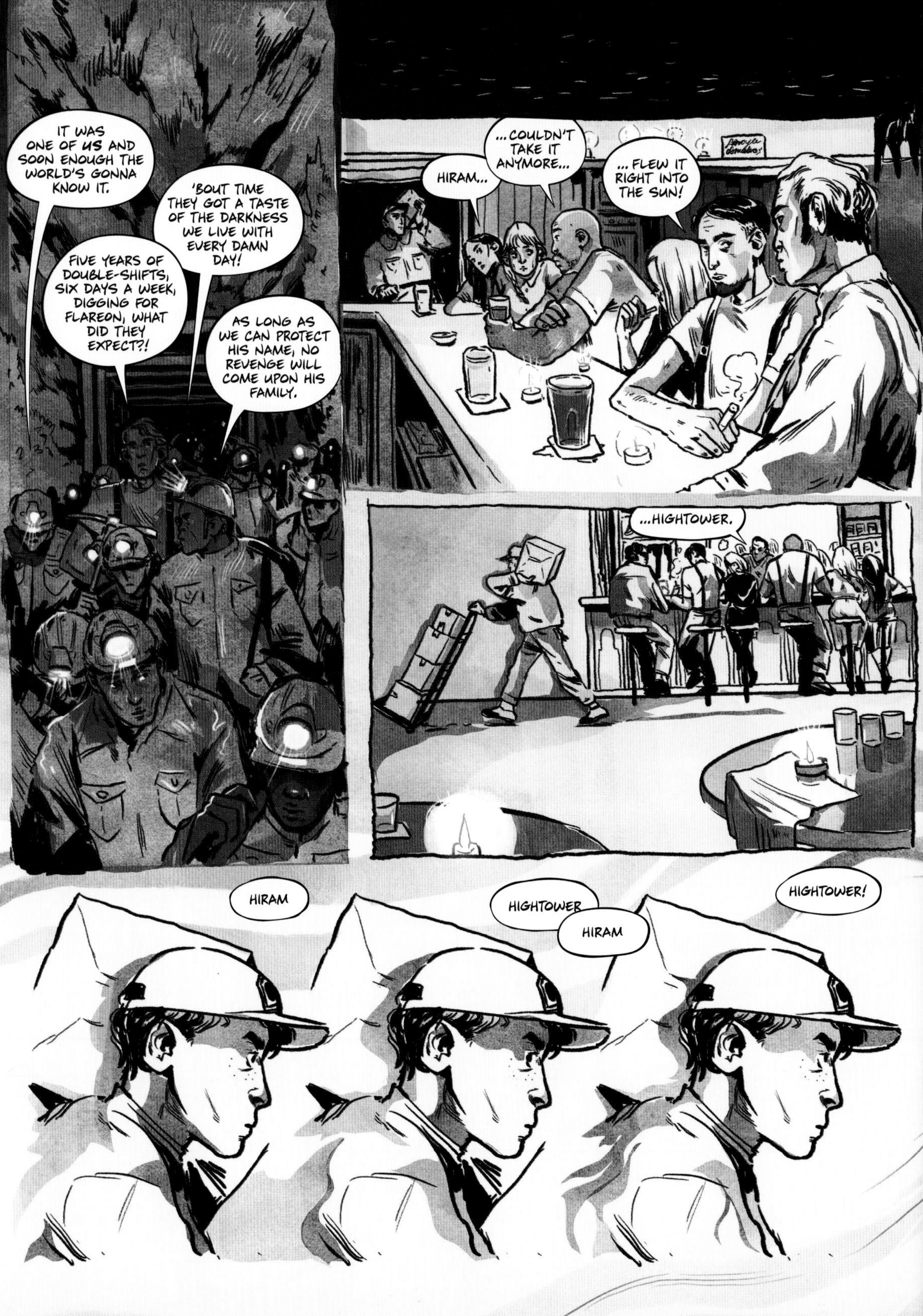
IT WAS ONE OF US AND SOON ENOUGH THE WORLD'S GONNA KNOW IT.
'BOUT TIME THEY GOT A TASTE OF THE DARKNESS WE LIVE WITH EVERY DAMN DAY!
FIVE YEARS OF DOUBLE-SHIFTS, SIX DAYS A WEEK, DIGGING FOR FLAREON, WHAT DID THEY EXPECT?!
AS LONG AS WE CAN PROTECT HIS NAME, NO REVENGE WILL COME UPON HIS FAMILY.
HIRAM...
...COULDN'T TAKE IT ANYMORE...
...FLEW IT RIGHT INTO THE SUN!
...HIGHTOWER.
HIRAM
HIGHTOWER
HIRAM
HIGHTOWER!

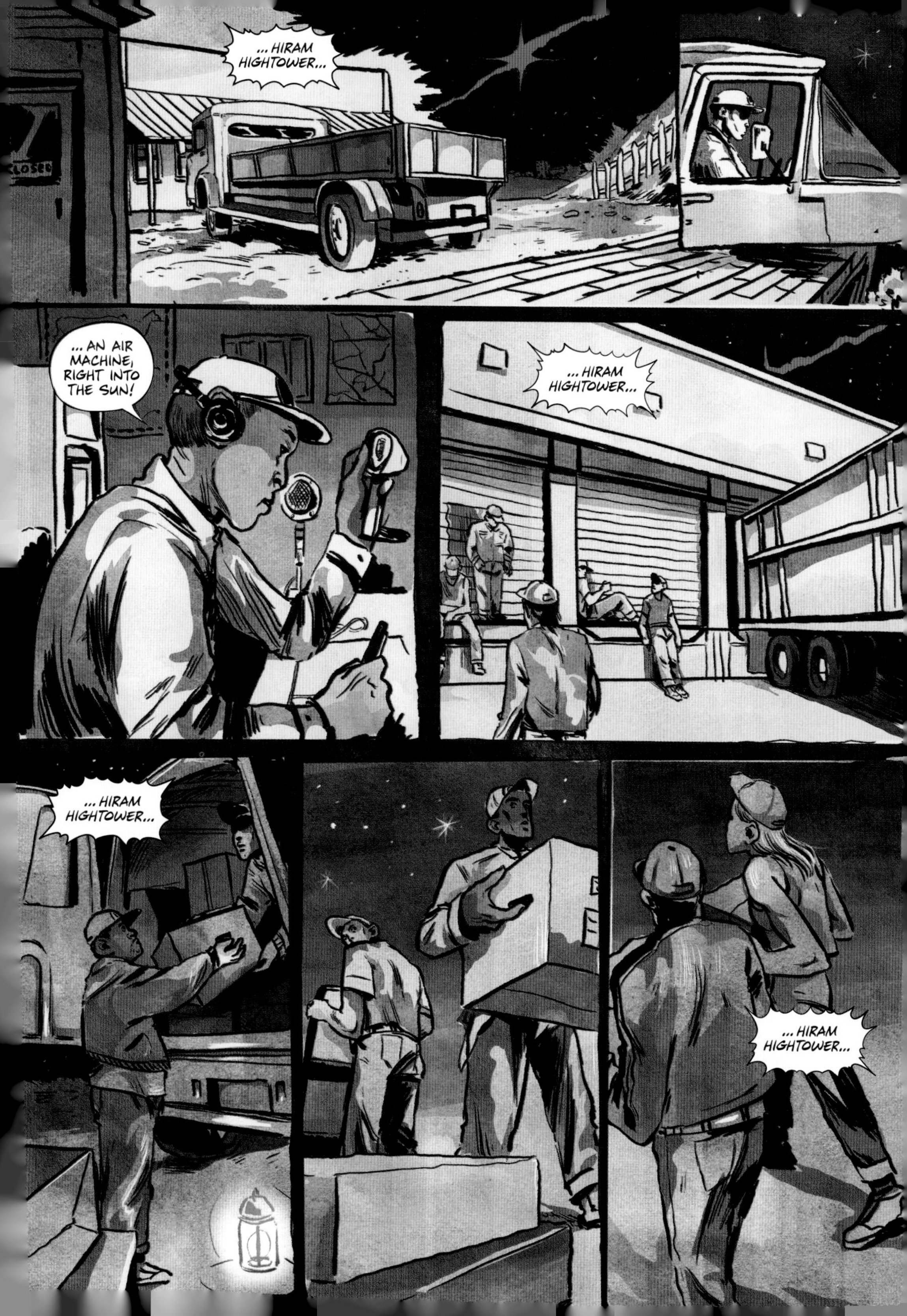

CLOSED
... HIRAM HIGHTOWER...
... AN AIR MACHINE, RIGHT INTO THE SUN!
... HIRAM HIGHTOWER...
... HIRAM HIGHTOWER...
... HIRAM HIGHTOWER...

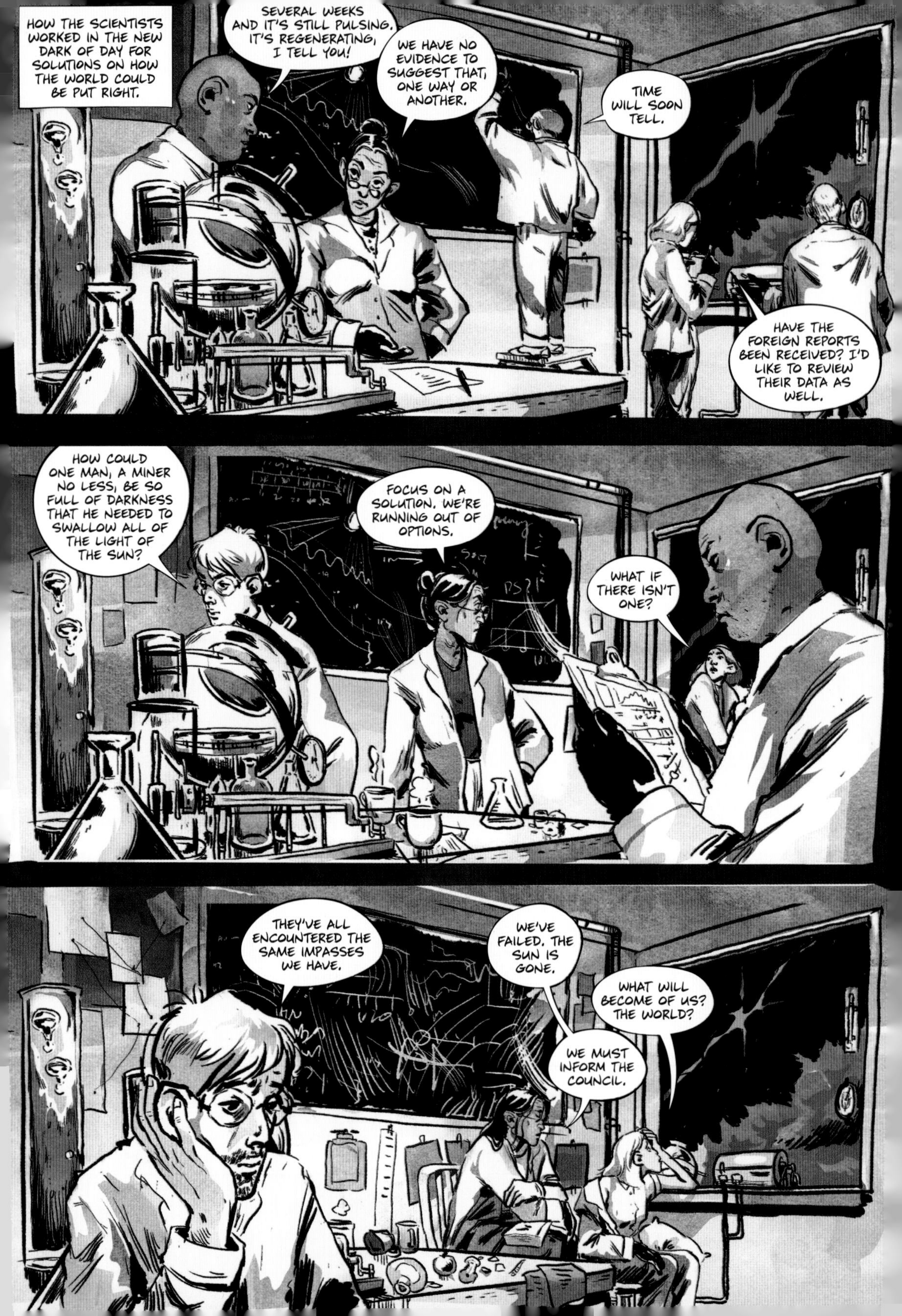
HOW THE SCIENTISTS WORKED IN THE NEW DARK OF DAY FOR SOLUTIONS ON HOW THE WORLD COULD BE PUT RIGHT.
SEVERAL WEEKS AND IT'S STILL PULSING. IT'S REGENERATING, I TELL YOU!
WE HAVE NO EVIDENCE TO SUGGEST THAT, ONE WAY OR ANOTHER.
TIME WILL SOON TELL.
HAVE THE FOREIGN REPORTS BEEN RECEIVED? I'D LIKE TO REVIEW THEIR DATA AS WELL.
HOW COULD ONE MAN, A MINER NO LESS, BE SO FULL OF DARKNESS THAT HE NEEDED TO SWALLOW ALL OF THE LIGHT OF THE SUN?
FOCUS ON A SOLUTION. WE'RE RUNNING OUT OF OPTIONS.
WHAT IF THERE ISN'T ONE?
THEY'VE ALL ENCOUNTERED THE SAME IMPASSES WE HAVE.
WE'VE FAILED. THE SUN IS GONE.
WHAT WILL BECOME OF US? THE WORLD?
WE MUST INFORM THE COUNCIL.

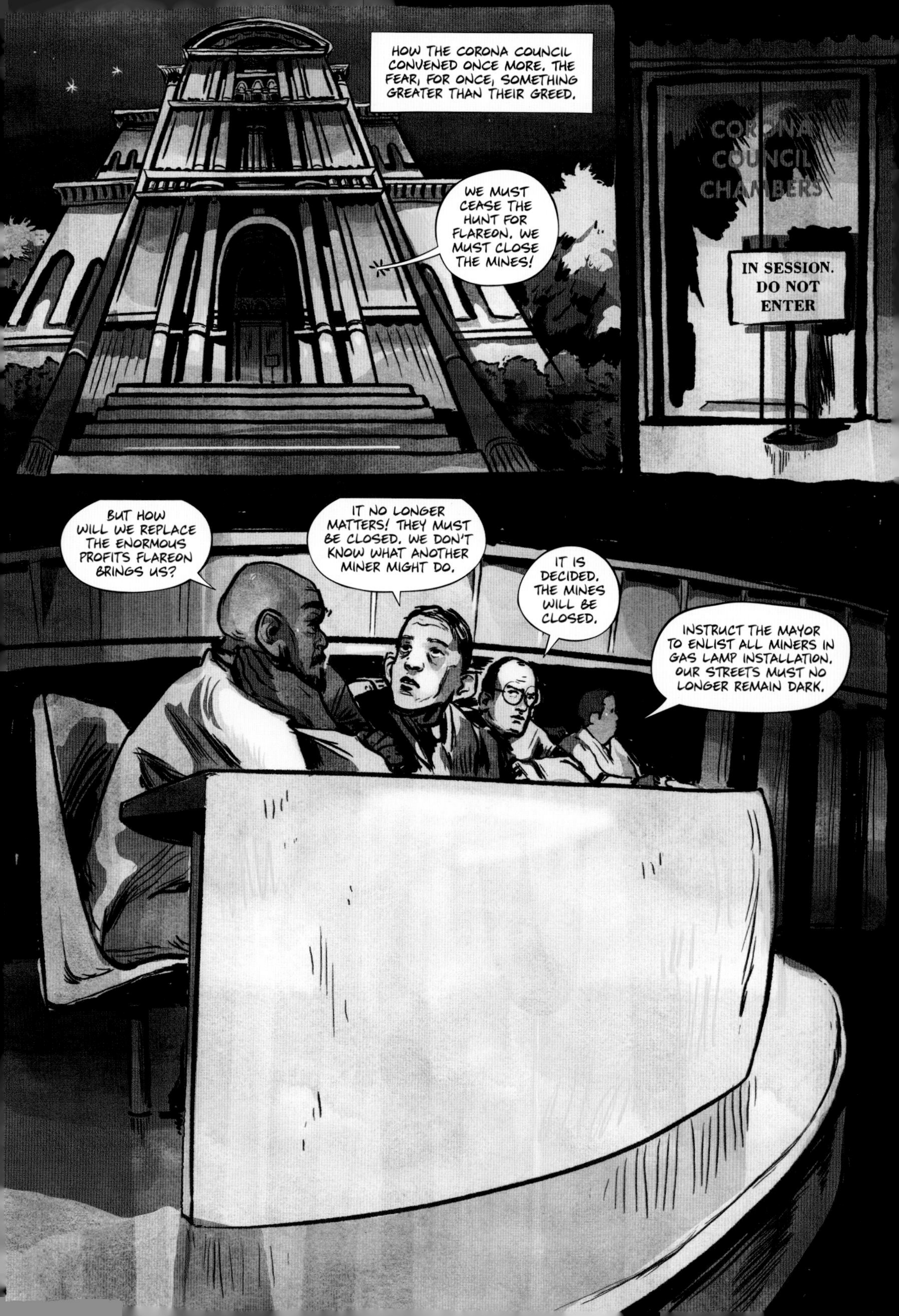
HOW THE CORONA COUNCIL CONVENED ONCE MORE. THE FEAR, FOR ONCE, SOMETHING GREATER THAN THEIR GREED.
WE MUST CEASE THE HUNT FOR FLAREON. WE MUST CLOSE THE MINES!
CORONA COUNCIL CHAMBERS
IN SESSION. DO NOT ENTER
BUT HOW WILL WE REPLACE THE ENORMOUS PROFITS FLAREON BRINGS US?
IT NO LONGER MATTERS! THEY MUST BE CLOSED. WE DON'T KNOW WHAT ANOTHER MINER MIGHT DO.
IT IS DECIDED. THE MINES WILL BE CLOSED.
INSTRUCT THE MAYOR TO ENLIST ALL MINERS IN GAS LAMP INSTALLATION. OUR STREETS MUST NO LONGER REMAIN DARK.

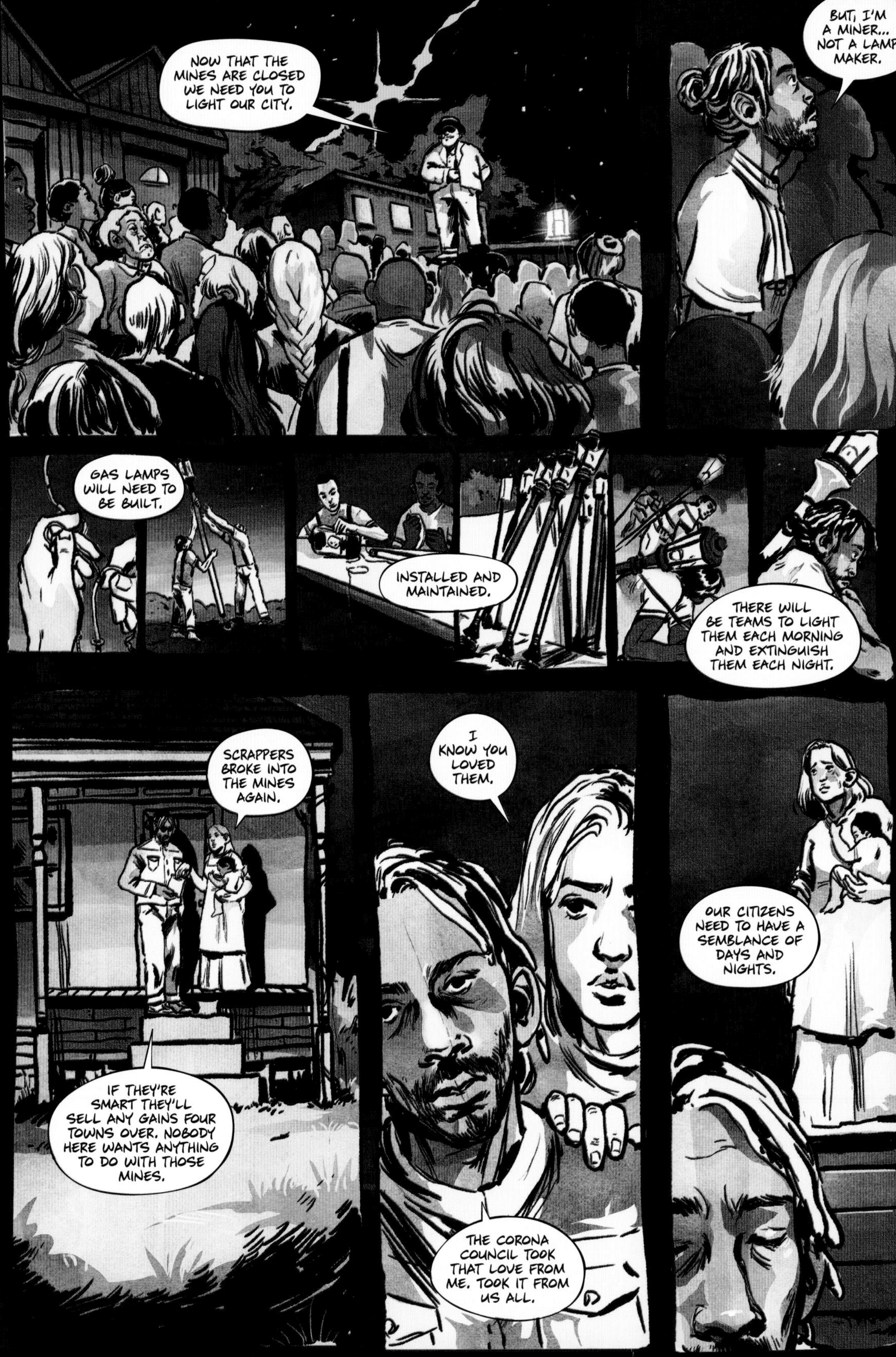
NOW THAT THE MINES ARE CLOSED WE NEED YOU TO LIGHT OUR CITY.
BUT, I'M A MINER... NOT A LAMP MAKER.
GAS LAMPS WILL NEED TO BE BUILT.
INSTALLED AND MAINTAINED.
THERE WILL BE TEAMS TO LIGHT THEM EACH MORNING AND EXTINGUISH THEM EACH NIGHT.
SCRAPPERS BROKE INTO THE MINES AGAIN.
IF THEY'RE SMART THEY'LL SELL ANY GAINS FOUR TOWNS OVER. NOBODY HERE WANTS ANYTHING TO DO WITH THOSE MINES.
I KNOW YOU LOVED THEM.
THE CORONA COUNCIL TOOK THAT LOVE FROM ME. TOOK IT FROM US ALL.
OUR CITIZENS NEED TO HAVE A SEMBLANCE OF DAYS AND NIGHTS.

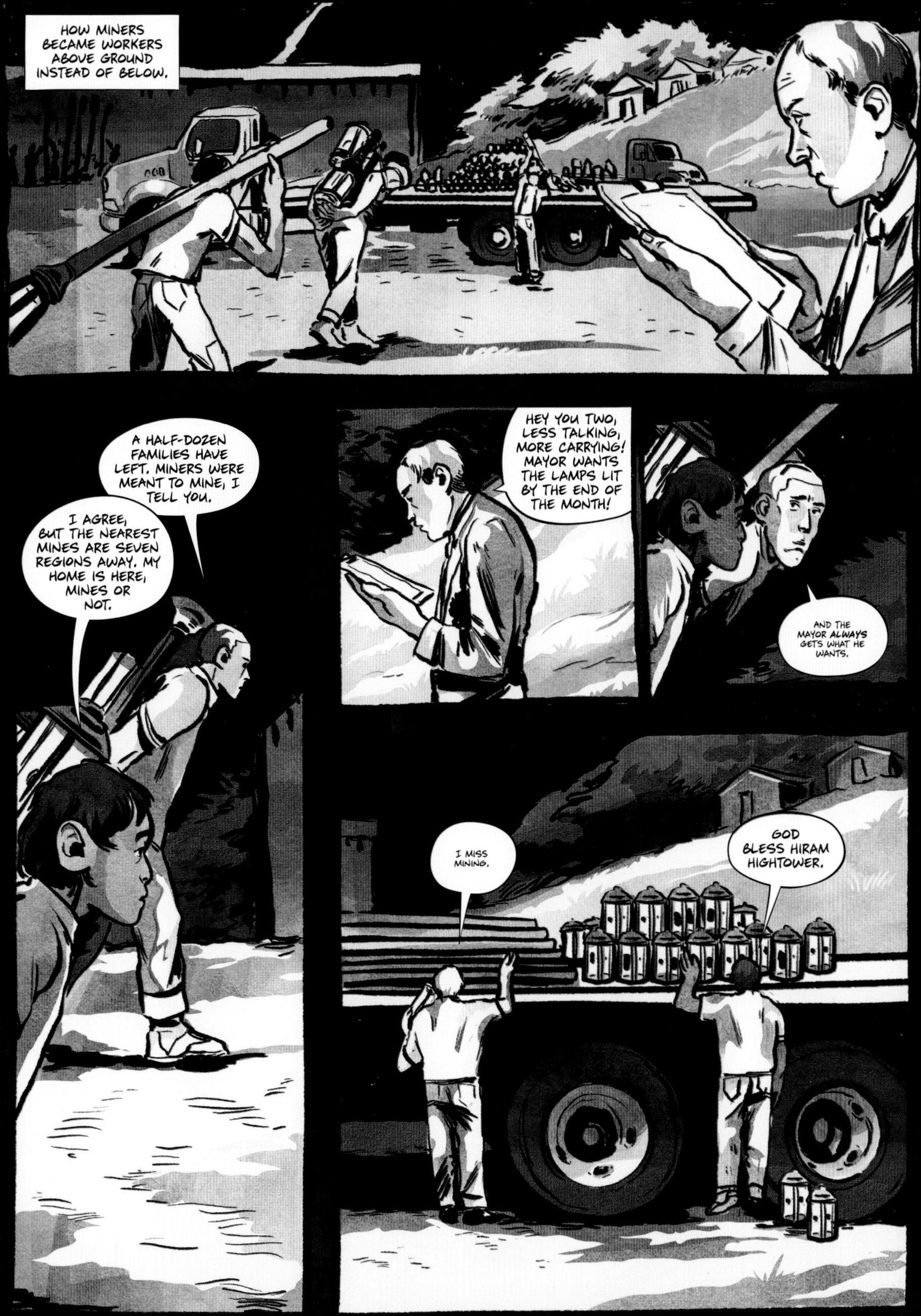
HOW MINERS BECAME WORKERS ABOVE GROUND INSTEAD OF BELOW.
A HALF-DOZEN FAMILIES HAVE LEFT. MINERS WERE MEANT TO MINE, I TELL YOU.
I AGREE, BUT THE NEAREST MINES ARE SEVEN REGIONS AWAY. MY HOME IS HERE, MINES OR NOT.
HEY YOU TWO, LESS TALKING, MORE CARRYING! MAYOR WANTS THE LAMPS LIT BY THE END OF THE MONTH!
AND THE MAYOR ALWAYS GETS WHAT HE WANTS.
I MISS MINING.
GOD BLESS HIRAM HIGHTOWER.

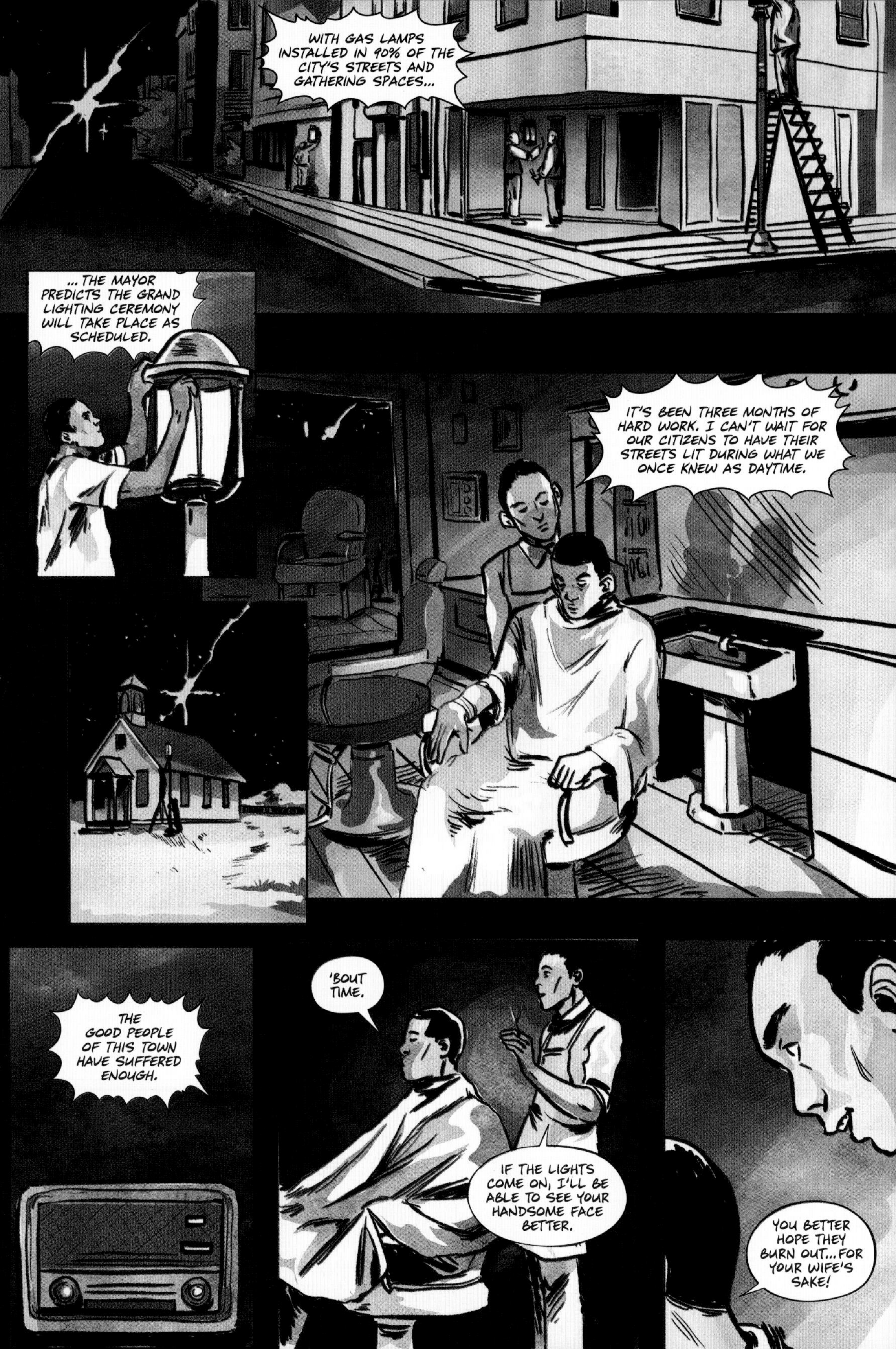
WITH GAS LAMPS INSTALLED IN 90% OF THE CITY'S STREETS AND GATHERING SPACES...
...THE MAYOR PREDICTS THE GRAND LIGHTING CEREMONY WILL TAKE PLACE AS SCHEDULED.
IT'S BEEN THREE MONTHS OF HARD WORK. I CAN'T WAIT FOR OUR CITIZENS TO HAVE THEIR STREETS LIT DURING WHAT WE ONCE KNEW AS DAYTIME.
THE GOOD PEOPLE OF THIS TOWN HAVE SUFFERED ENOUGH.
'BOUT TIME.
IF THE LIGHTS COME ON, I'LL BE ABLE TO SEE YOUR HANDSOME FACE BETTER.
YOU BETTER HOPE THEY BURN OUT...FOR YOUR WIFE'S SAKE!

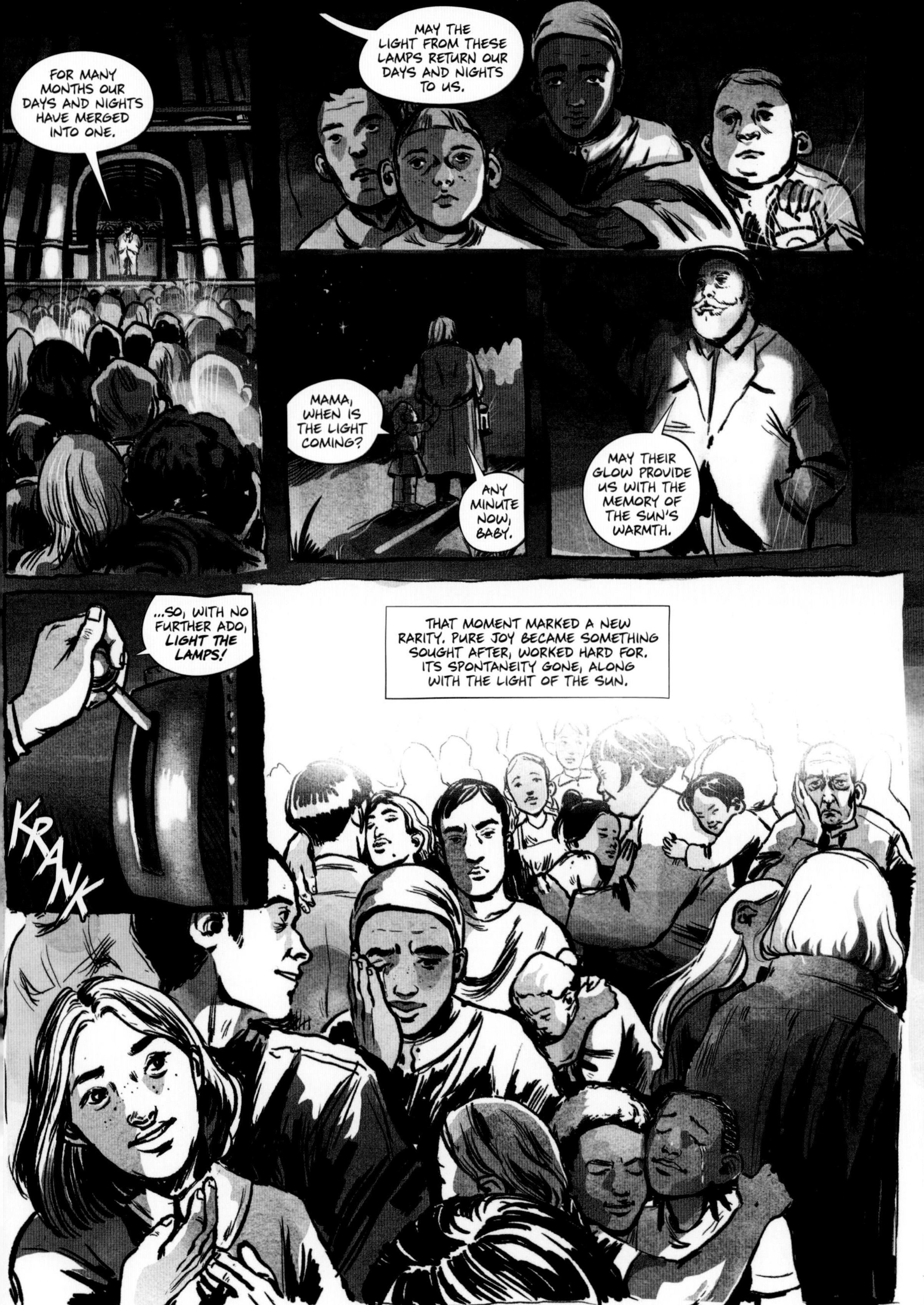
FOR MANY MONTHS OUR DAYS AND NIGHTS HAVE MERGED INTO ONE.
MAY THE LIGHT FROM THESE LAMPS RETURN OUR DAYS AND NIGHTS TO US.
MAMA, WHEN IS THE LIGHT COMING?
ANY MINUTE NOW, BABY.
MAY THEIR GLOW PROVIDE US WITH THE MEMORY OF THE SUN'S WARMTH.
...SO, WITH NO FURTHER ADO, LIGHT THE LAMPS!
KRANK
THAT MOMENT MARKED A NEW RARITY. PURE JOY BECAME SOMETHING SOUGHT AFTER, WORKED HARD FOR. ITS SPONTANEITY GONE, ALONG WITH THE LIGHT OF THE SUN.

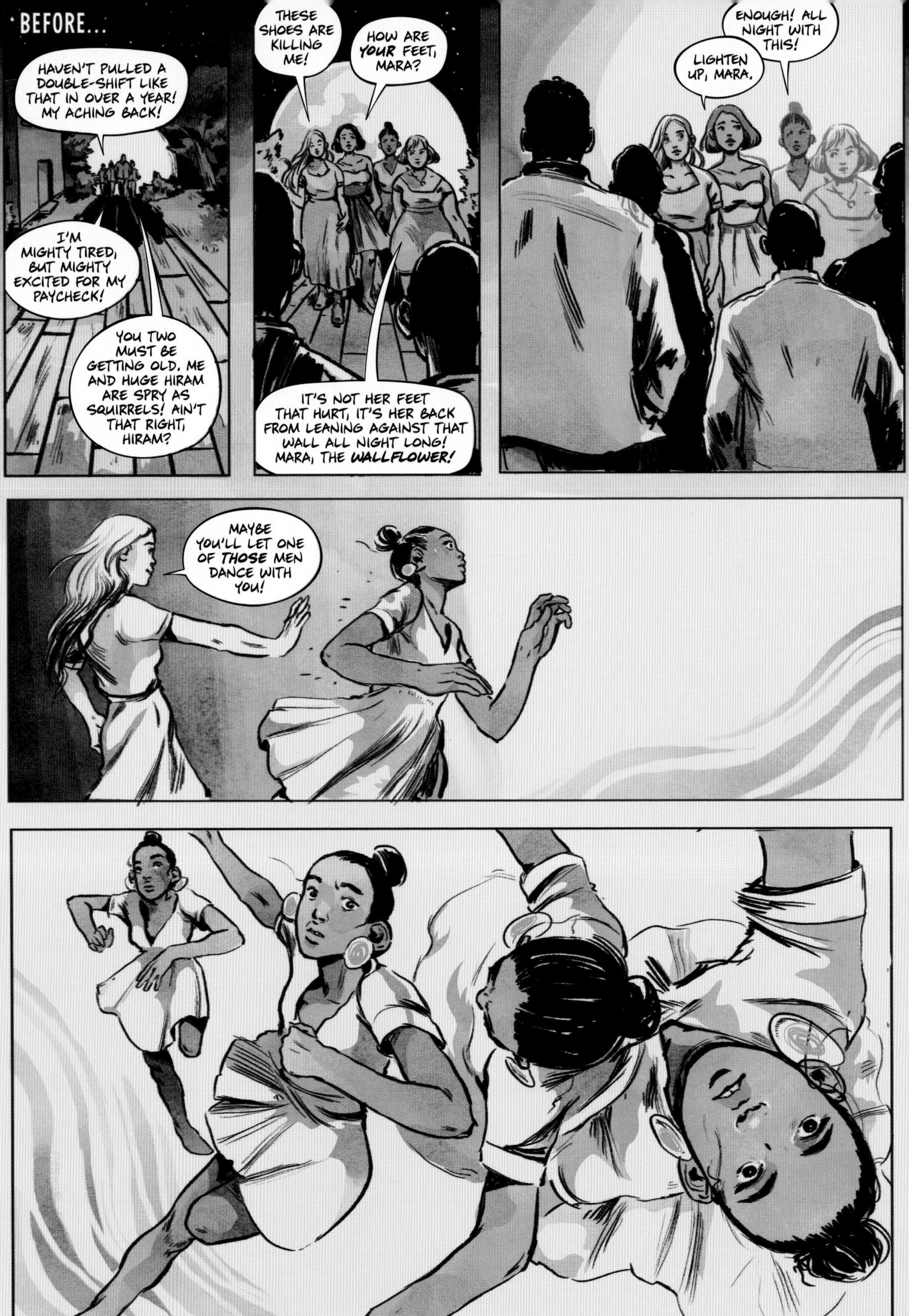
BEFORE...
HAVEN'T PULLED A DOUBLE-SHIFT LIKE THAT IN OVER A YEAR! MY ACHING BACK!
I'M MIGHTY TIRED, BUT MIGHTY EXCITED FOR MY PAYCHECK!
YOU TWO MUST BE GETTING OLD. ME AND HUGE HIRAM ARE SPRY AS SQUIRRELS! AIN'T THAT RIGHT, HIRAM?
THESE SHOES ARE KILLING ME!
HOW ARE YOUR FEET, MARA?
IT'S NOT HER FEET THAT HURT, IT'S HER BACK FROM LEANING AGAINST THAT WALL ALL NIGHT LONG! MARA, THE WALLFLOWER!
LIGHTEN UP, MARA.
ENOUGH! ALL NIGHT WITH THIS!
MAYBE YOU'LL LET ONE OF THOSE MEN DANCE WITH YOU!

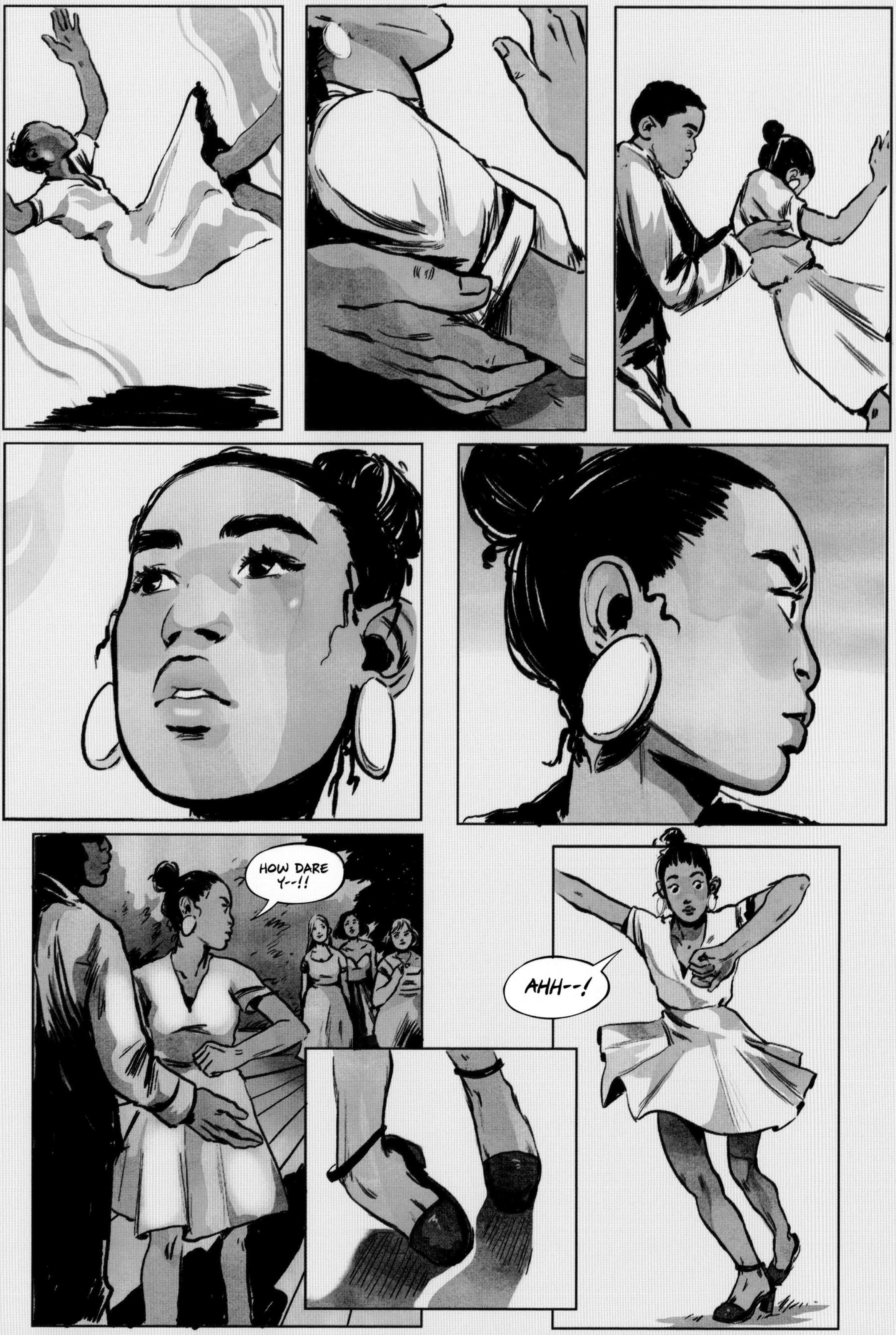
HOW DARE Y--!!
AHH--!

SORRY, MARA!

SEE YOU AT LUNCH TOMORROW!

HAVE FUN!

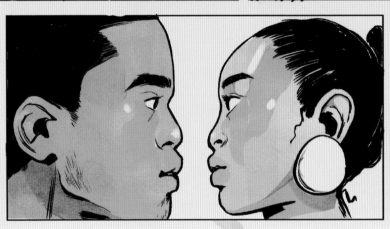

HIRAM? YOU COMING BACK TO THE BARRACKS?

I THINK HE'S GOT HIS HANDS FULL, FELLAS.

YEAH, LET'S GO. SEE YA, HIRAM!

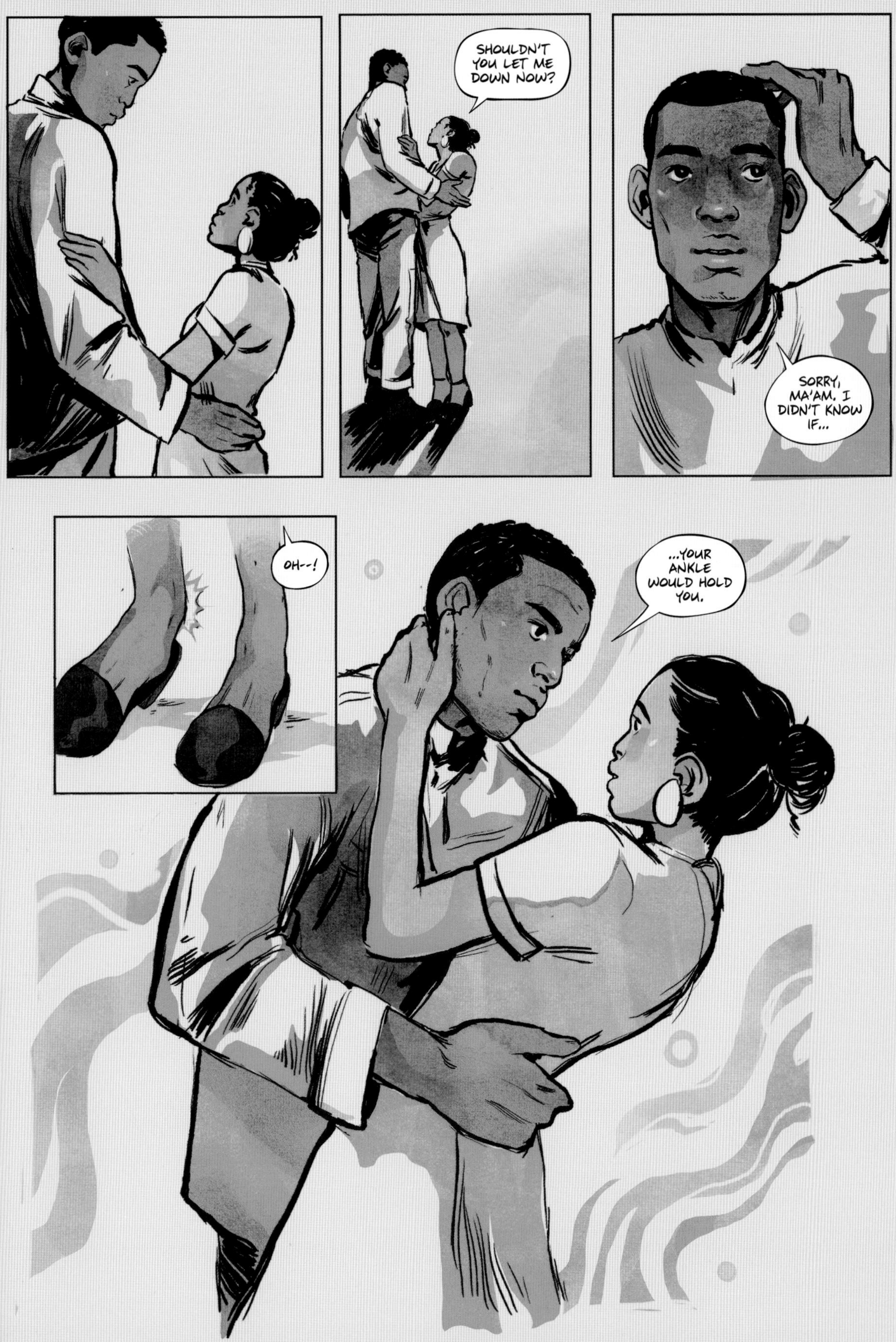
SHOULDN'T YOU LET ME DOWN NOW?
SORRY, MA'AM. I DIDN'T KNOW IF...
OH--!
...YOUR ANKLE WOULD HOLD YOU.

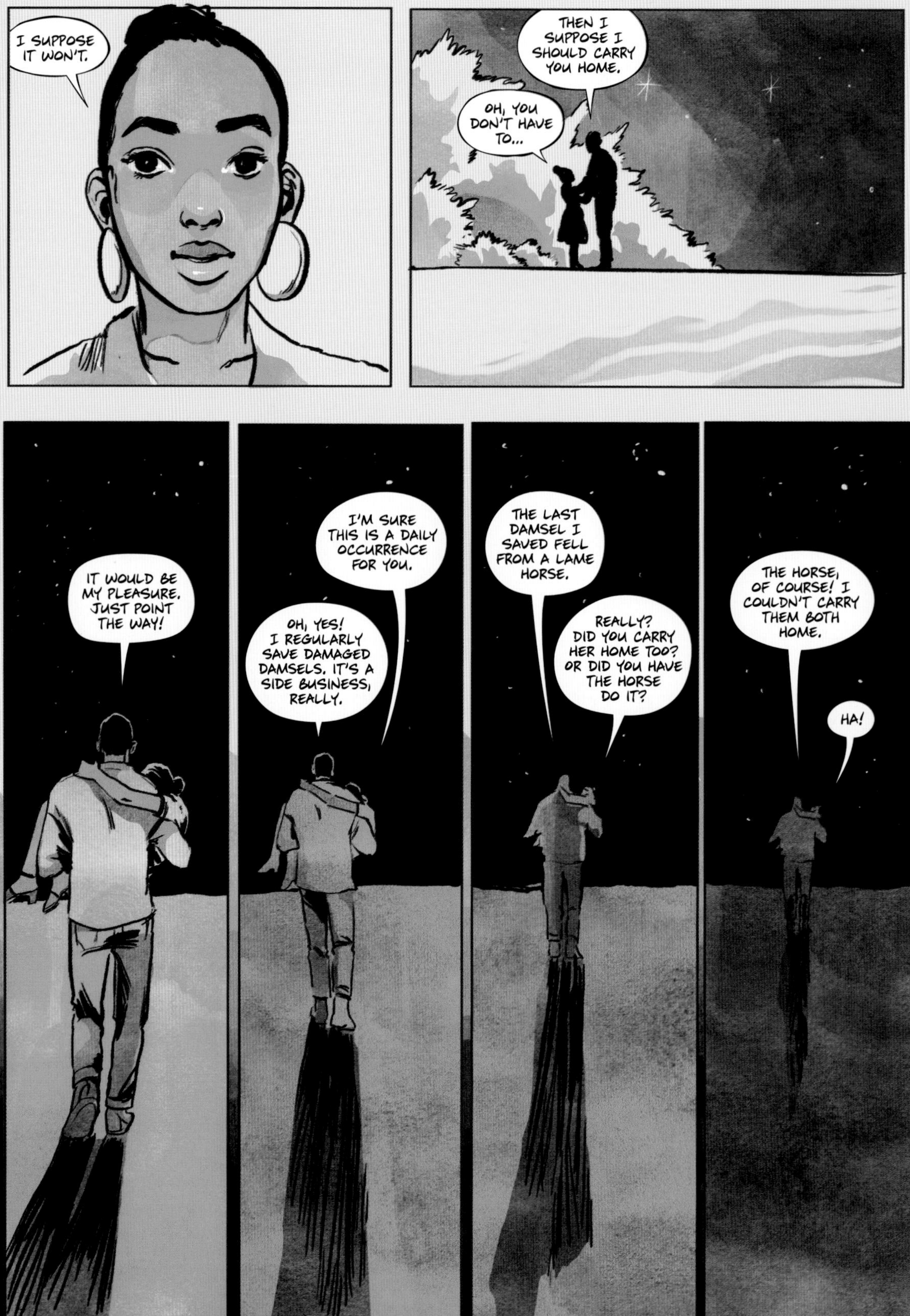
I SUPPOSE IT WON'T.
THEN I SUPPOSE I SHOULD CARRY YOU HOME.
OH, YOU DON'T HAVE TO...
IT WOULD BE MY PLEASURE. JUST POINT THE WAY!
I'M SURE THIS IS A DAILY OCCURRENCE FOR YOU.
OH, YES! I REGULARLY SAVE DAMAGED DAMSELS. IT'S A SIDE BUSINESS, REALLY.
THE LAST DAMSEL I SAVED FELL FROM A LAME HORSE.
REALLY? DID YOU CARRY HER HOME TOO? OR DID YOU HAVE THE HORSE DO IT?
THE HORSE, OF COURSE! I COULDN'T CARRY THEM BOTH HOME.
HA!

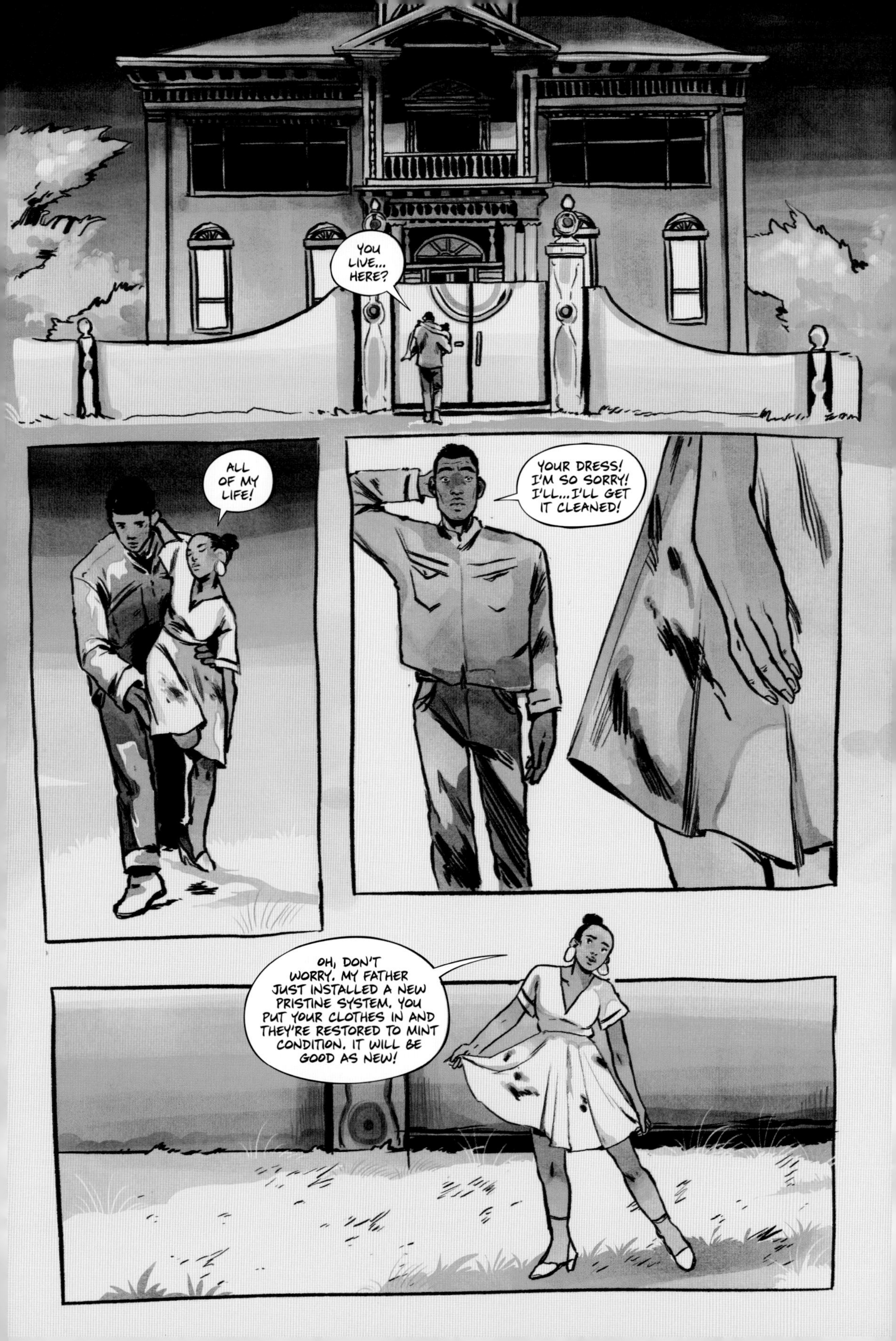
YOU LIVE... HERE?
ALL OF MY LIFE!
YOUR DRESS! I'M SO SORRY! I'LL...I'LL GET IT CLEANED!
OH, DON'T WORRY. MY FATHER JUST INSTALLED A NEW PRISTINE SYSTEM. YOU PUT YOUR CLOTHES IN AND THEY'RE RESTORED TO MINT CONDITION. IT WILL BE GOOD AS NEW!

HOW'S YOUR ANKLE?

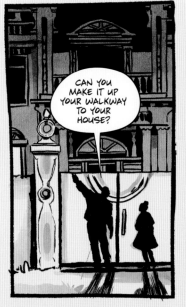

CAN YOU MAKE IT UP YOUR WALKWAY TO YOUR HOUSE?

IT FEELS MUCH BETTER. I SHOULD BE FINE.

ARE YOU SURE?

NO.

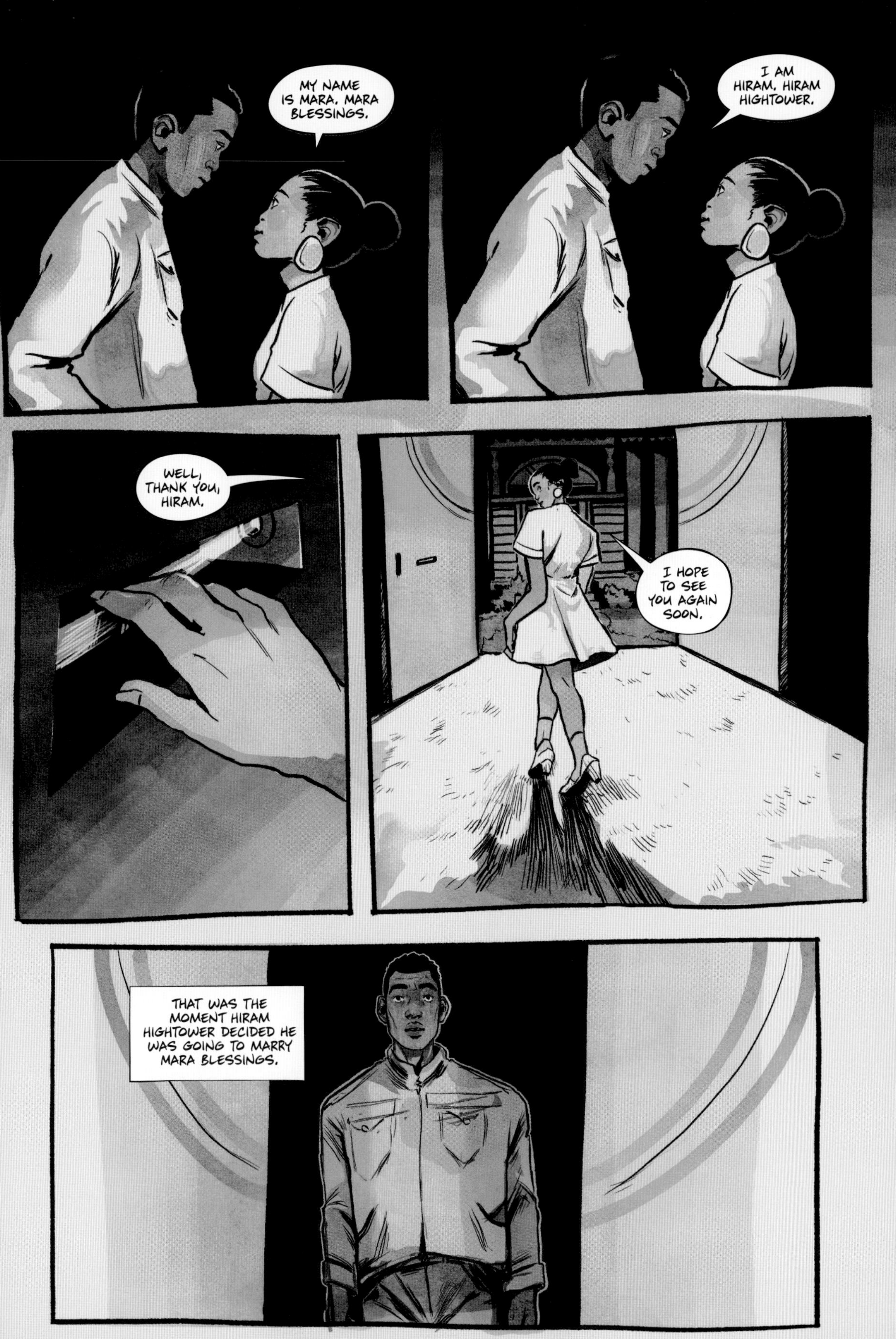
MY NAME IS MARA. MARA BLESSINGS.
I AM HIRAM. HIRAM HIGHTOWER.
WELL, THANK YOU, HIRAM.
I HOPE TO SEE YOU AGAIN SOON.
THAT WAS THE MOMENT HIRAM HIGHTOWER DECIDED HE WAS GOING TO MARRY MARA BLESSINGS.

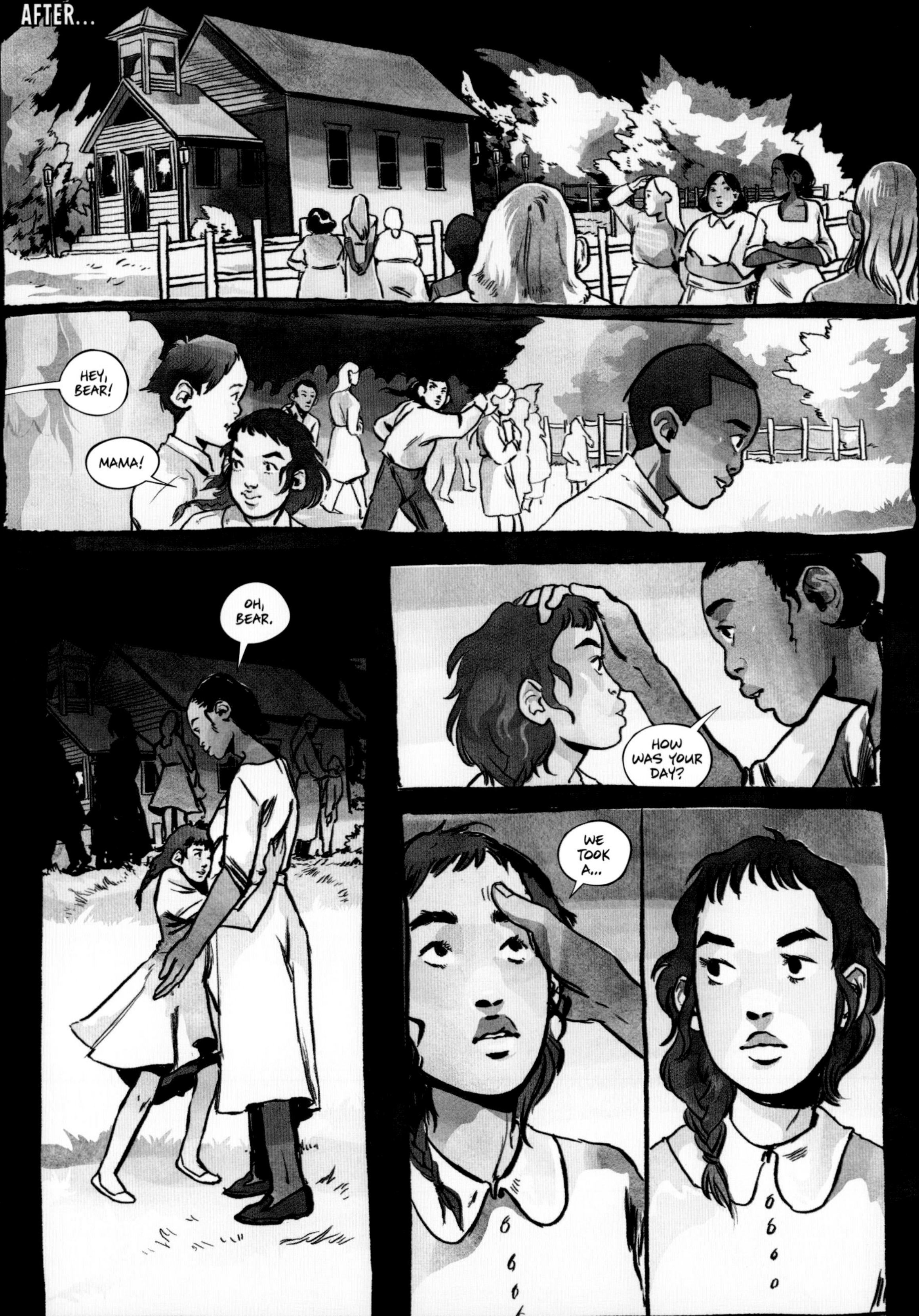
AFTER...
HEY, BEAR!
MAMA!
OH, BEAR.
HOW WAS YOUR DAY?
WE TOOK A...

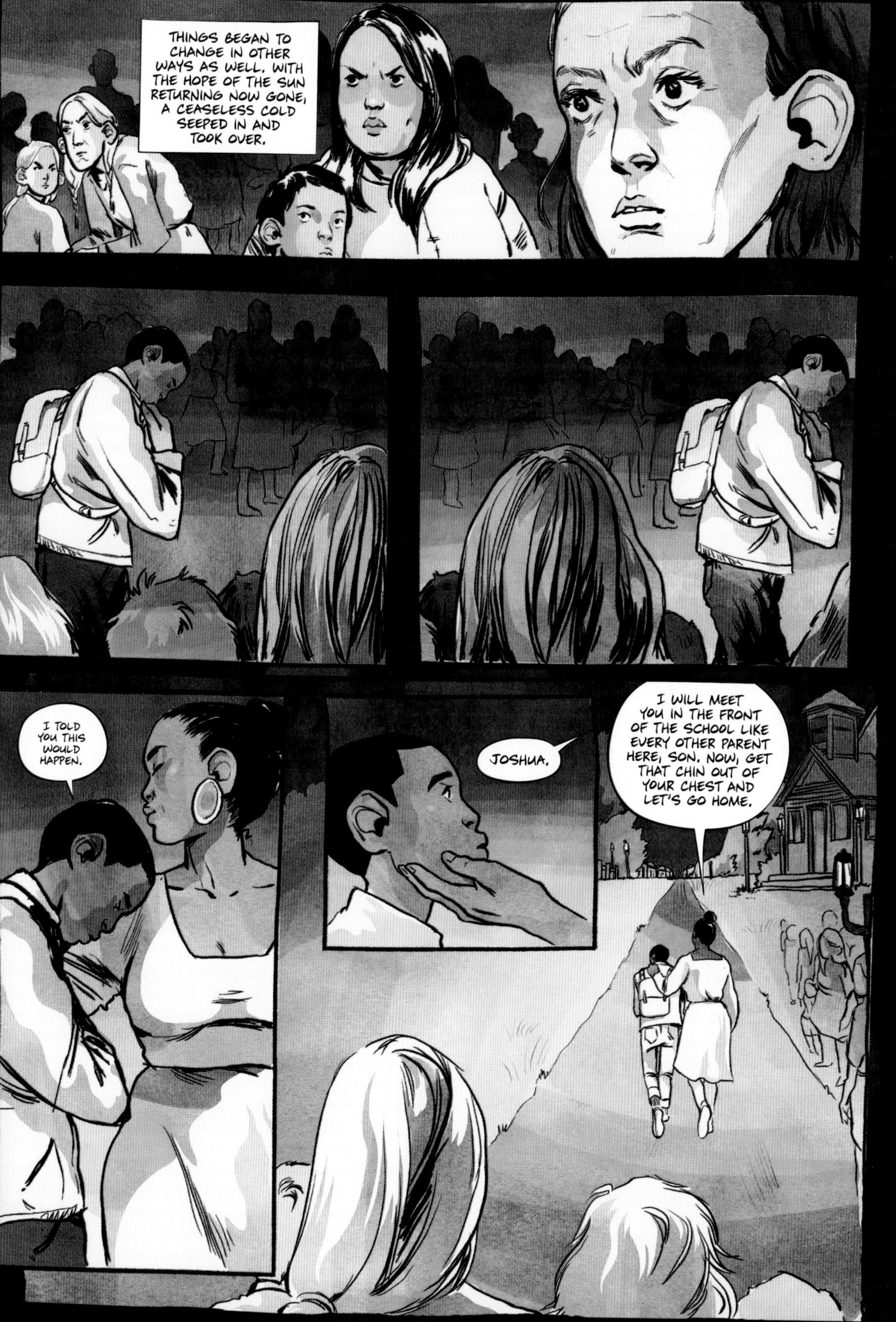
THINGS BEGAN TO CHANGE IN OTHER WAYS AS WELL. WITH THE HOPE OF THE SUN RETURNING NOW GONE, A CEASELESS COLD SEEPED IN AND TOOK OVER.
I TOLD YOU THIS WOULD HAPPEN.
JOSHUA.
I WILL MEET YOU IN THE FRONT OF THE SCHOOL LIKE EVERY OTHER PARENT HERE, SON. NOW, GET THAT CHIN OUT OF YOUR CHEST AND LET'S GO HOME.

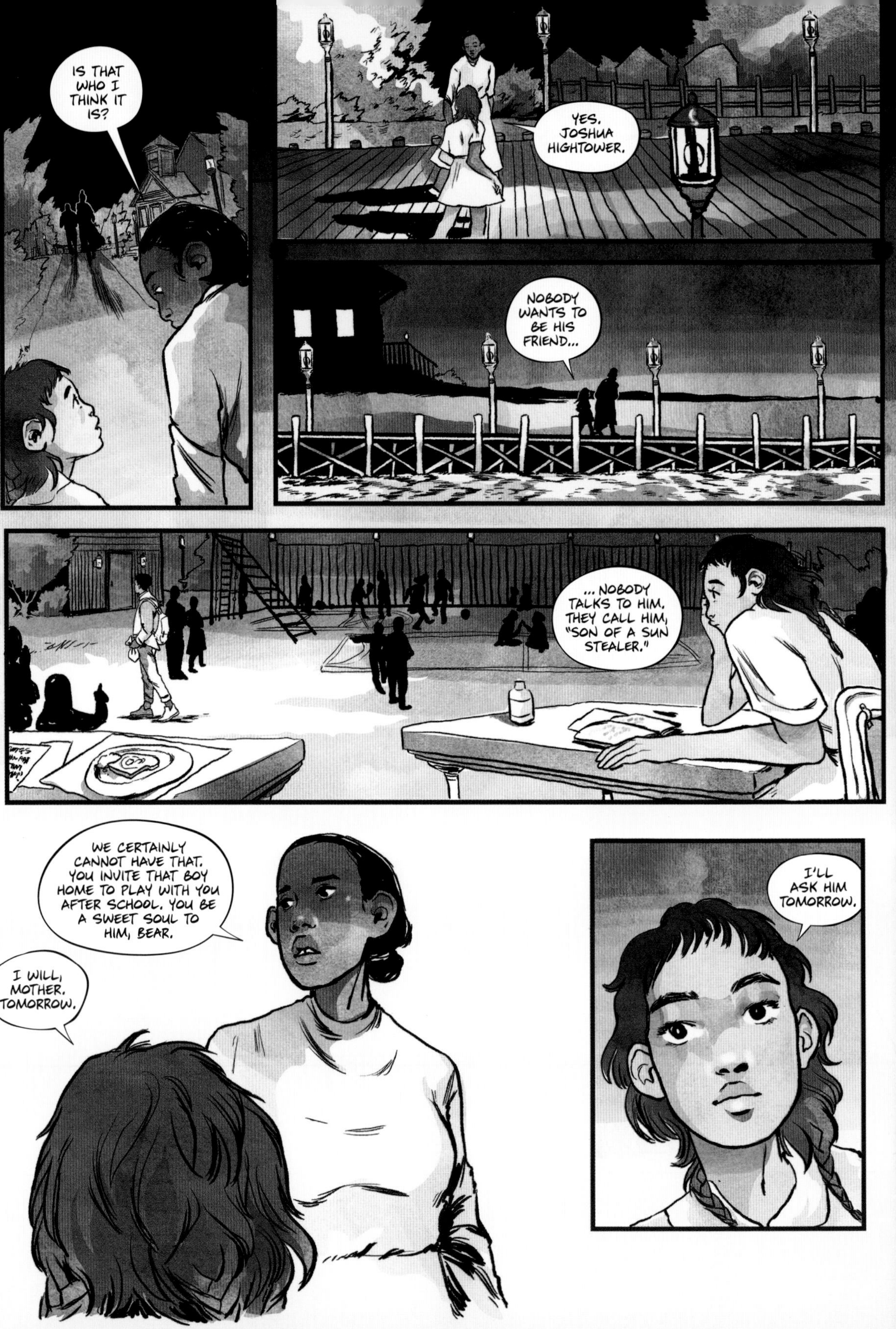
IS THAT WHO I THINK IT IS?
YES. JOSHUA HIGHTOWER.
NOBODY WANTS TO BE HIS FRIEND...
...NOBODY TALKS TO HIM. THEY CALL HIM, "SON OF A SUN STEALER."
WE CERTAINLY CANNOT HAVE THAT. YOU INVITE THAT BOY HOME TO PLAY WITH YOU AFTER SCHOOL. YOU BE A SWEET SOUL TO HIM, BEAR.
I WILL, MOTHER. TOMORROW.
I'LL ASK HIM TOMORROW.

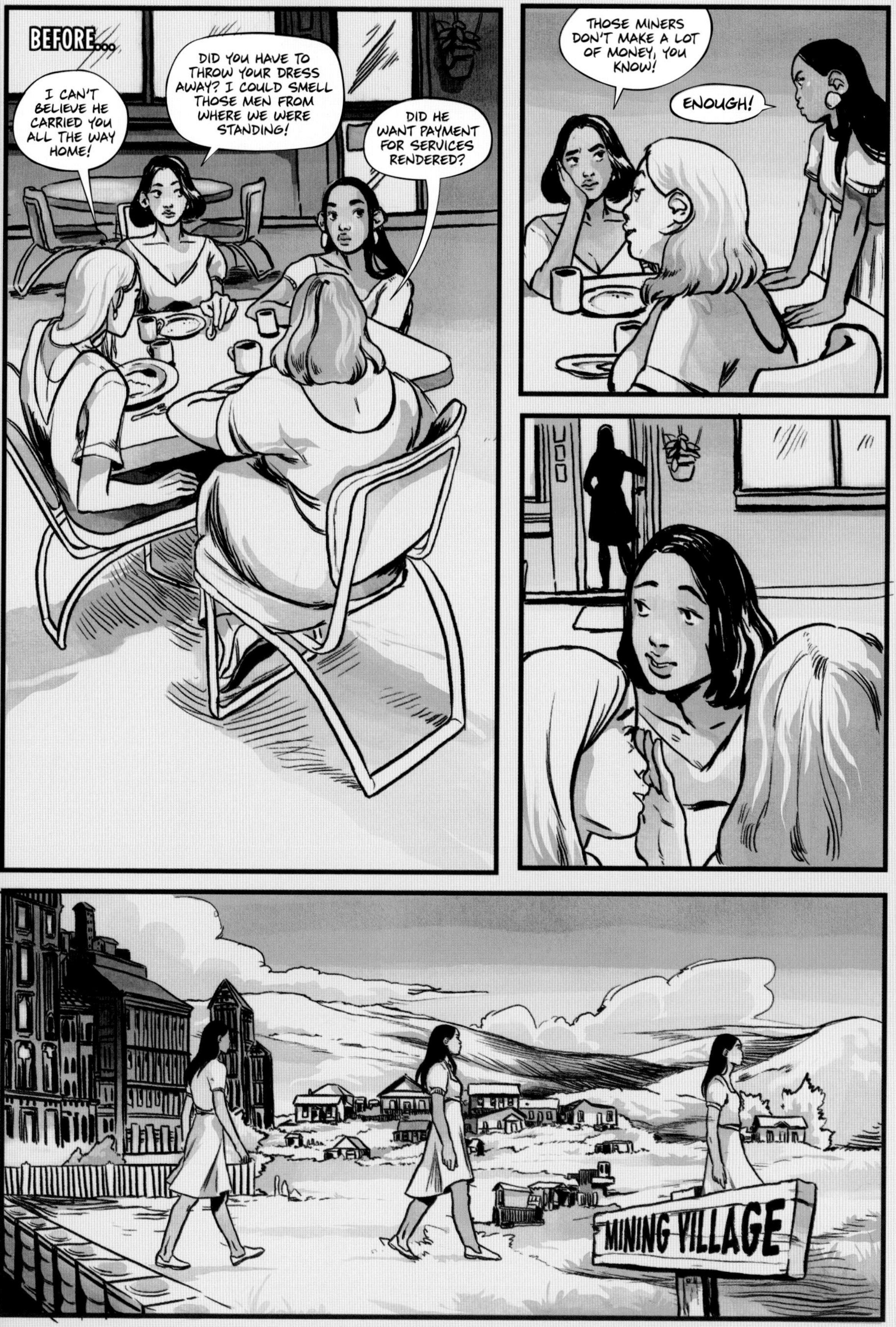
BEFORE...
I CAN'T BELIEVE HE CARRIED YOU ALL THE WAY HOME!
DID YOU HAVE TO THROW YOUR DRESS AWAY? I COULD SMELL THOSE MEN FROM WHERE WE WERE STANDING!
DID HE WANT PAYMENT FOR SERVICES RENDERED?
THOSE MINERS DON'T MAKE A LOT OF MONEY, YOU KNOW!
ENOUGH!
MINING VILLAGE

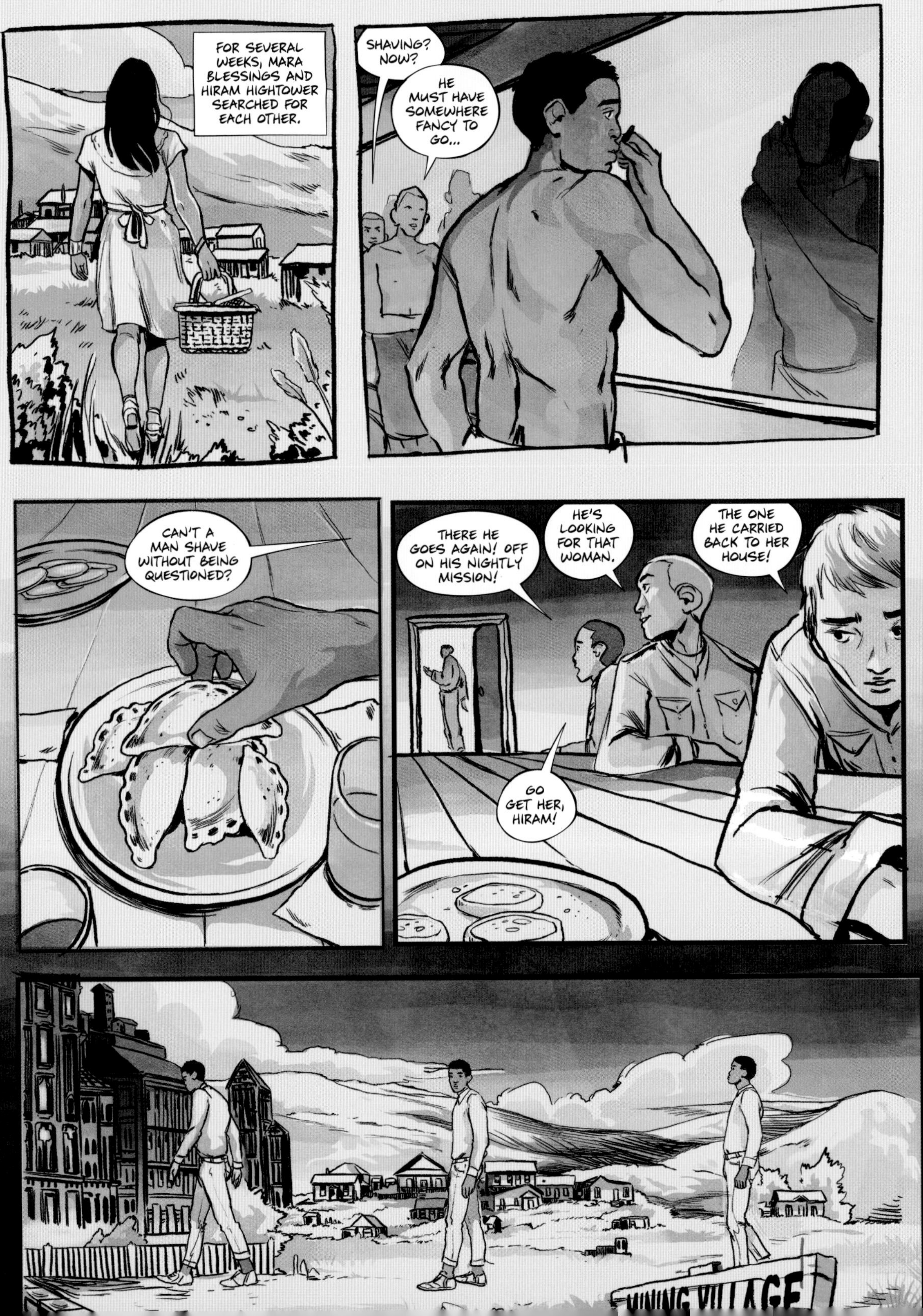
FOR SEVERAL WEEKS, MARA BLESSINGS AND HIRAM HIGHTOWER SEARCHED FOR EACH OTHER.
SHAVING? NOW?
HE MUST HAVE SOMEWHERE FANCY TO GO...
CAN'T A MAN SHAVE WITHOUT BEING QUESTIONED?
THERE HE GOES AGAIN! OFF ON HIS NIGHTLY MISSION!
HE'S LOOKING FOR THAT WOMAN.
THE ONE HE CARRIED BACK TO HER HOUSE!
GO GET HER, HIRAM!

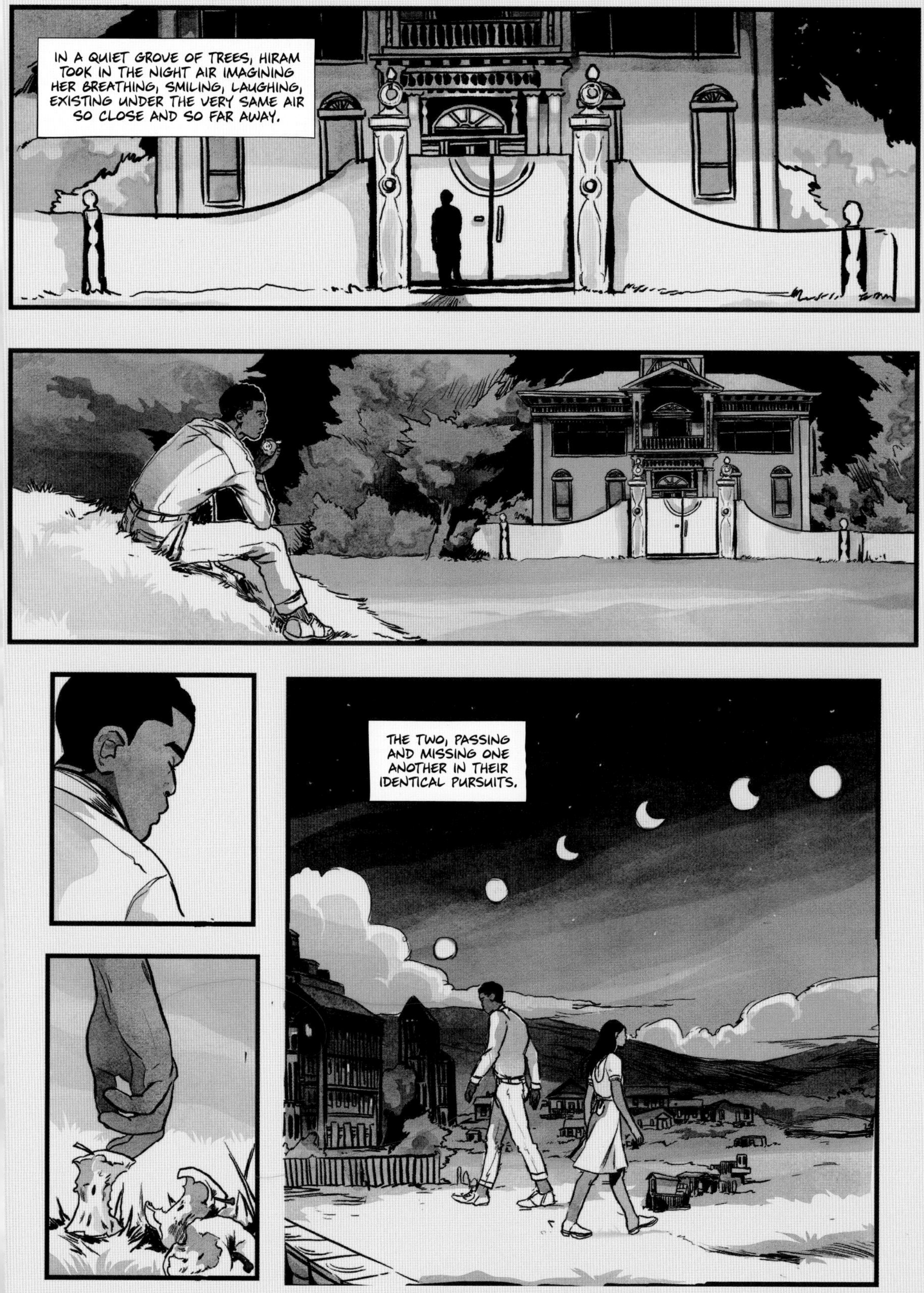
IN A QUIET GROVE OF TREES, HIRAM TOOK IN THE NIGHT AIR IMAGINING HER BREATHING, SMILING, LAUGHING, EXISTING UNDER THE VERY SAME AIR SO CLOSE AND SO FAR AWAY.
THE TWO, PASSING AND MISSING ONE ANOTHER IN THEIR IDENTICAL PURSUITS.

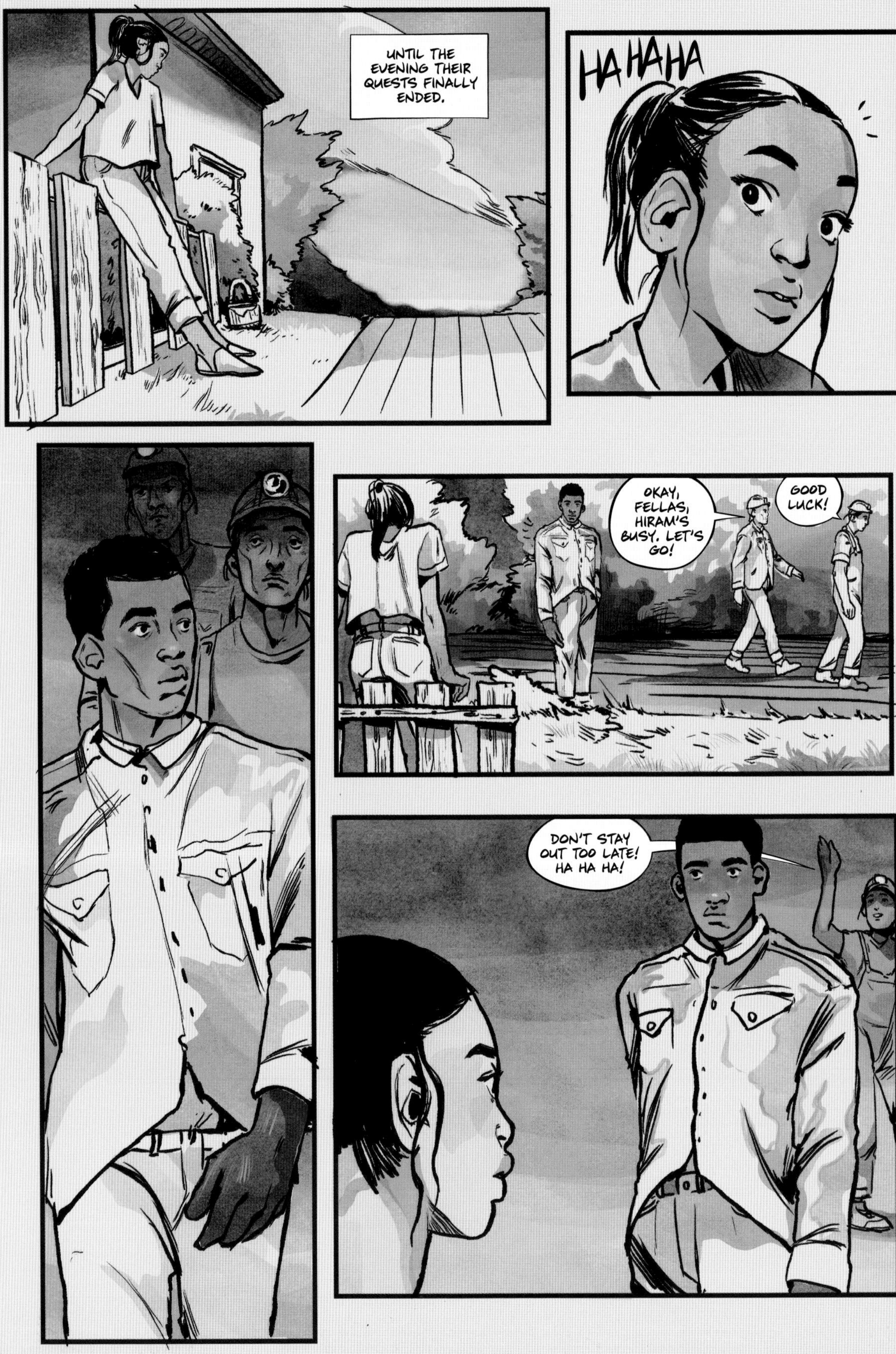
UNTIL THE EVENING THEIR QUESTS FINALLY ENDED.
HAHAHA
OKAY, FELLAS, HIRAM'S BUSY. LET'S GO!
GOOD LUCK!
DON'T STAY OUT TOO LATE! HA HA HA!

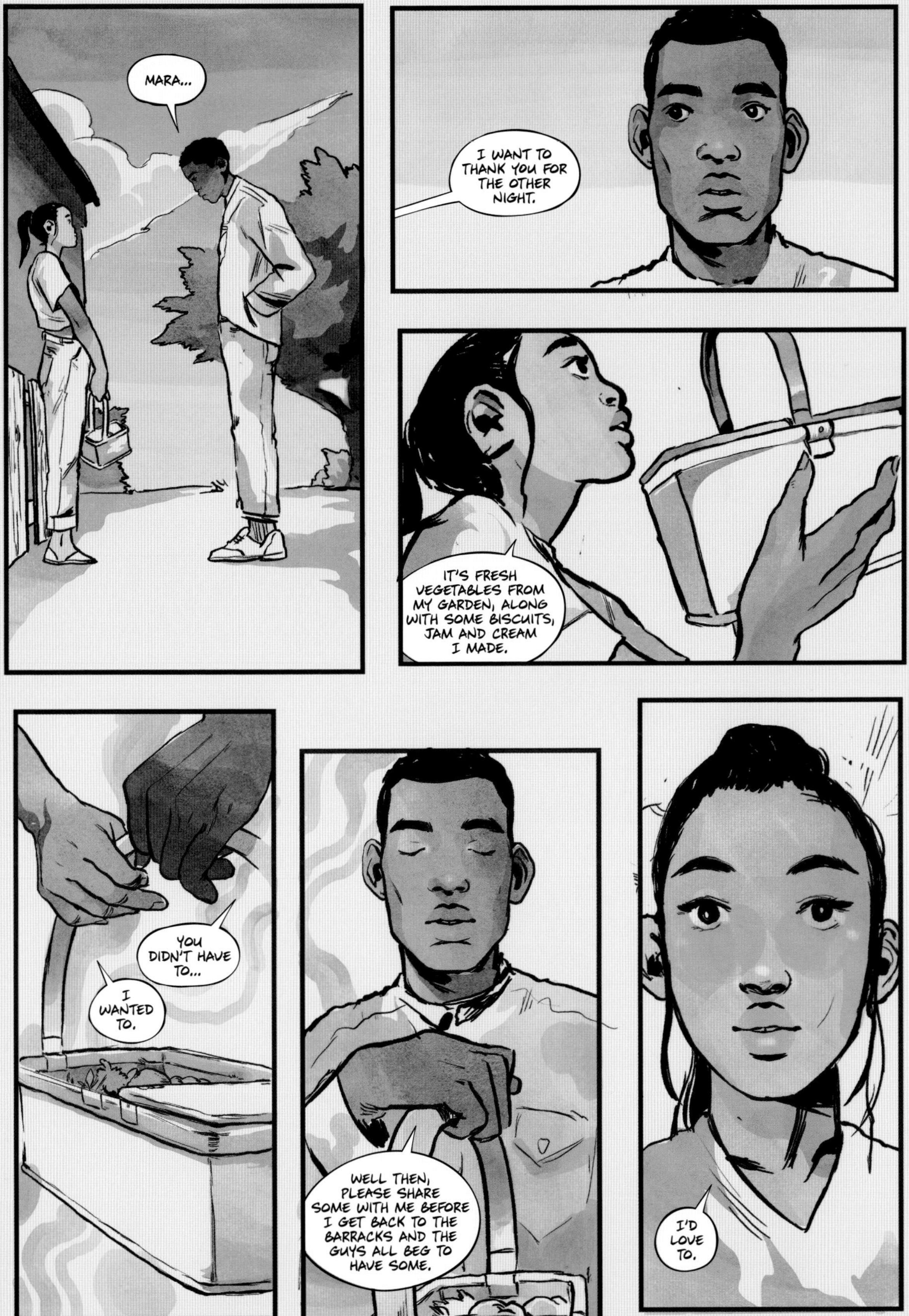
MARA...
I WANT TO THANK YOU FOR THE OTHER NIGHT.
IT'S FRESH VEGETABLES FROM MY GARDEN, ALONG WITH SOME BISCUITS, JAM AND CREAM I MADE.
YOU DIDN'T HAVE TO...
I WANTED TO.
WELL THEN, PLEASE SHARE SOME WITH ME BEFORE I GET BACK TO THE BARRACKS AND THE GUYS ALL BEG TO HAVE SOME.
I'D LOVE TO.

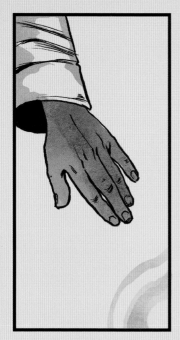

HERE YOU GO.

THIS LOOKS DELICIOUS!

THANK YOU.

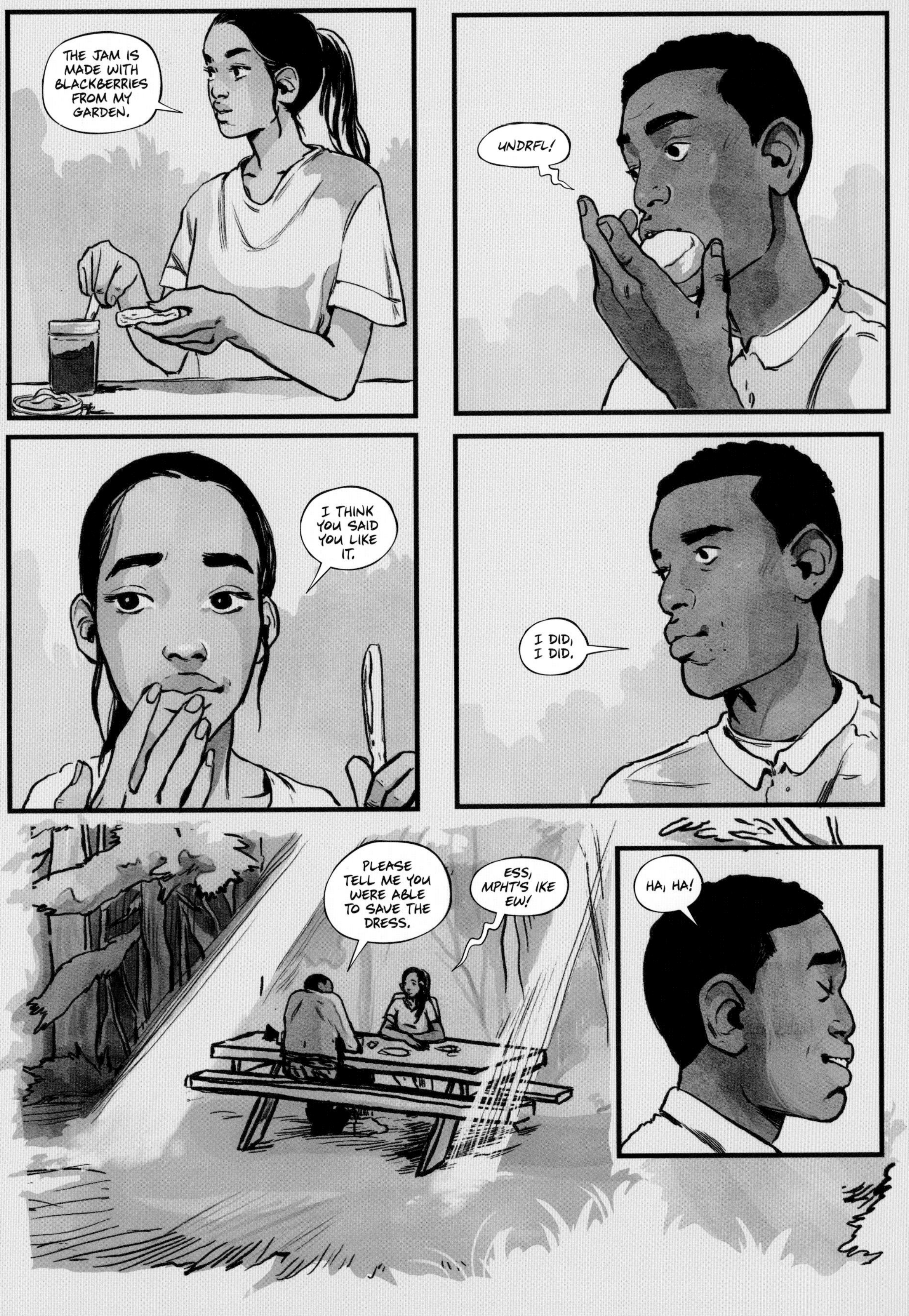
THE JAM IS MADE WITH BLACKBERRIES FROM MY GARDEN.
UNDRFL!
I THINK YOU SAID YOU LIKE IT.
I DID, I DID.
PLEASE TELL ME YOU WERE ABLE TO SAVE THE DRESS.
ESS, MPHT'S IKE EW!
HA, HA!

I THINK YOU SAID YOU SAVED IT.
I DID, I DID.
WOULD YOU LIKE SOME CREAM FOR YOUR BISCUIT?
OF COURSE. YES, PLEASE!
MMMMM...

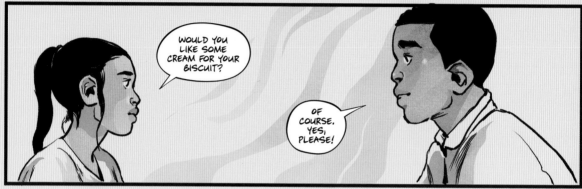

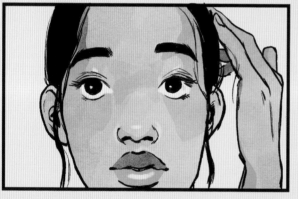

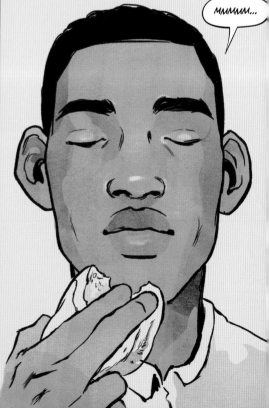

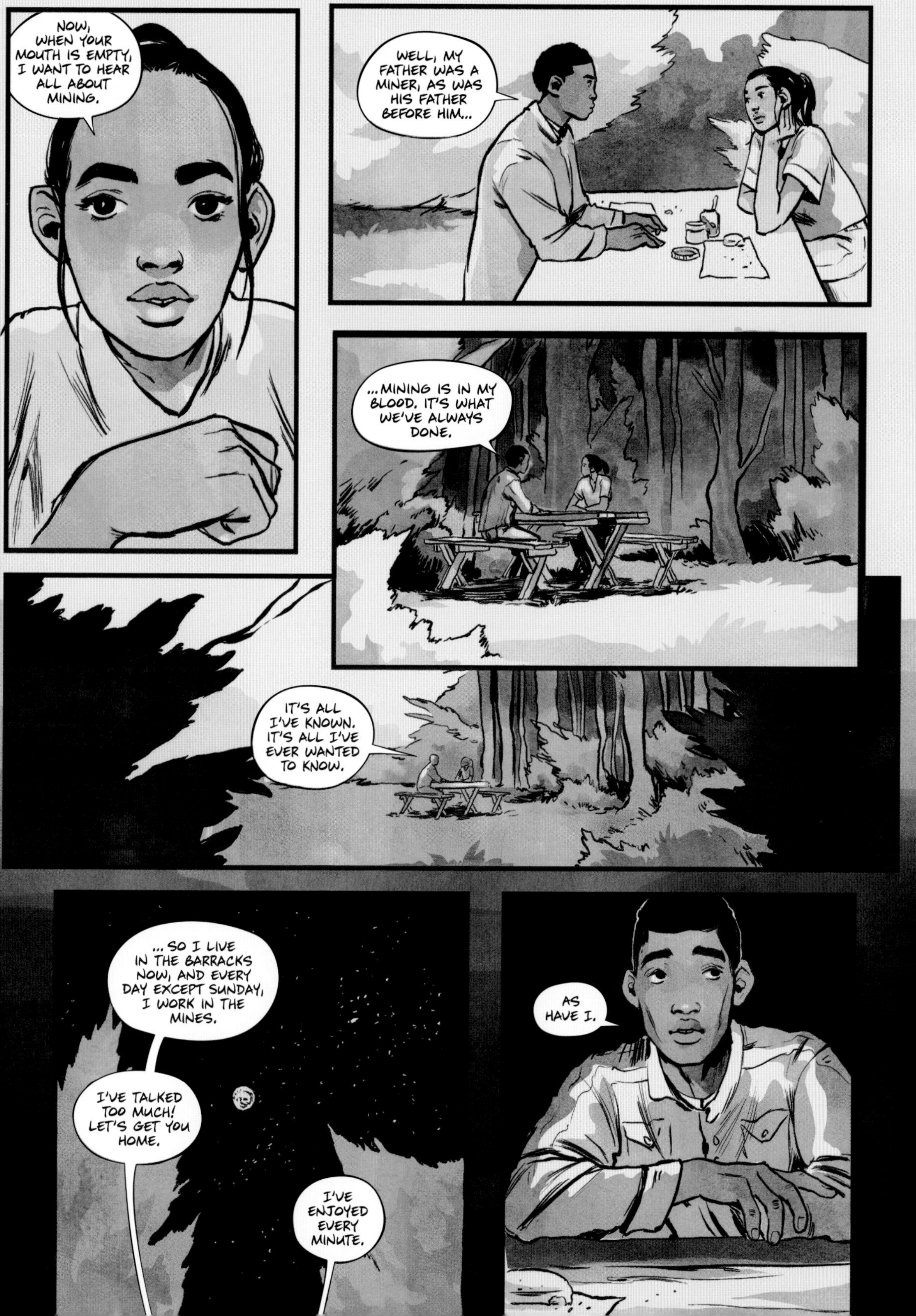
NOW, WHEN YOUR MOUTH IS EMPTY, I WANT TO HEAR ALL ABOUT MINING.
WELL, MY FATHER WAS A MINER, AS WAS HIS FATHER BEFORE HIM...
...MINING IS IN MY BLOOD. IT'S WHAT WE'VE ALWAYS DONE.
IT'S ALL I'VE KNOWN. IT'S ALL I'VE EVER WANTED TO KNOW.
... SO I LIVE IN THE BARRACKS NOW, AND EVERY DAY EXCEPT SUNDAY, I WORK IN THE MINES.
I'VE TALKED TOO MUCH! LET'S GET YOU HOME.
I'VE ENJOYED EVERY MINUTE.
AS HAVE I.

THE AWKWARD SILENCE STILLED BETWEEN THEM...

...UNTIL THE NIGHT AIR SLID IT ASIDE...

...BRINGING THE TWO...

...TOGETHER...

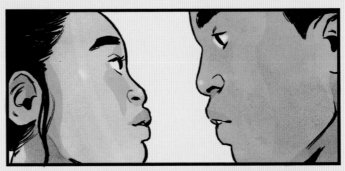

...IN A BEGINNING THAT WOULD CHANGE THE WORLD.

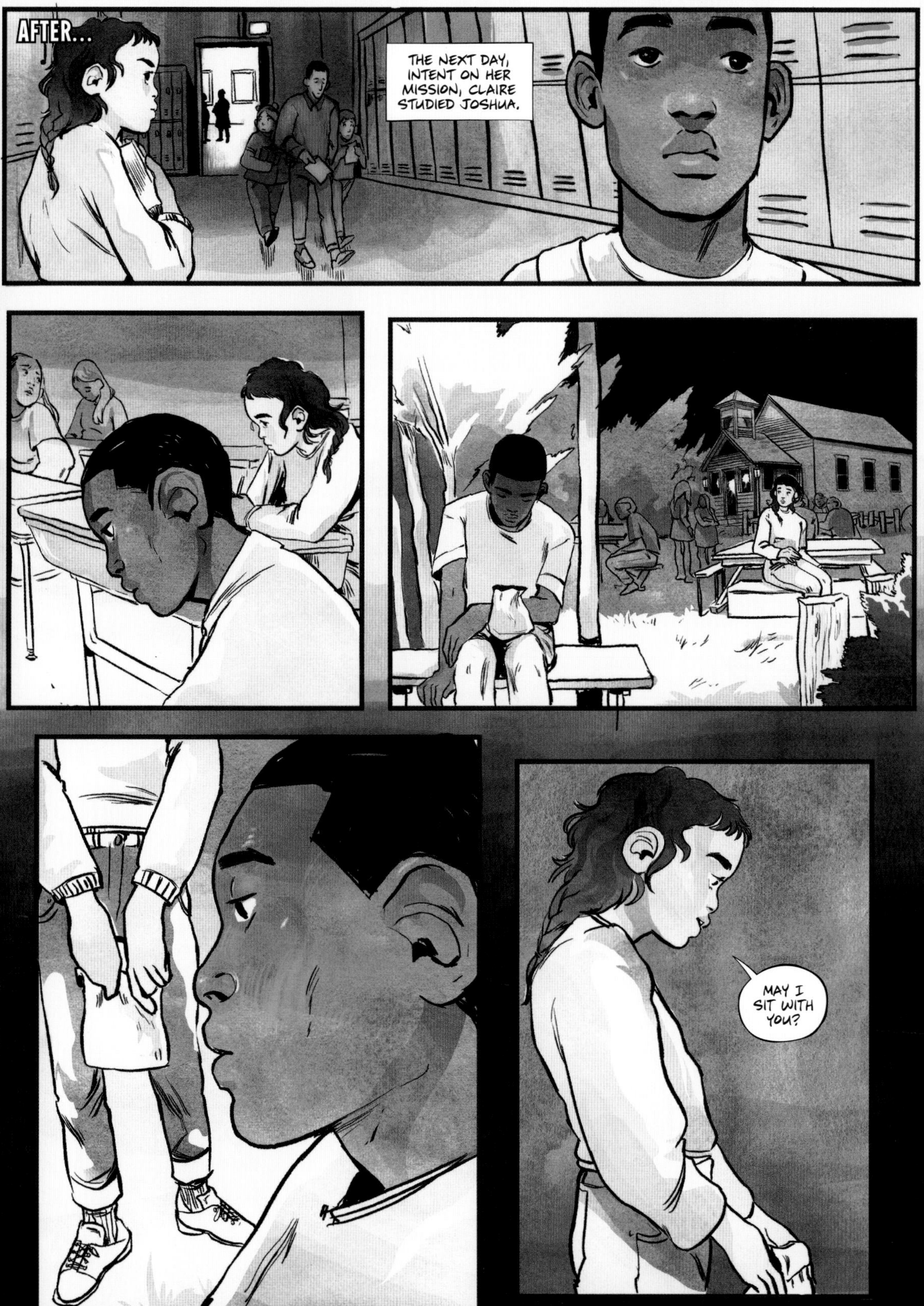
AFTER...
THE NEXT DAY, INTENT ON HER MISSION, CLAIRE STUDIED JOSHUA.
MAY I SIT WITH YOU?

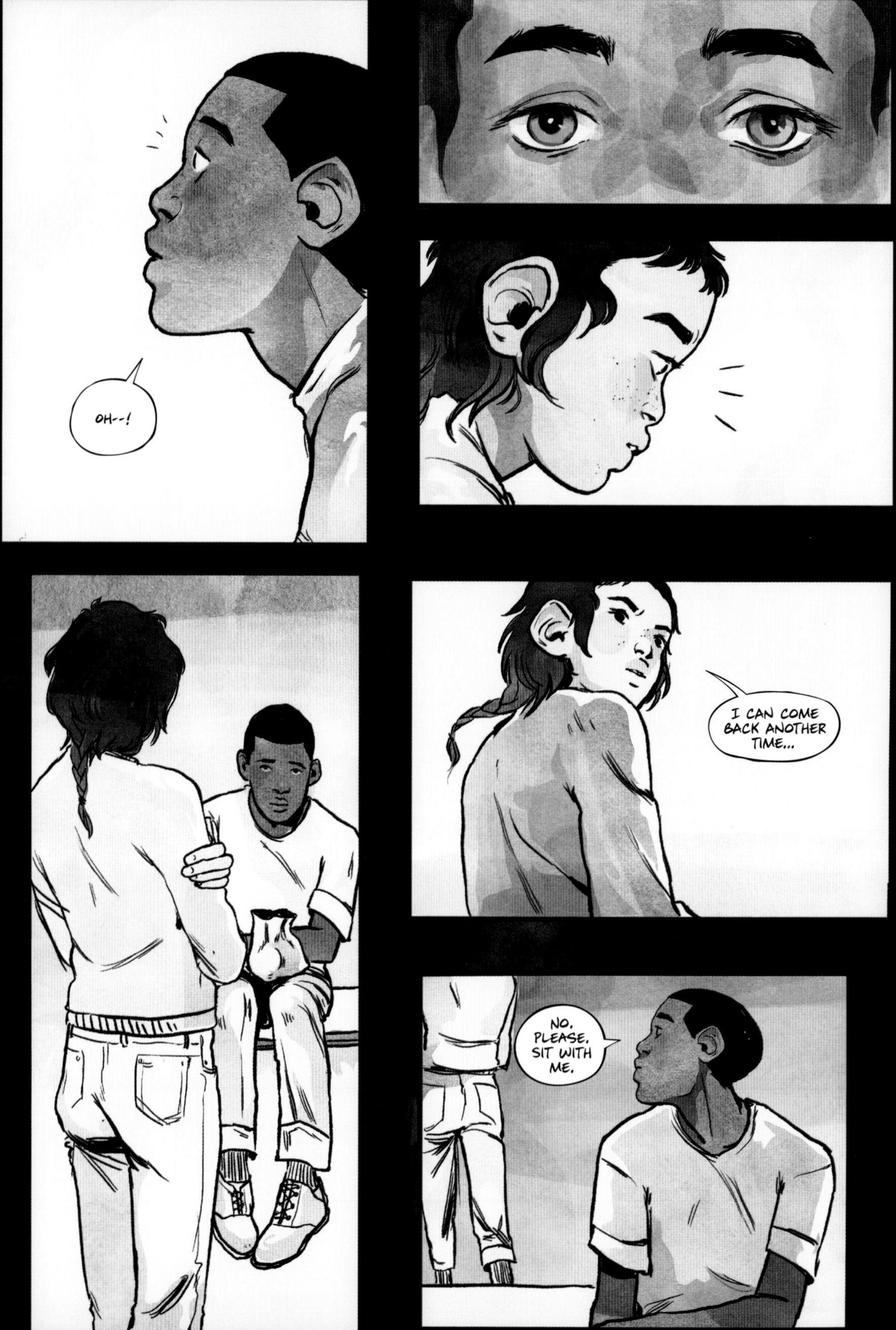
OH--!
I CAN COME BACK ANOTHER TIME...
NO. PLEASE. SIT WITH ME.

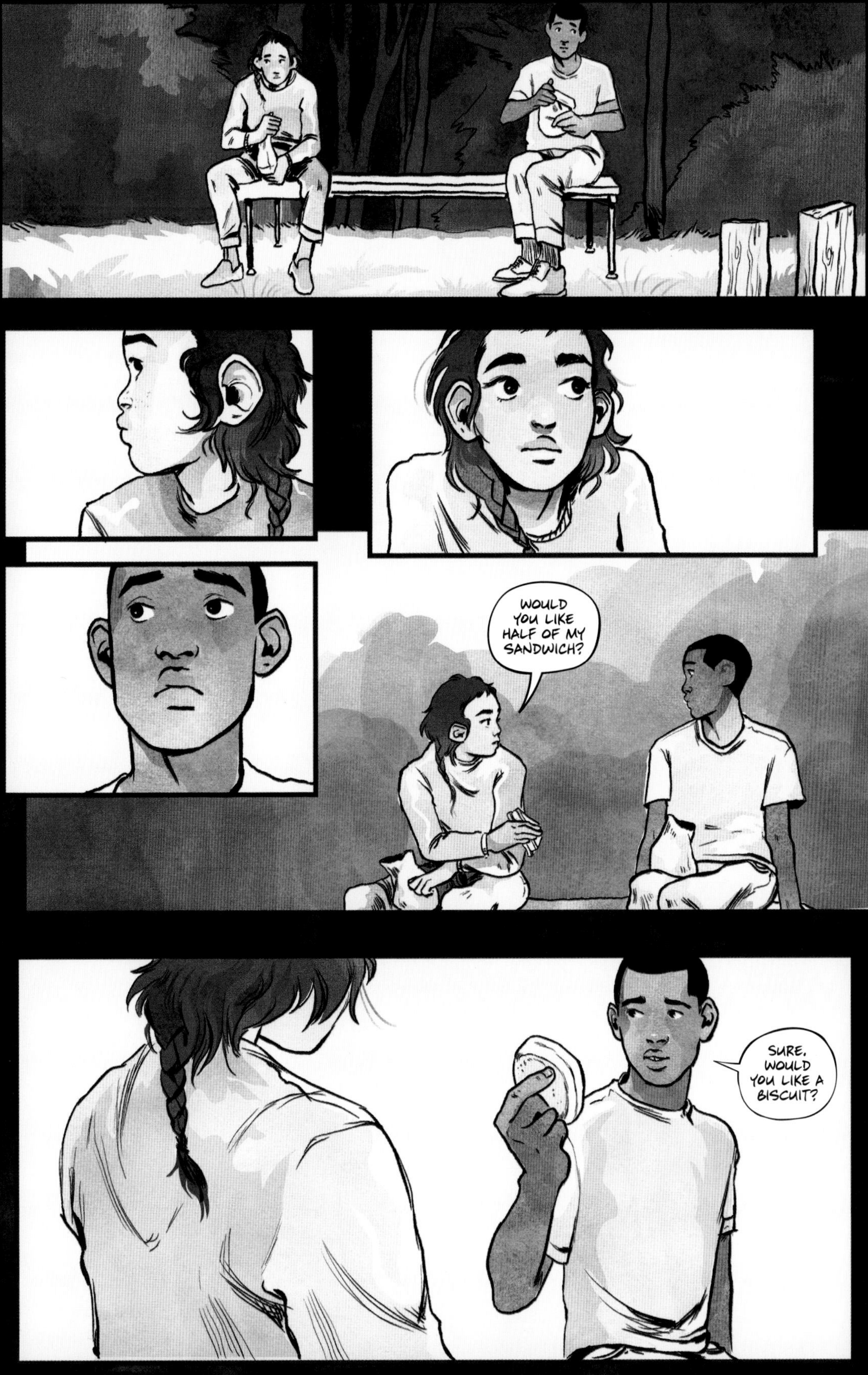
WOULD YOU LIKE HALF OF MY SANDWICH?
SURE. WOULD YOU LIKE A BISCUIT?

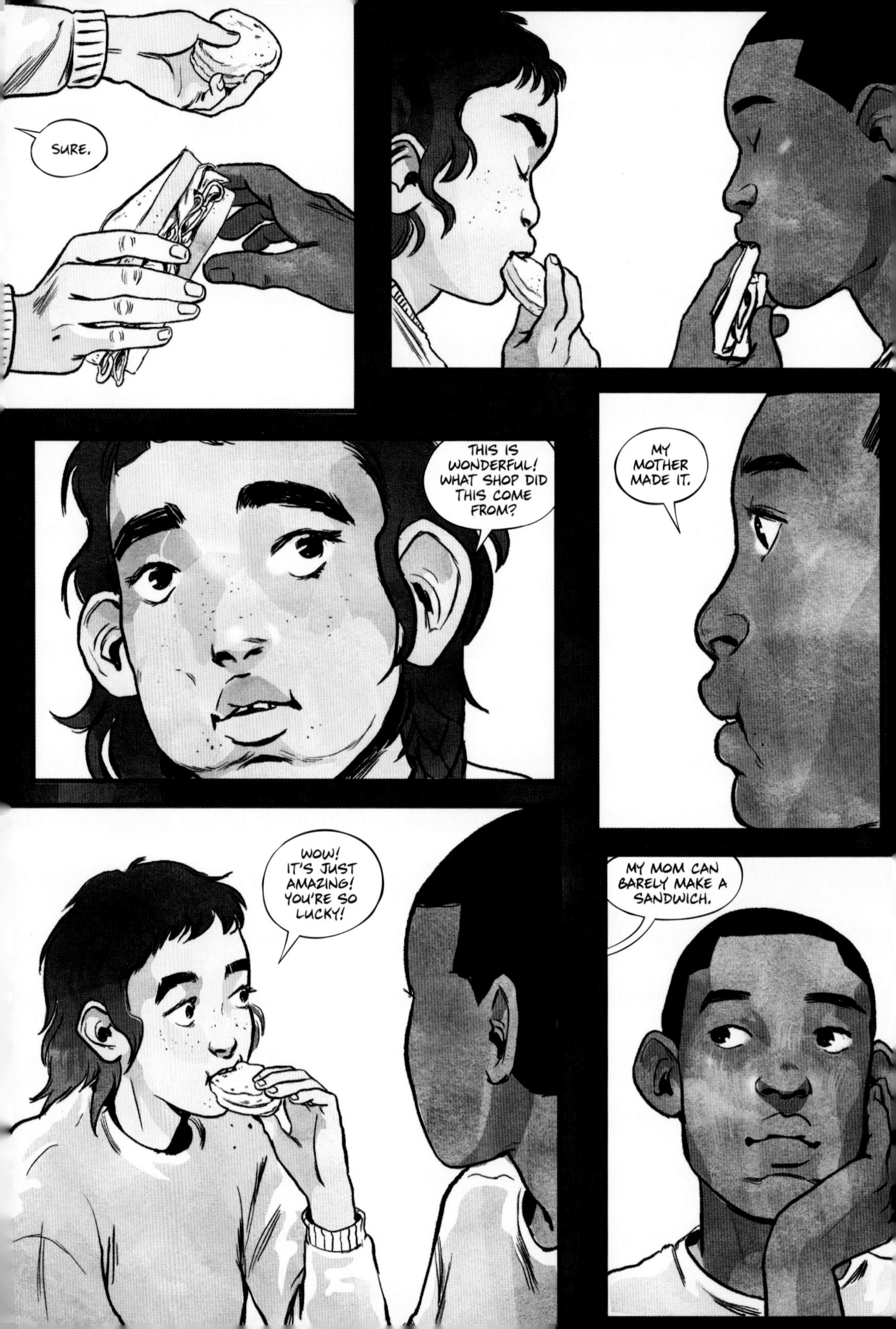
SURE.
THIS IS WONDERFUL! WHAT SHOP DID THIS COME FROM?
MY MOTHER MADE IT.
WOW! IT'S JUST AMAZING! YOU'RE SO LUCKY!
MY MOM CAN BARELY MAKE A SANDWICH.

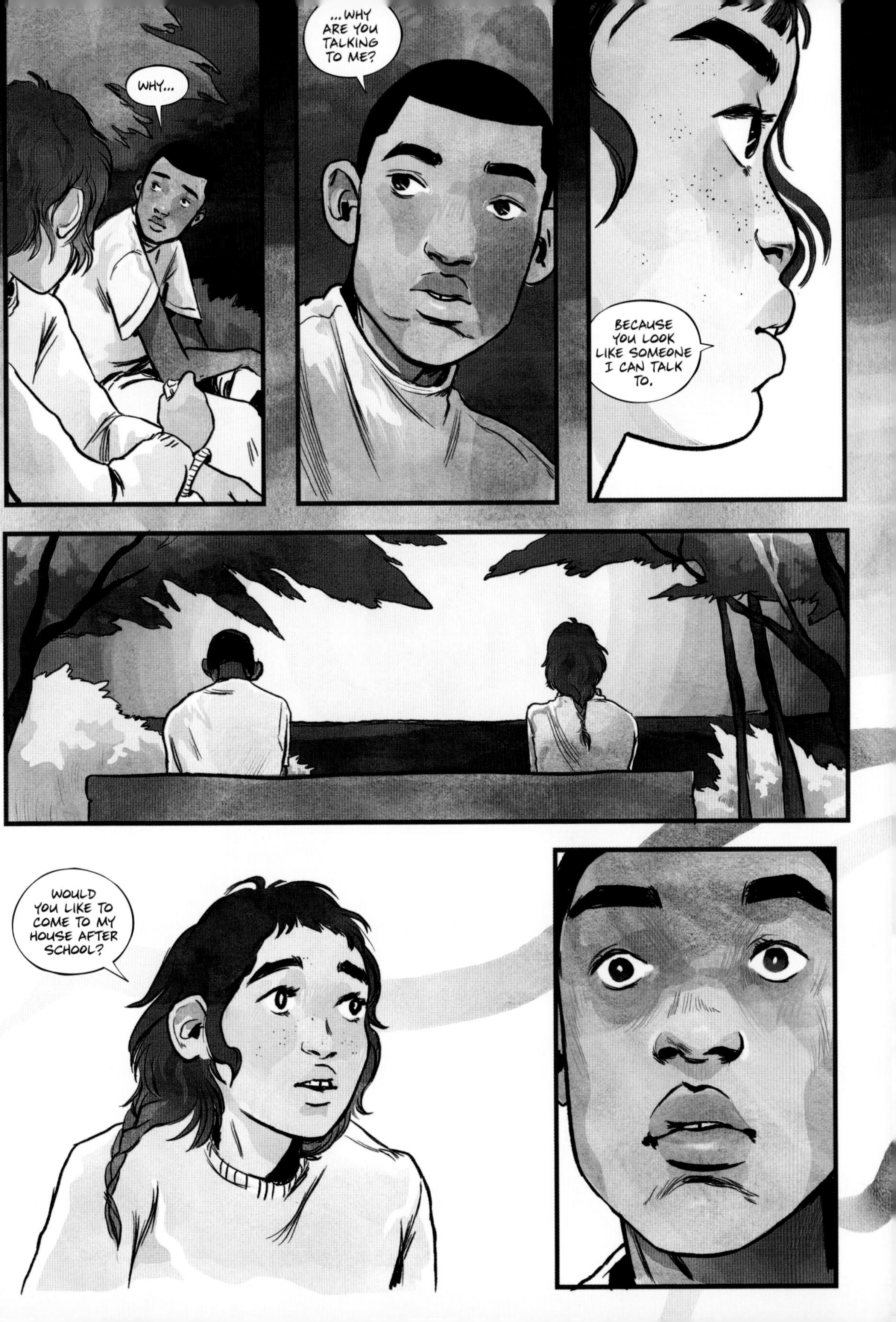
WHY...
...WHY ARE YOU TALKING TO ME?
BECAUSE YOU LOOK LIKE SOMEONE I CAN TALK TO.
WOULD YOU LIKE TO COME TO MY HOUSE AFTER SCHOOL?

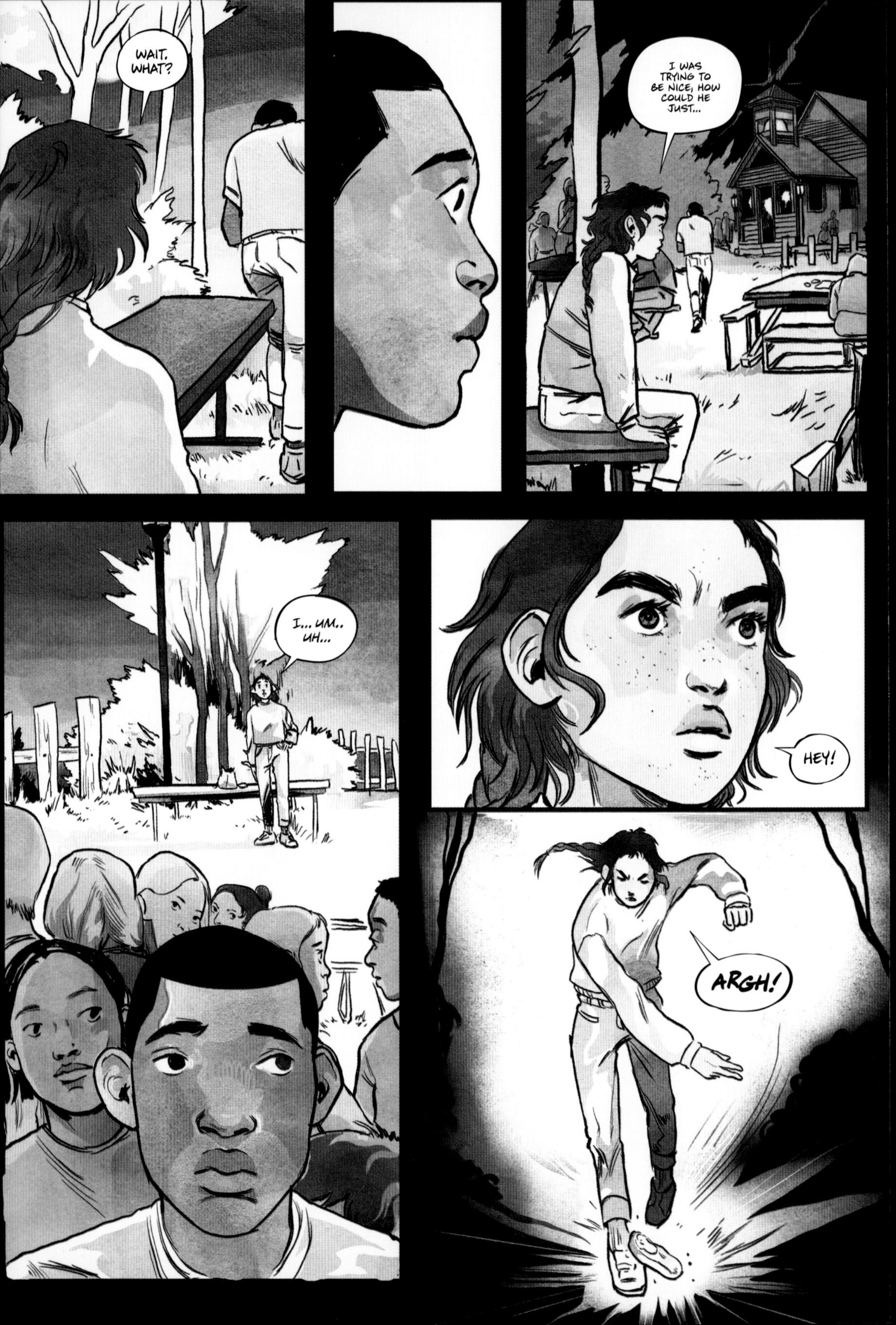
WAIT. WHAT?
I WAS TRYING TO BE NICE, HOW COULD HE JUST...
I... UM.. UH...
HEY!
ARGH!

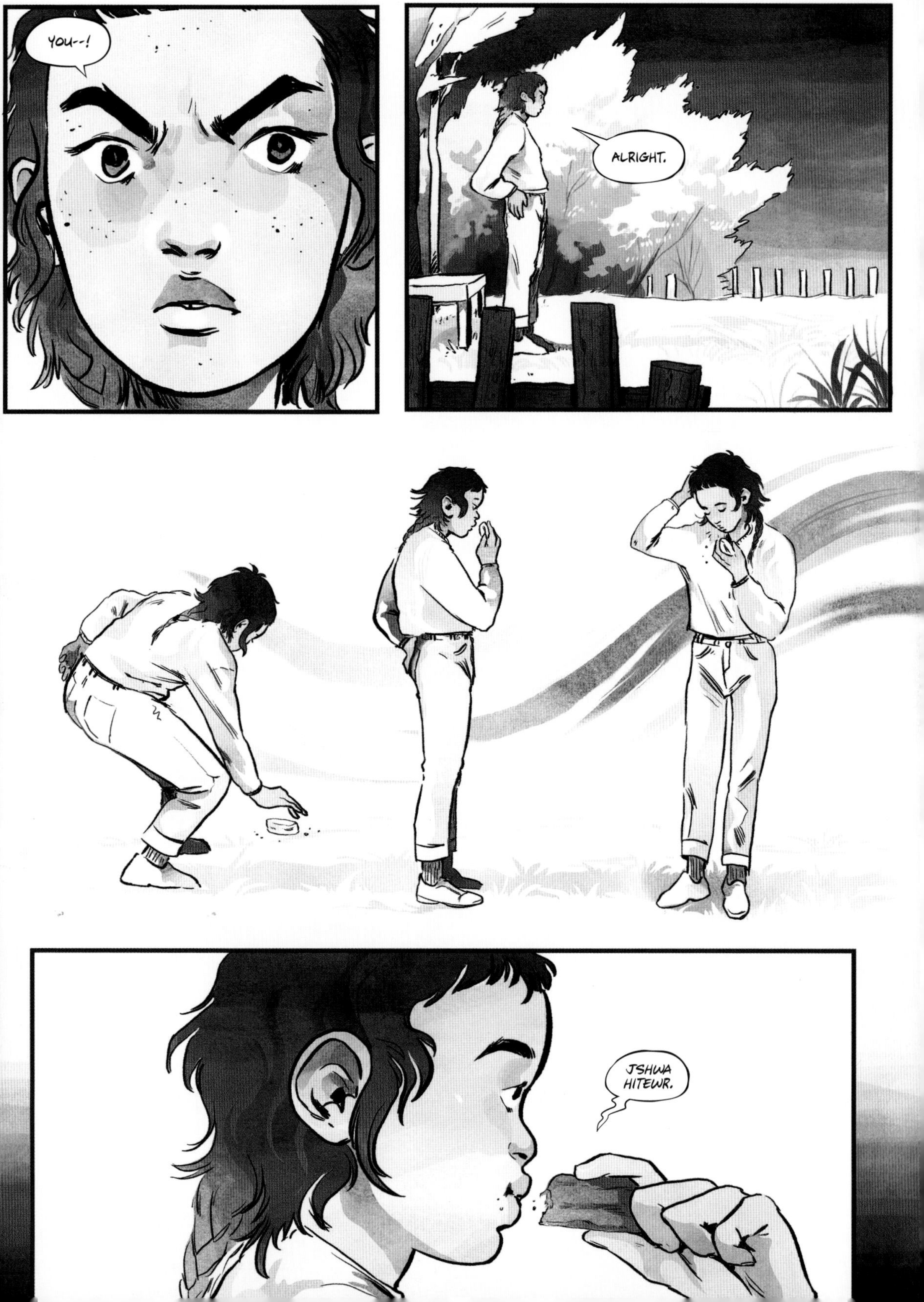
YOU--!
ALRIGHT.
JSHWA HITEWR.

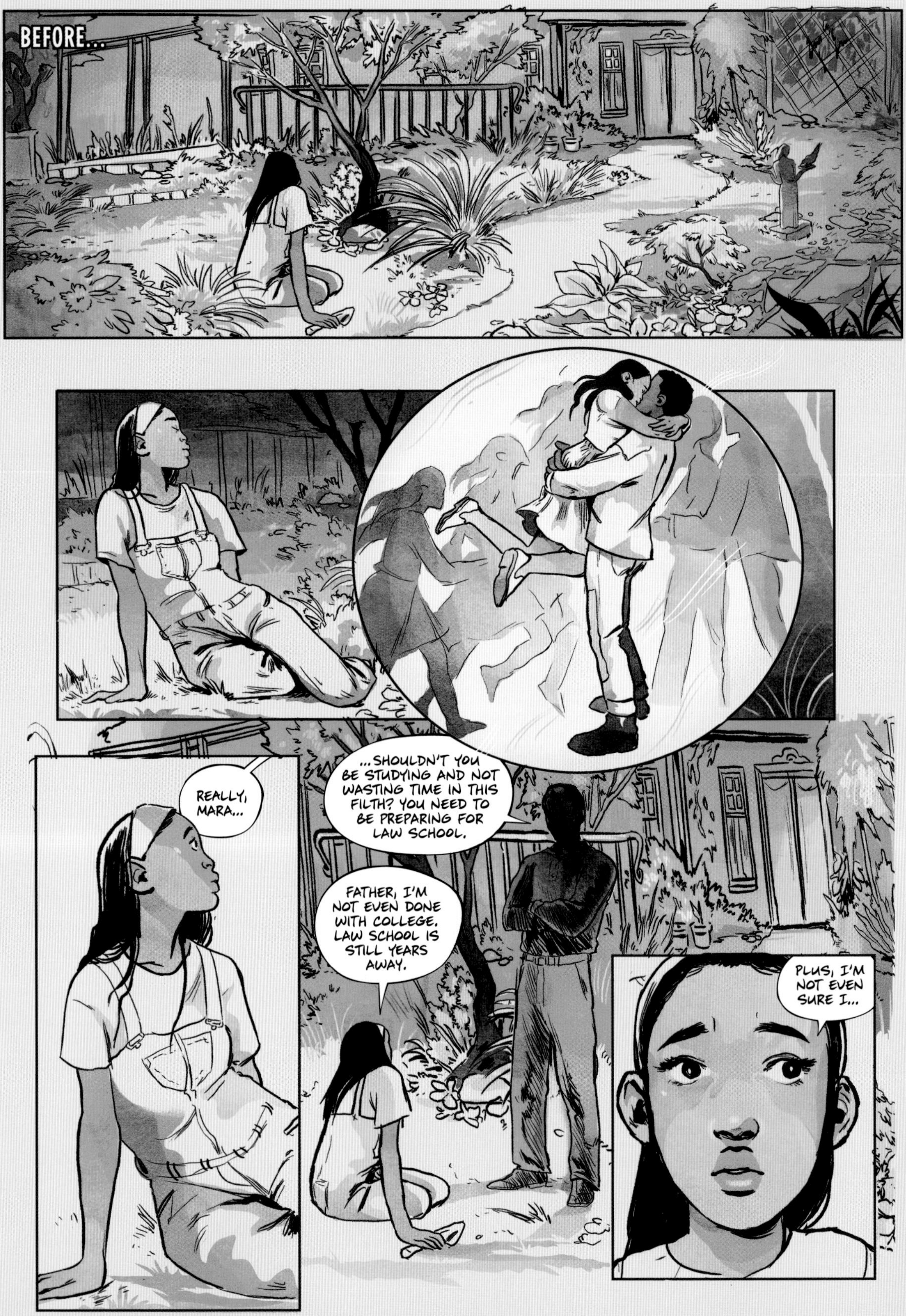
BEFORE...
REALLY, MARA...
...SHOULDN'T YOU BE STUDYING AND NOT WASTING TIME IN THIS FILTH? YOU NEED TO BE PREPARING FOR LAW SCHOOL.
FATHER, I'M NOT EVEN DONE WITH COLLEGE. LAW SCHOOL IS STILL YEARS AWAY.
PLUS, I'M NOT EVEN SURE I...

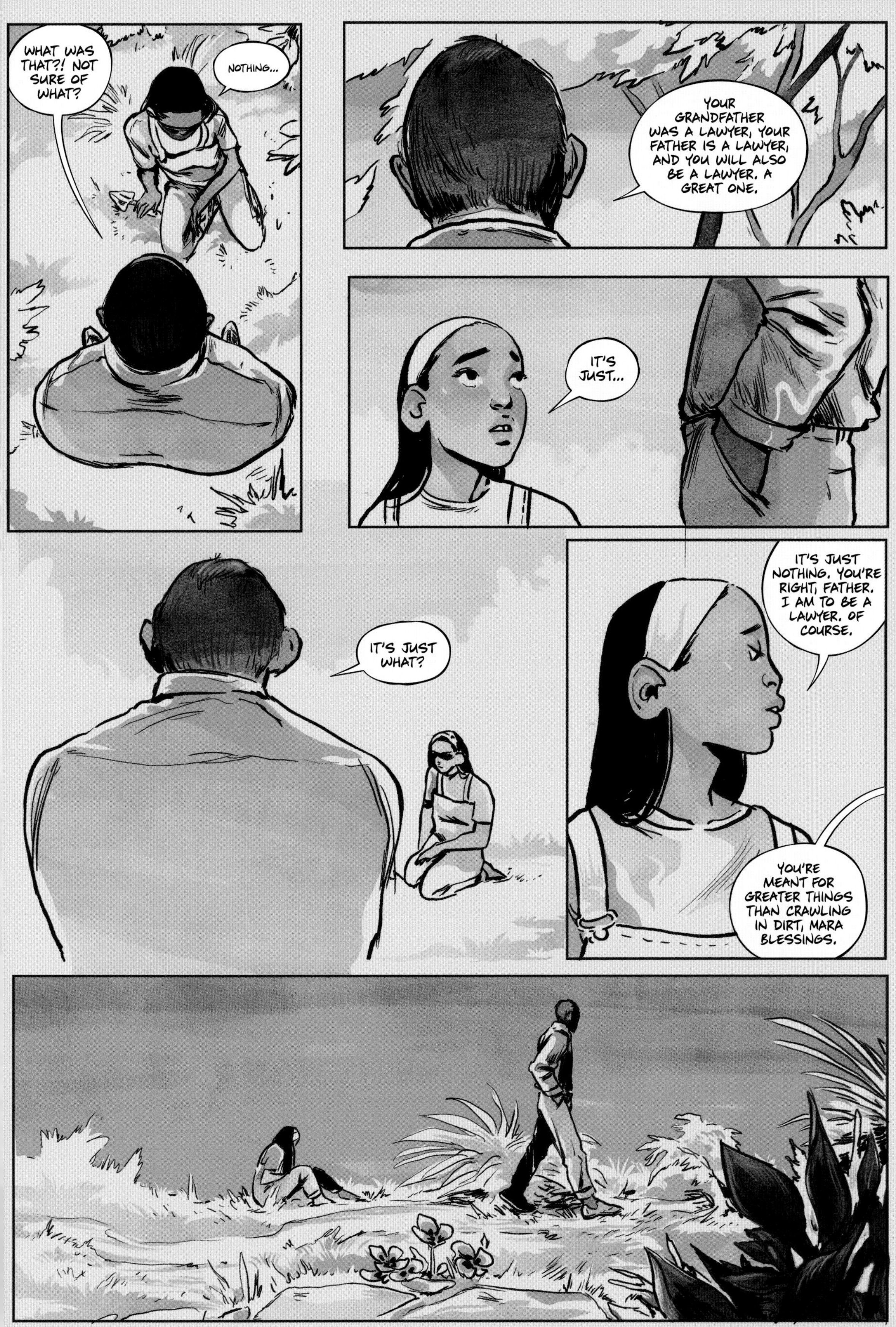
WHAT WAS THAT?! NOT SURE OF WHAT?
NOTHING...
YOUR GRANDFATHER WAS A LAWYER, YOUR FATHER IS A LAWYER, AND YOU WILL ALSO BE A LAWYER. A GREAT ONE.
IT'S JUST...
IT'S JUST WHAT?
IT'S JUST NOTHING. YOU'RE RIGHT, FATHER. I AM TO BE A LAWYER. OF COURSE.
YOU'RE MEANT FOR GREATER THINGS THAN CRAWLING IN DIRT, MARA BLESSINGS.

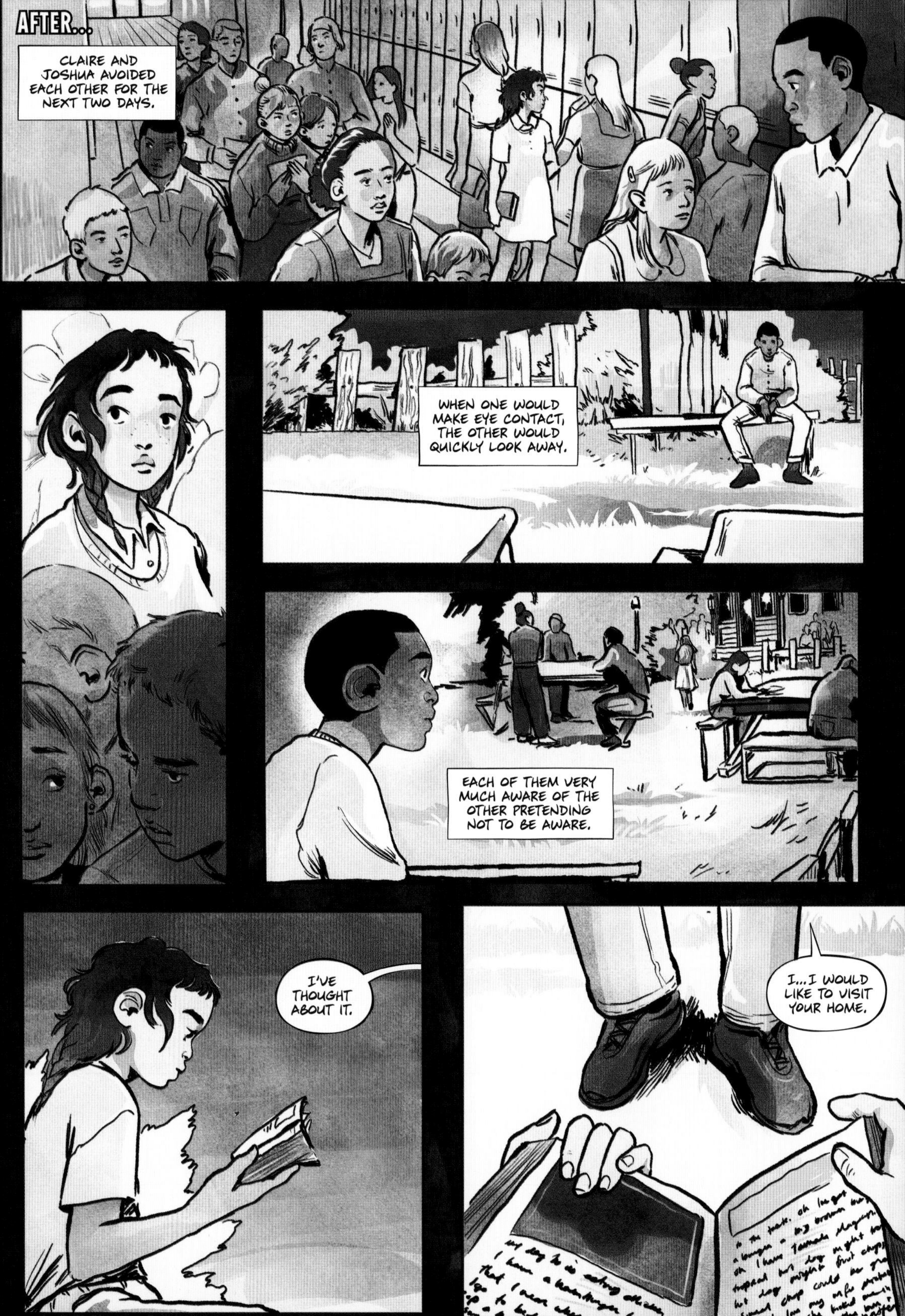
AFTER...
CLAIRE AND JOSHUA AVOIDED EACH OTHER FOR THE NEXT TWO DAYS.
WHEN ONE WOULD MAKE EYE CONTACT, THE OTHER WOULD QUICKLY LOOK AWAY.
EACH OF THEM VERY MUCH AWARE OF THE OTHER PRETENDING NOT TO BE AWARE.
I'VE THOUGHT ABOUT IT.
I... I WOULD LIKE TO VISIT YOUR HOME.

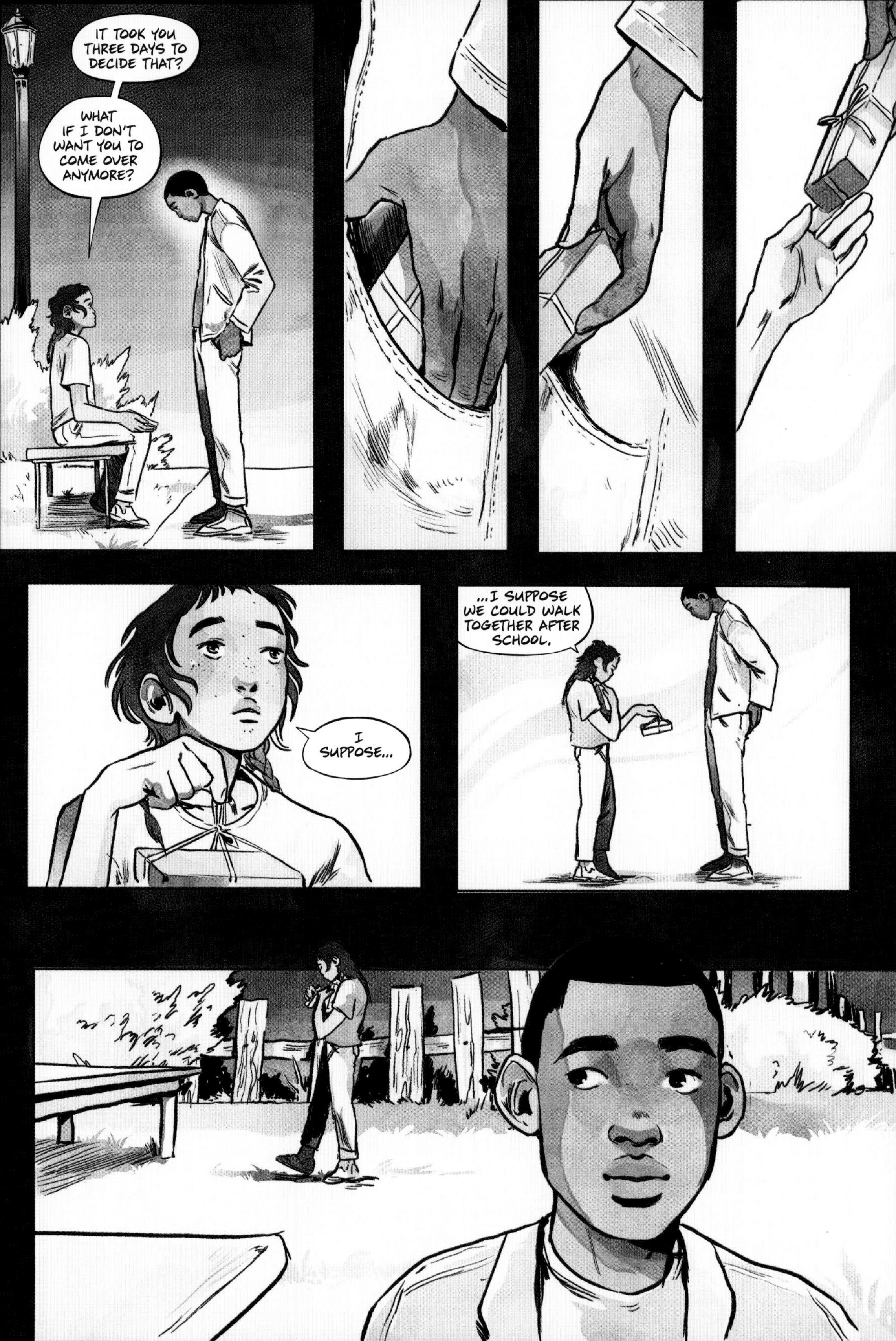
IT TOOK YOU THREE DAYS TO DECIDE THAT?
WHAT IF I DON'T WANT YOU TO COME OVER ANYMORE?
I SUPPOSE...
...I SUPPOSE WE COULD WALK TOGETHER AFTER SCHOOL.

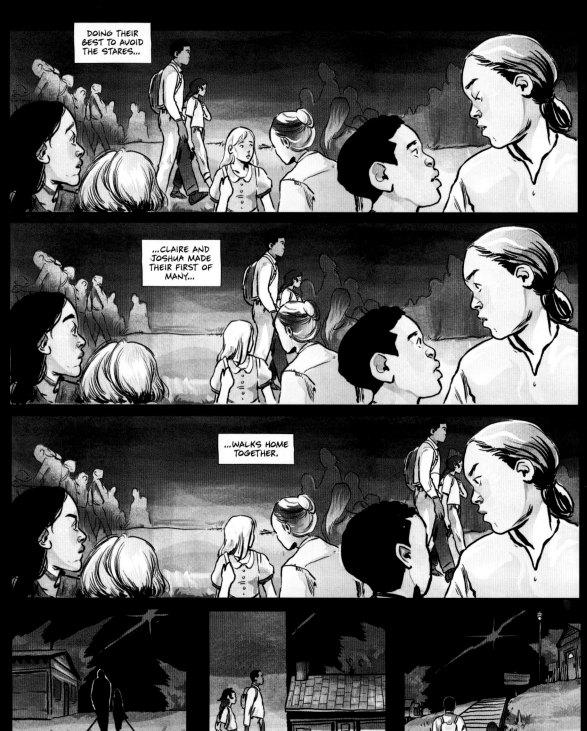

DOING THEIR BEST TO AVOID THE STARES...

...CLAIRE AND JOSHUA MADE THEIR FIRST OF MANY...

...WALKS HOME TOGETHER.

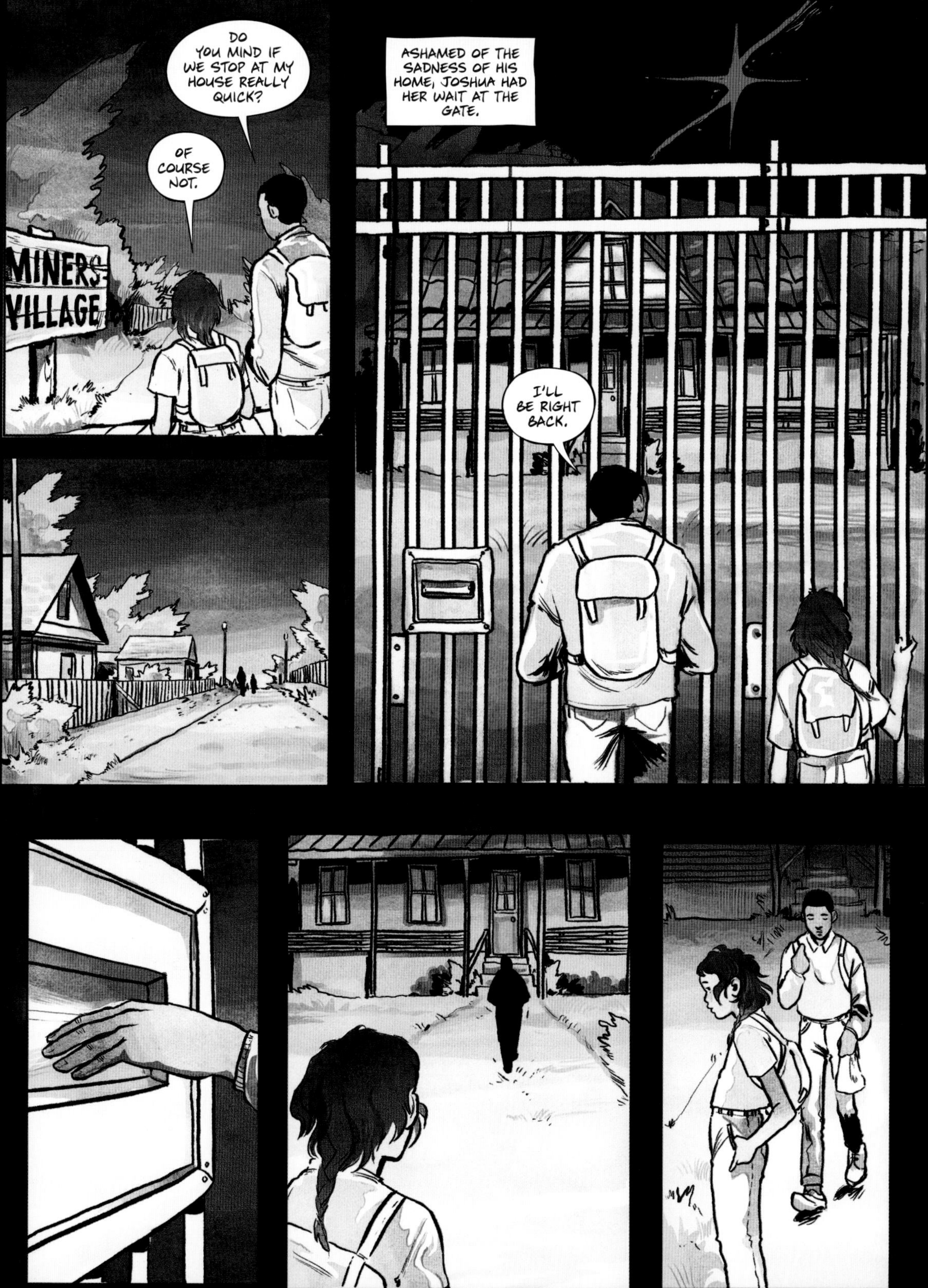
DO YOU MIND IF WE STOP AT MY HOUSE REALLY QUICK?
OF COURSE NOT.
MINERS VILLAGE
ASHAMED OF THE SADNESS OF HIS HOME, JOSHUA HAD HER WAIT AT THE GATE.
I'LL BE RIGHT BACK.

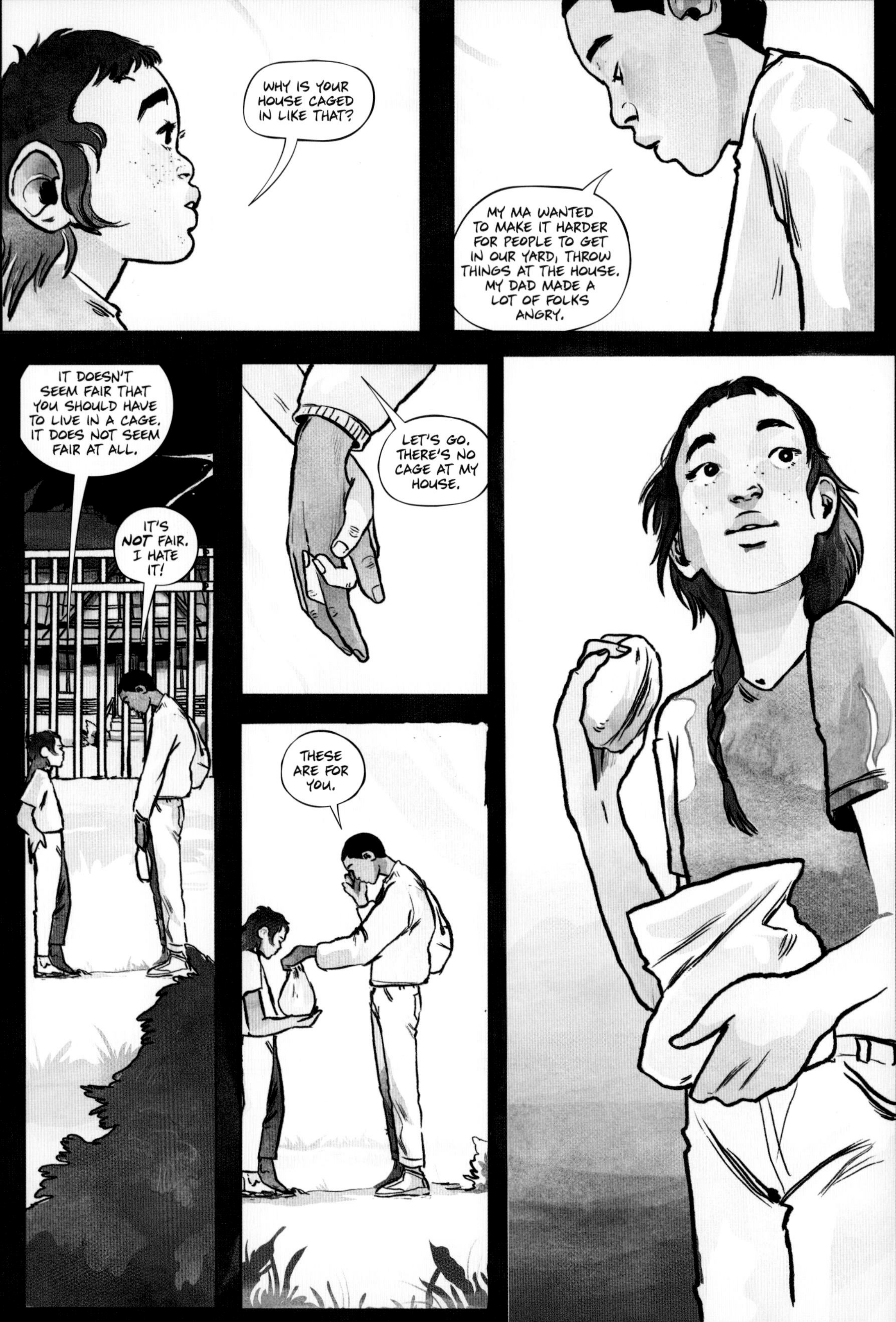
WHY IS YOUR HOUSE CAGED IN LIKE THAT?
MY MA WANTED TO MAKE IT HARDER FOR PEOPLE TO GET IN OUR YARD, THROW THINGS AT THE HOUSE. MY DAD MADE A LOT OF FOLKS ANGRY.
IT DOESN'T SEEM FAIR THAT YOU SHOULD HAVE TO LIVE IN A CAGE. IT DOES NOT SEEM FAIR AT ALL.
IT'S NOT FAIR. I HATE IT!
LET'S GO. THERE'S NO CAGE AT MY HOUSE.
THESE ARE FOR YOU.

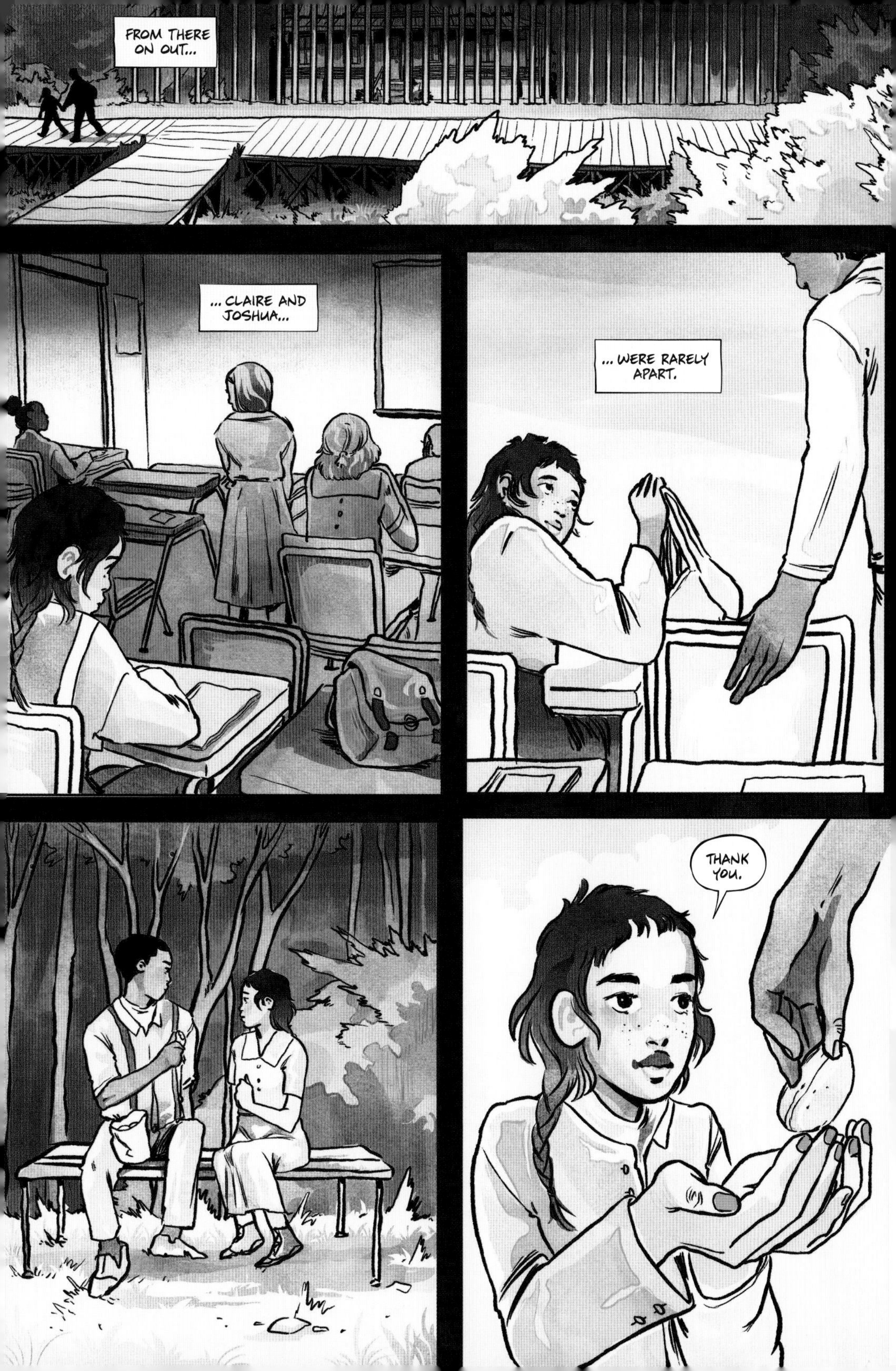
FROM THERE ON OUT...
...CLAIRE AND JOSHUA...
...WERE RARELY APART.
THANK YOU.

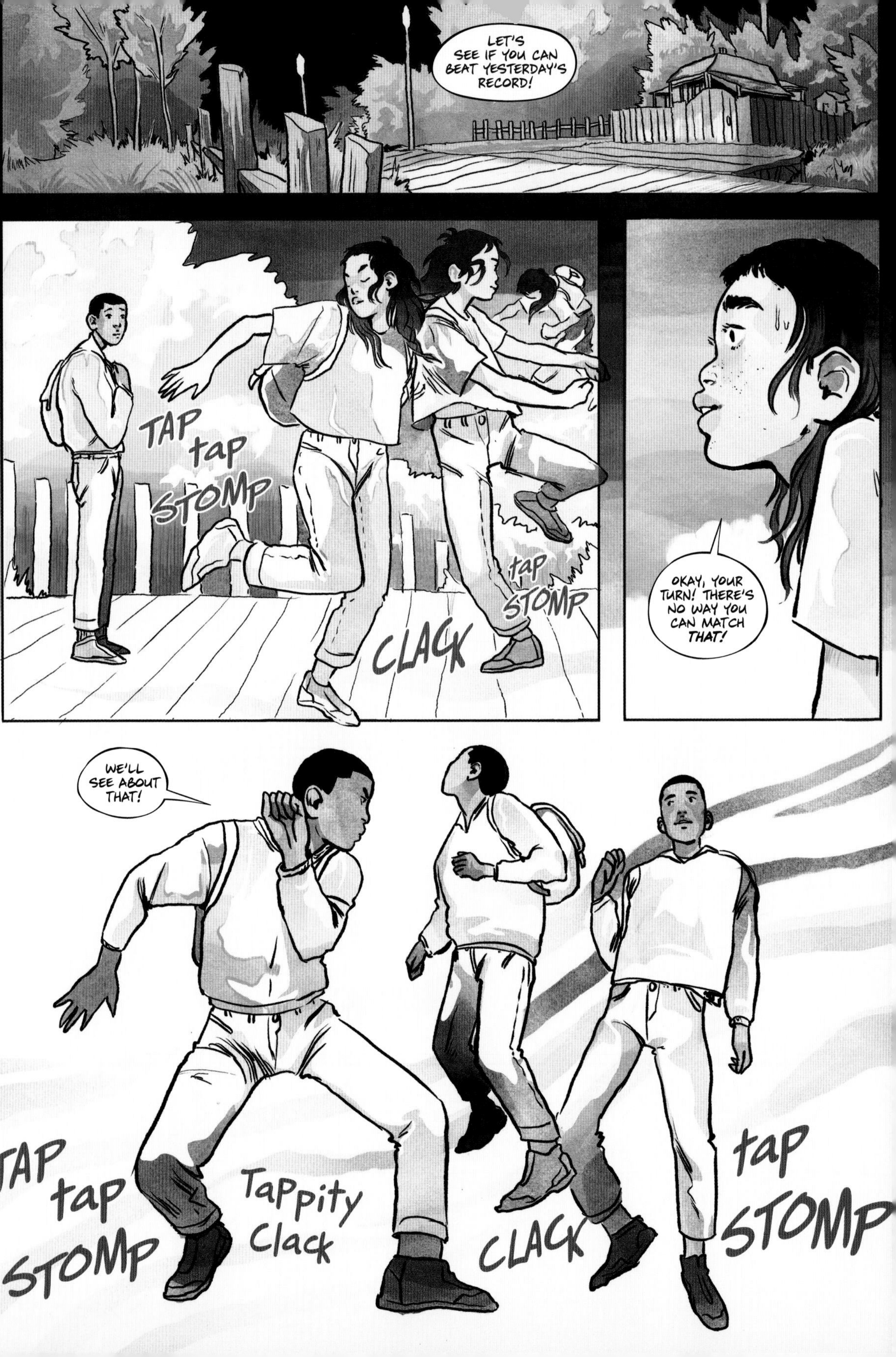
LET'S SEE IF YOU CAN BEAT YESTERDAY'S RECORD!
TAP tap STOMP
tap STOMP
CLACK
OKAY, YOUR TURN! THERE'S NO WAY YOU CAN MATCH THAT!
WE'LL SEE ABOUT THAT!
TAP tap STOMP
Tappity Clack
CLACK
tap STOMP

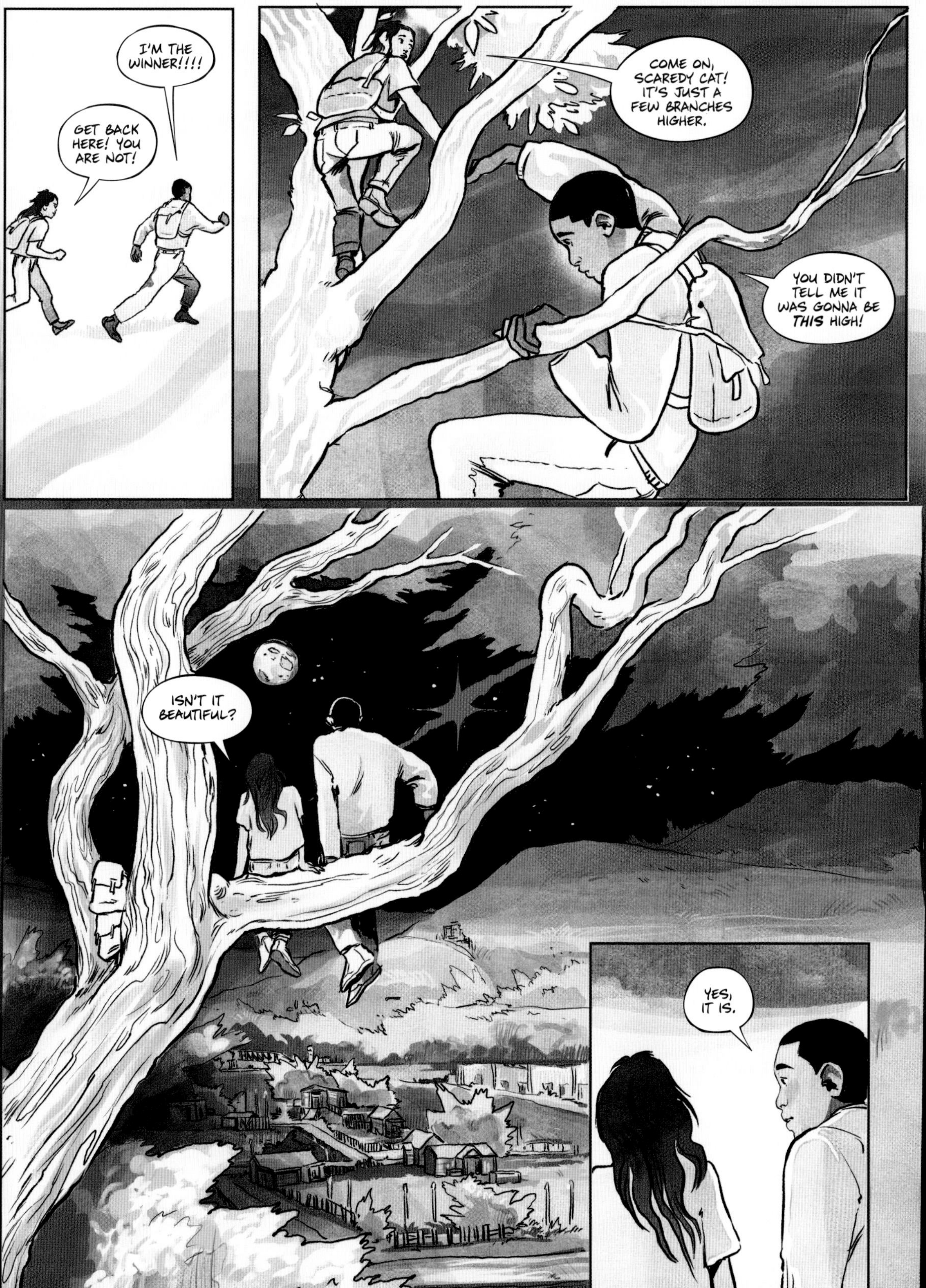
I'M THE WINNER!!!!
GET BACK HERE! YOU ARE NOT!
COME ON, SCAREDY CAT! IT'S JUST A FEW BRANCHES HIGHER.
YOU DIDN'T TELL ME IT WAS GONNA BE THIS HIGH!
ISN'T IT BEAUTIFUL?
YES, IT IS.

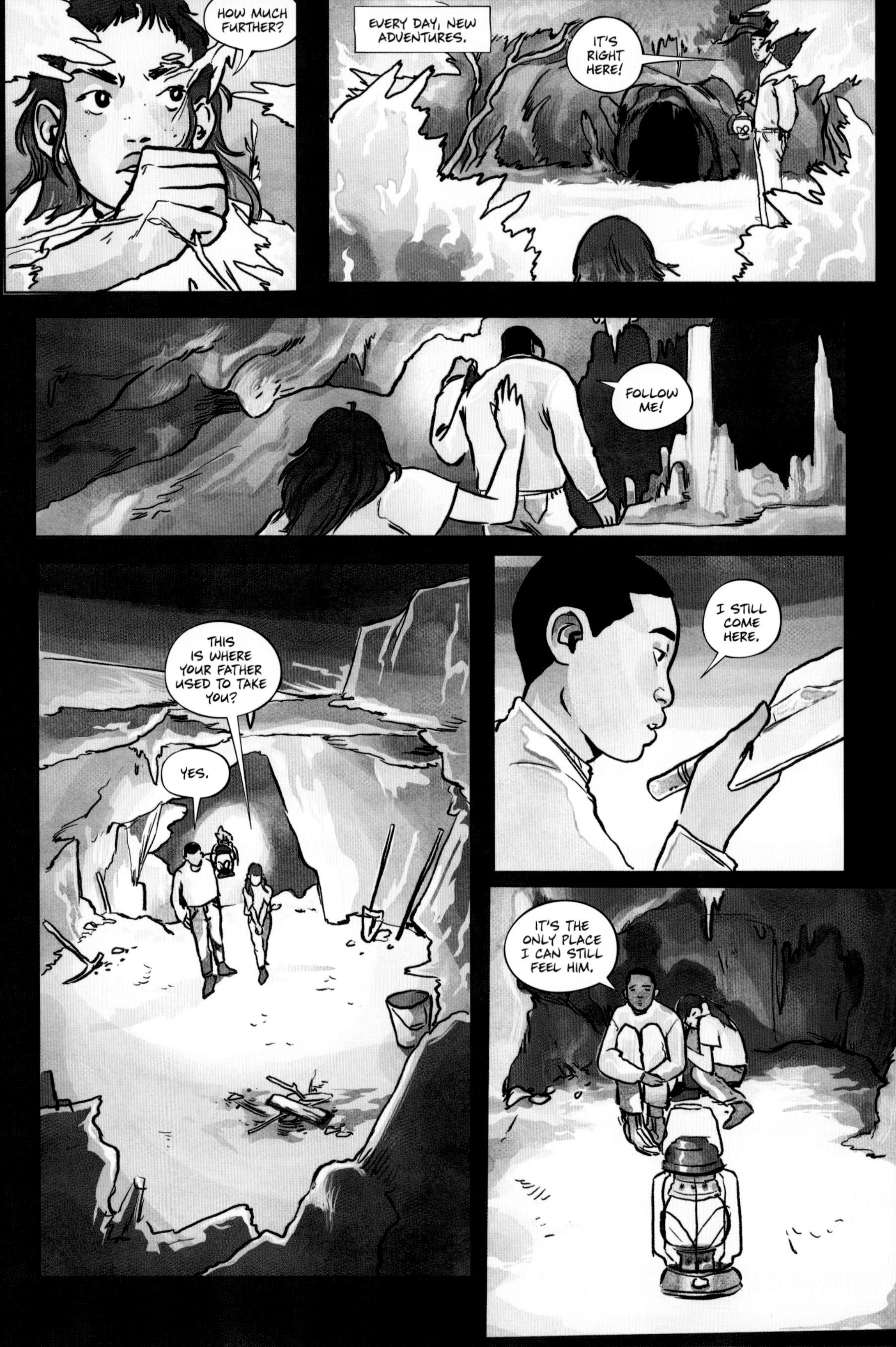
HOW MUCH FURTHER?
EVERY DAY, NEW ADVENTURES.
IT'S RIGHT HERE!
FOLLOW ME!
THIS IS WHERE YOUR FATHER USED TO TAKE YOU?
YES.
I STILL COME HERE.
IT'S THE ONLY PLACE I CAN STILL FEEL HIM.

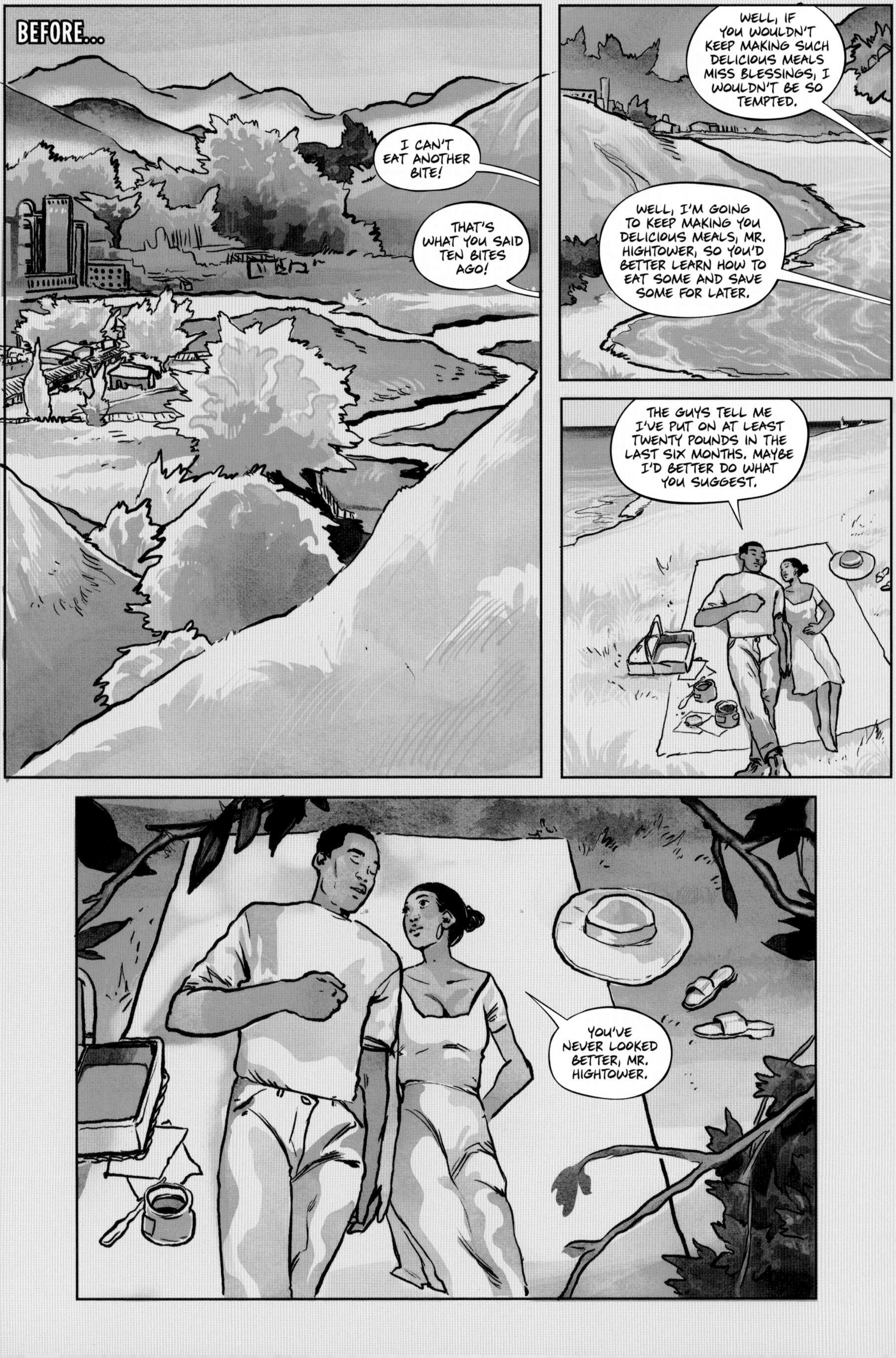
BEFORE...
I CAN'T EAT ANOTHER BITE!
THAT'S WHAT YOU SAID TEN BITES AGO!
WELL, IF YOU WOULDN'T KEEP MAKING SUCH DELICIOUS MEALS MISS BLESSINGS, I WOULDN'T BE SO TEMPTED.
WELL, I'M GOING TO KEEP MAKING YOU DELICIOUS MEALS, MR. HIGHTOWER, SO YOU'D BETTER LEARN HOW TO EAT SOME AND SAVE SOME FOR LATER.
THE GUYS TELL ME I'VE PUT ON AT LEAST TWENTY POUNDS IN THE LAST SIX MONTHS. MAYBE I'D BETTER DO WHAT YOU SUGGEST.
YOU'VE NEVER LOOKED BETTER, MR. HIGHTOWER.

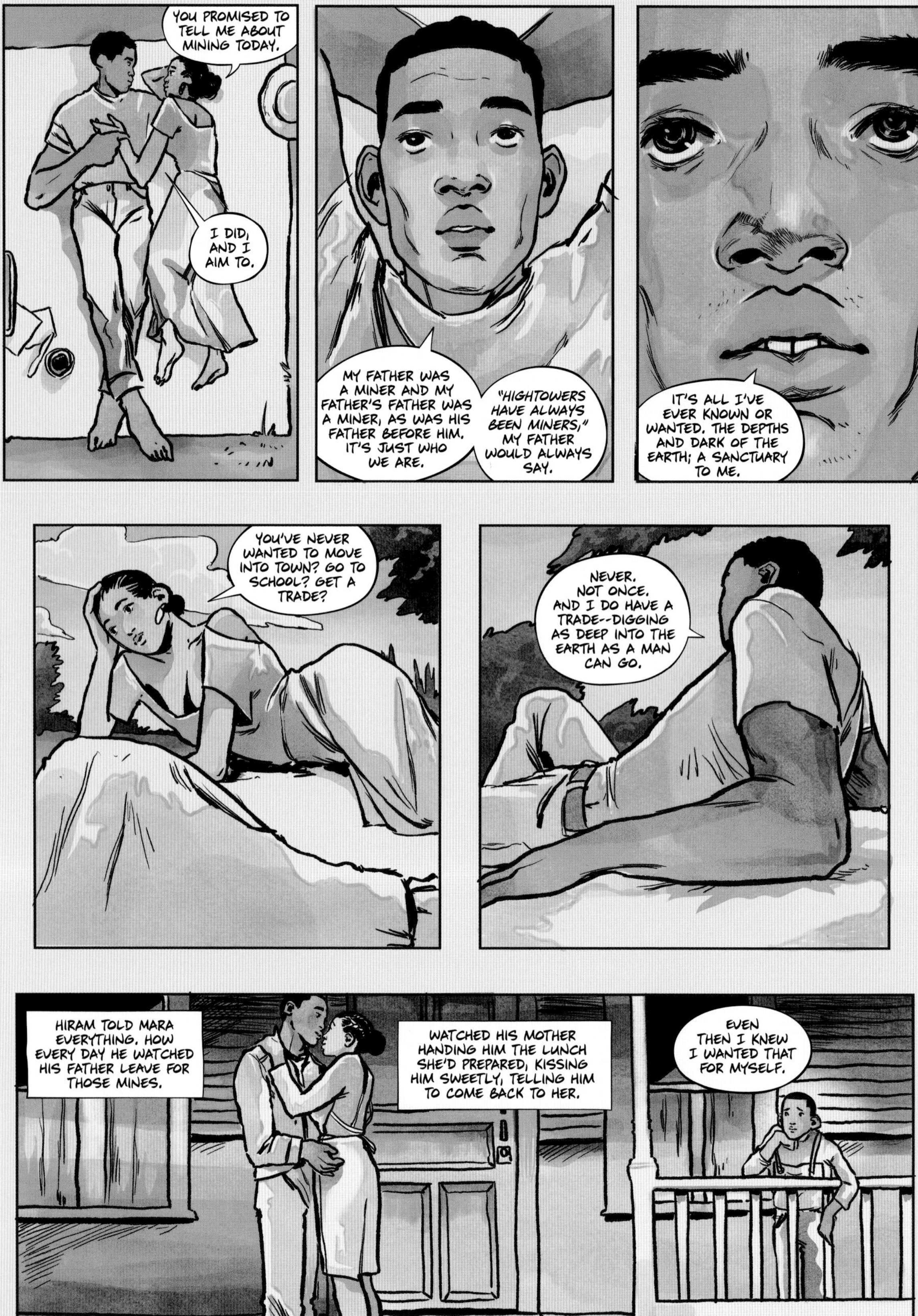
YOU PROMISED TO TELL ME ABOUT MINING TODAY.
I DID, AND I AIM TO.
MY FATHER WAS A MINER AND MY FATHER'S FATHER WAS A MINER, AS WAS HIS FATHER BEFORE HIM. IT'S JUST WHO WE ARE.
"HIGHTOWERS HAVE ALWAYS BEEN MINERS," MY FATHER WOULD ALWAYS SAY.
IT'S ALL I'VE EVER KNOWN OR WANTED. THE DEPTHS AND DARK OF THE EARTH; A SANCTUARY TO ME.
YOU'VE NEVER WANTED TO MOVE INTO TOWN? GO TO SCHOOL? GET A TRADE?
NEVER. NOT ONCE. AND I DO HAVE A TRADE--DIGGING AS DEEP INTO THE EARTH AS A MAN CAN GO.
HIRAM TOLD MARA EVERYTHING. HOW EVERY DAY HE WATCHED HIS FATHER LEAVE FOR THOSE MINES.
WATCHED HIS MOTHER HANDING HIM THE LUNCH SHE'D PREPARED, KISSING HIM SWEETLY, TELLING HIM TO COME BACK TO HER.
EVEN THEN I KNEW I WANTED THAT FOR MYSELF.

HIRAM TOLD MARA HOW EVERY DAY HE WATCHED HIS FATHER RETURN FROM THOSE MINES, DIRTY, SMELLY, TIRED AND HUNGRY, BUT SO VERY HAPPY.

HOW, OVER DINNER, HE WOULD TELL HIS FAMILY ABOUT WHAT HAPPENED THAT DAY; ALL THE THINGS THEY'D UNCOVERED, HOW DEEP THEY DUG, ANY FUNNY STORIES ABOUT HIS WORK MATES.

WE LOVED HIS STORIES. WE LOOKED FORWARD TO IT EVERY DAY.

AND NOW I AM MAKING MY OWN STORIES! EVERY DAY I GO INTO THOSE MINES IT'S AN ADVENTURE.

EVERY SO OFTEN, MY FATHER WOULD BRING HOME SMALL TREASURES TO MY MOTHER. THINGS HE'D UNEARTHED, POCKETED AND POLISHED TO A SHINE.

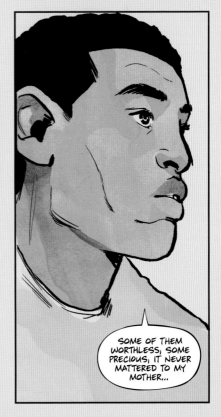

SOME OF THEM WORTHLESS, SOME PRECIOUS, IT NEVER MATTERED TO MY MOTHER...

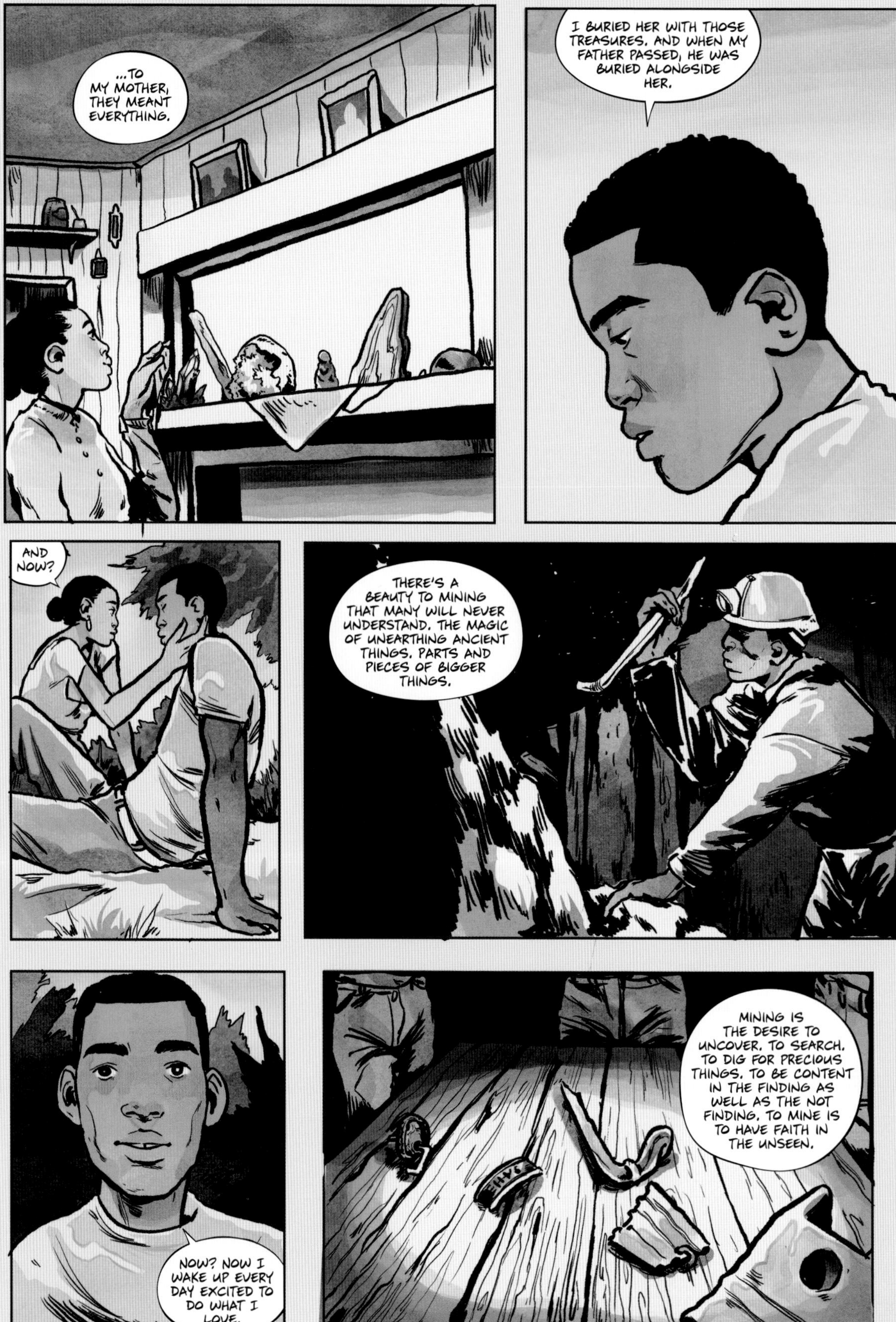
...TO MY MOTHER, THEY MEANT EVERYTHING.
I BURIED HER WITH THOSE TREASURES. AND WHEN MY FATHER PASSED, HE WAS BURIED ALONGSIDE HER.
AND NOW?
THERE'S A BEAUTY TO MINING THAT MANY WILL NEVER UNDERSTAND. THE MAGIC OF UNEARTHING ANCIENT THINGS. PARTS AND PIECES OF BIGGER THINGS.
NOW? NOW I WAKE UP EVERY DAY EXCITED TO DO WHAT I LOVE.
MINING IS THE DESIRE TO UNCOVER. TO SEARCH. TO DIG FOR PRECIOUS THINGS. TO BE CONTENT IN THE FINDING AS WELL AS THE NOT FINDING. TO MINE IS TO HAVE FAITH IN THE UNSEEN.

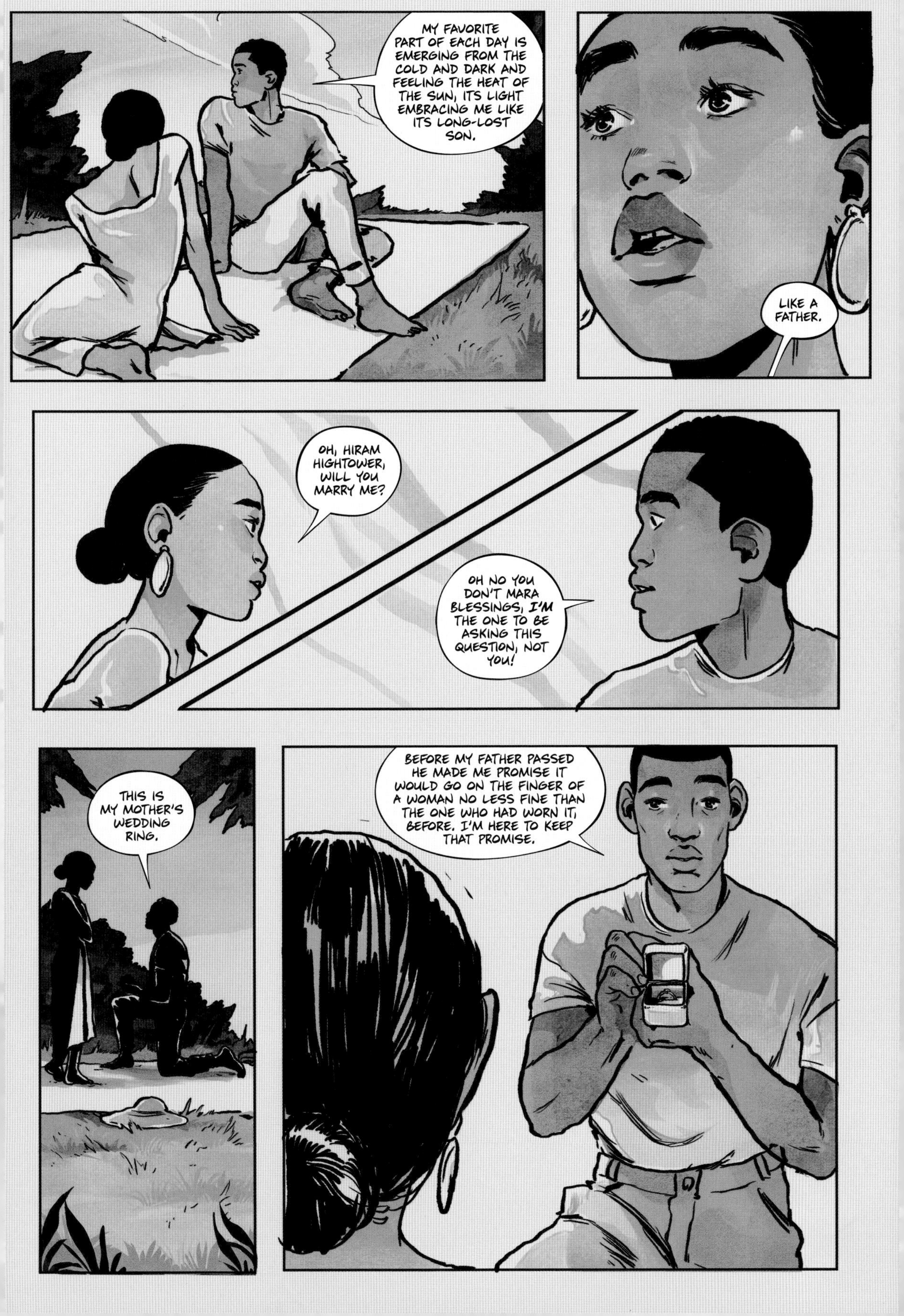
MY FAVORITE PART OF EACH DAY IS EMERGING FROM THE COLD AND DARK AND FEELING THE HEAT OF THE SUN, ITS LIGHT EMBRACING ME LIKE ITS LONG-LOST SON.
LIKE A FATHER.
OH, HIRAM HIGHTOWER, WILL YOU MARRY ME?
OH NO YOU DON'T MARA BLESSINGS, I'M THE ONE TO BE ASKING THIS QUESTION, NOT YOU!
THIS IS MY MOTHER'S WEDDING RING.
BEFORE MY FATHER PASSED HE MADE ME PROMISE IT WOULD GO ON THE FINGER OF A WOMAN NO LESS FINE THAN THE ONE WHO HAD WORN IT, BEFORE. I'M HERE TO KEEP THAT PROMISE.

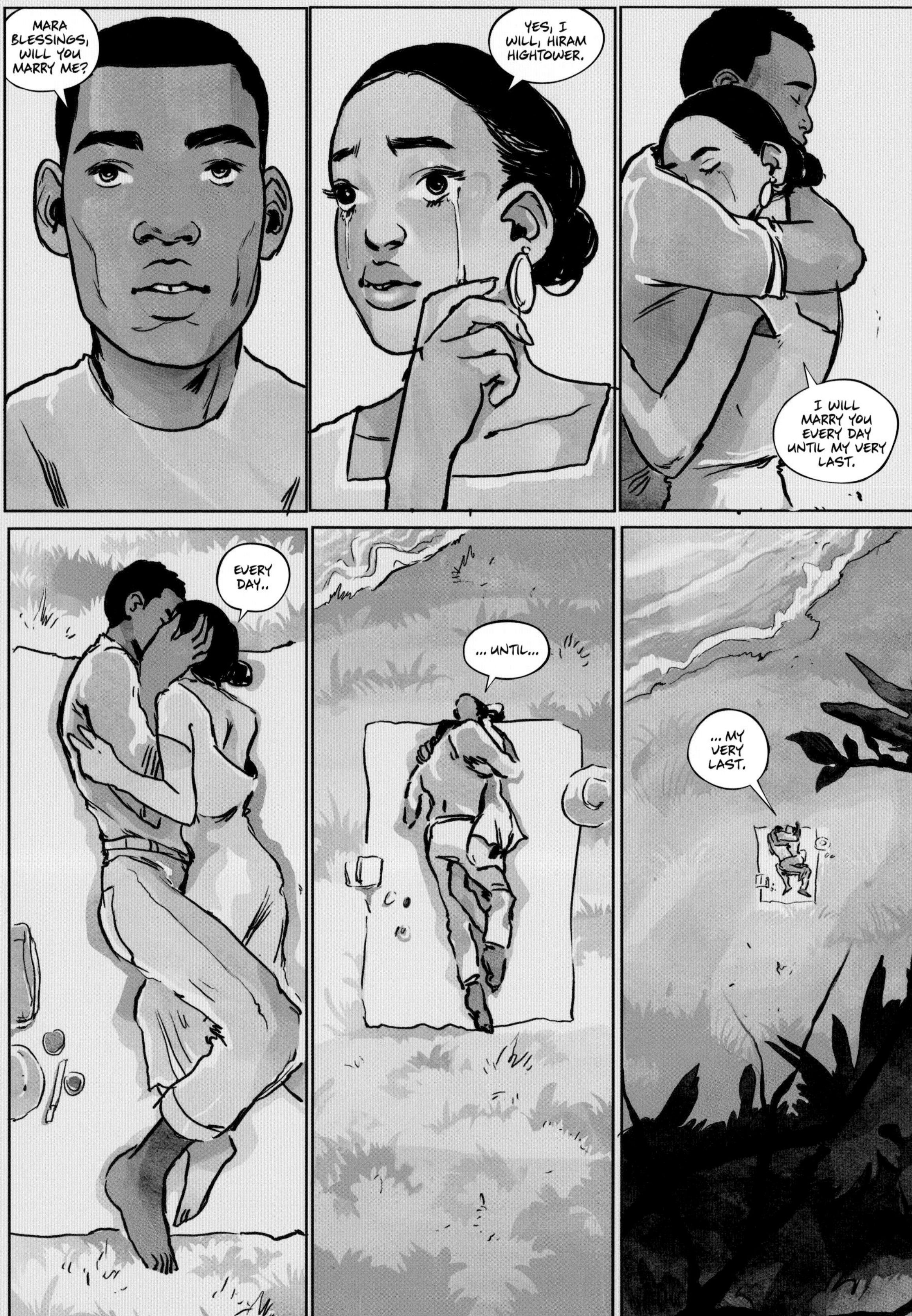

MARA BLESSINGS, WILL YOU MARRY ME?
YES, I WILL, HIRAM HIGHTOWER.
I WILL MARRY YOU EVERY DAY UNTIL MY VERY LAST.
EVERY DAY..
... UNTIL...
... MY VERY LAST.

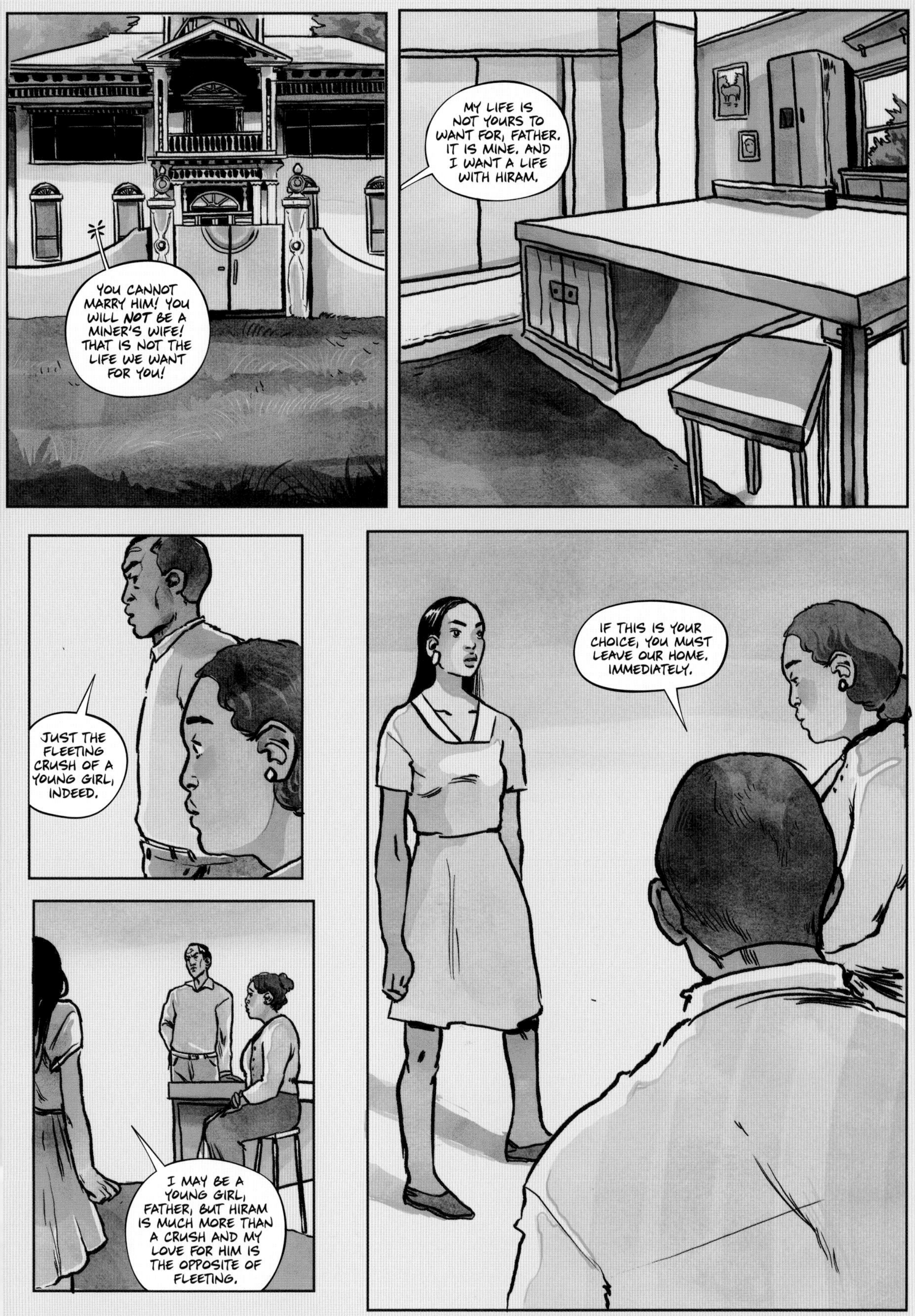
YOU CANNOT MARRY HIM! YOU WILL NOT BE A MINER'S WIFE! THAT IS NOT THE LIFE WE WANT FOR YOU!
MY LIFE IS NOT YOURS TO WANT FOR, FATHER. IT IS MINE. AND I WANT A LIFE WITH HIRAM.
JUST THE FLEETING CRUSH OF A YOUNG GIRL, INDEED.
I MAY BE A YOUNG GIRL, FATHER, BUT HIRAM IS MUCH MORE THAN A CRUSH AND MY LOVE FOR HIM IS THE OPPOSITE OF FLEETING.
IF THIS IS YOUR CHOICE, YOU MUST LEAVE OUR HOME. IMMEDIATELY.

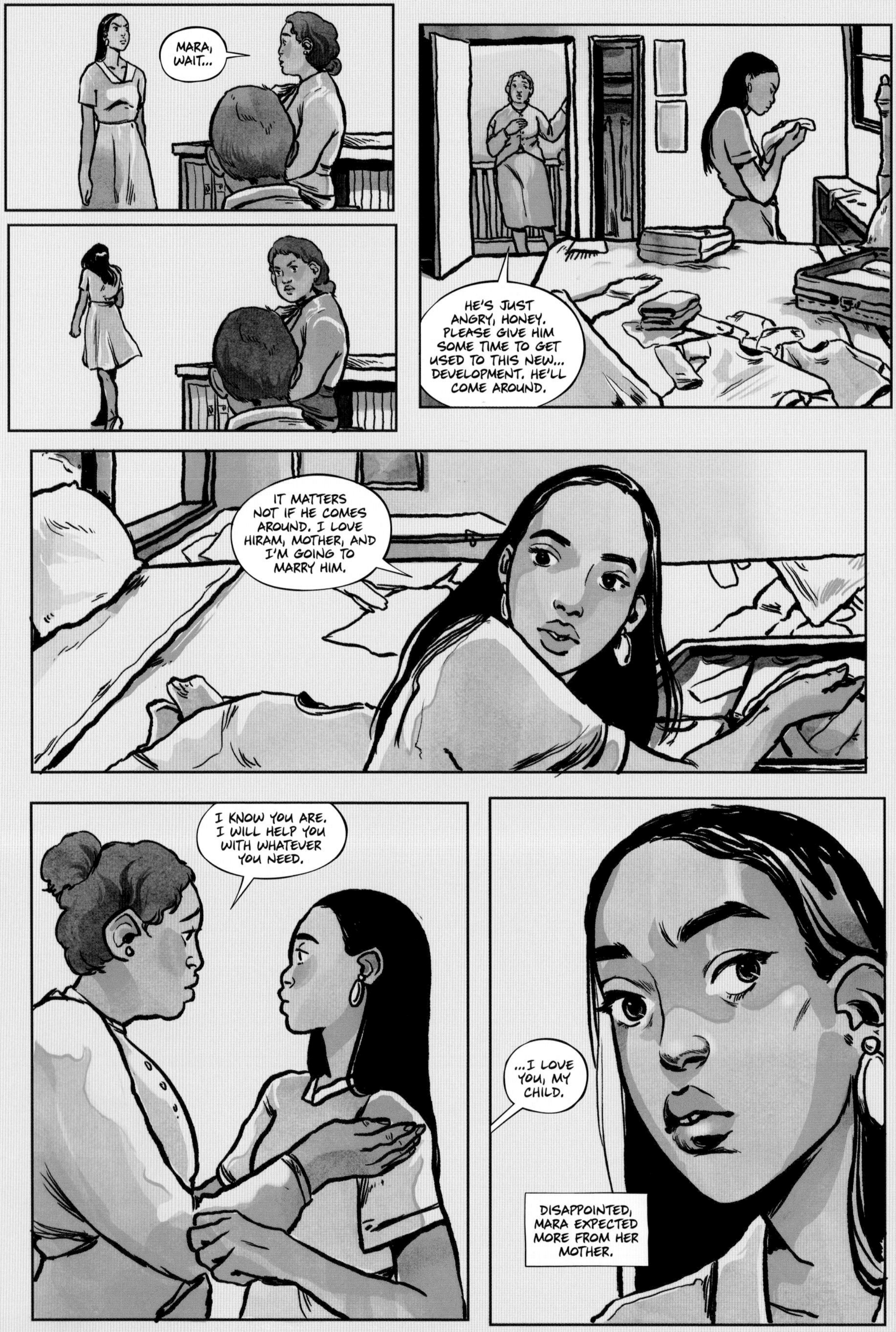
MARA, WAIT...
HE'S JUST ANGRY, HONEY. PLEASE GIVE HIM SOME TIME TO GET USED TO THIS NEW... DEVELOPMENT. HE'LL COME AROUND.
IT MATTERS NOT IF HE COMES AROUND. I LOVE HIRAM, MOTHER, AND I'M GOING TO MARRY HIM.
I KNOW YOU ARE. I WILL HELP YOU WITH WHATEVER YOU NEED.
...I LOVE YOU, MY CHILD.
DISAPPOINTED, MARA EXPECTED MORE FROM HER MOTHER.

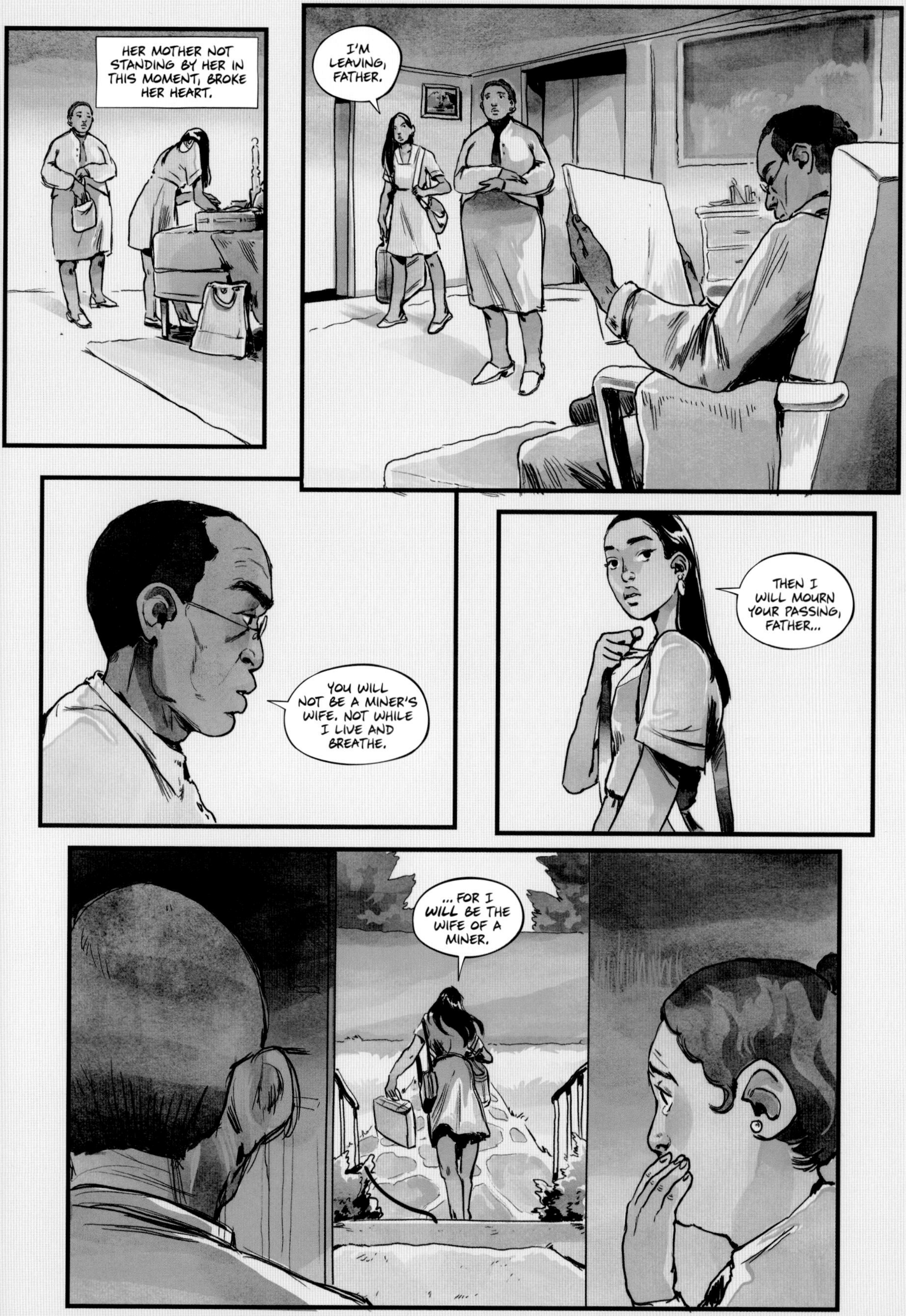
HER MOTHER NOT STANDING BY HER IN THIS MOMENT, BROKE HER HEART.
I'M LEAVING, FATHER.
YOU WILL NOT BE A MINER'S WIFE. NOT WHILE I LIVE AND BREATHE.
THEN I WILL MOURN YOUR PASSING, FATHER...
...FOR I WILL BE THE WIFE OF A MINER.

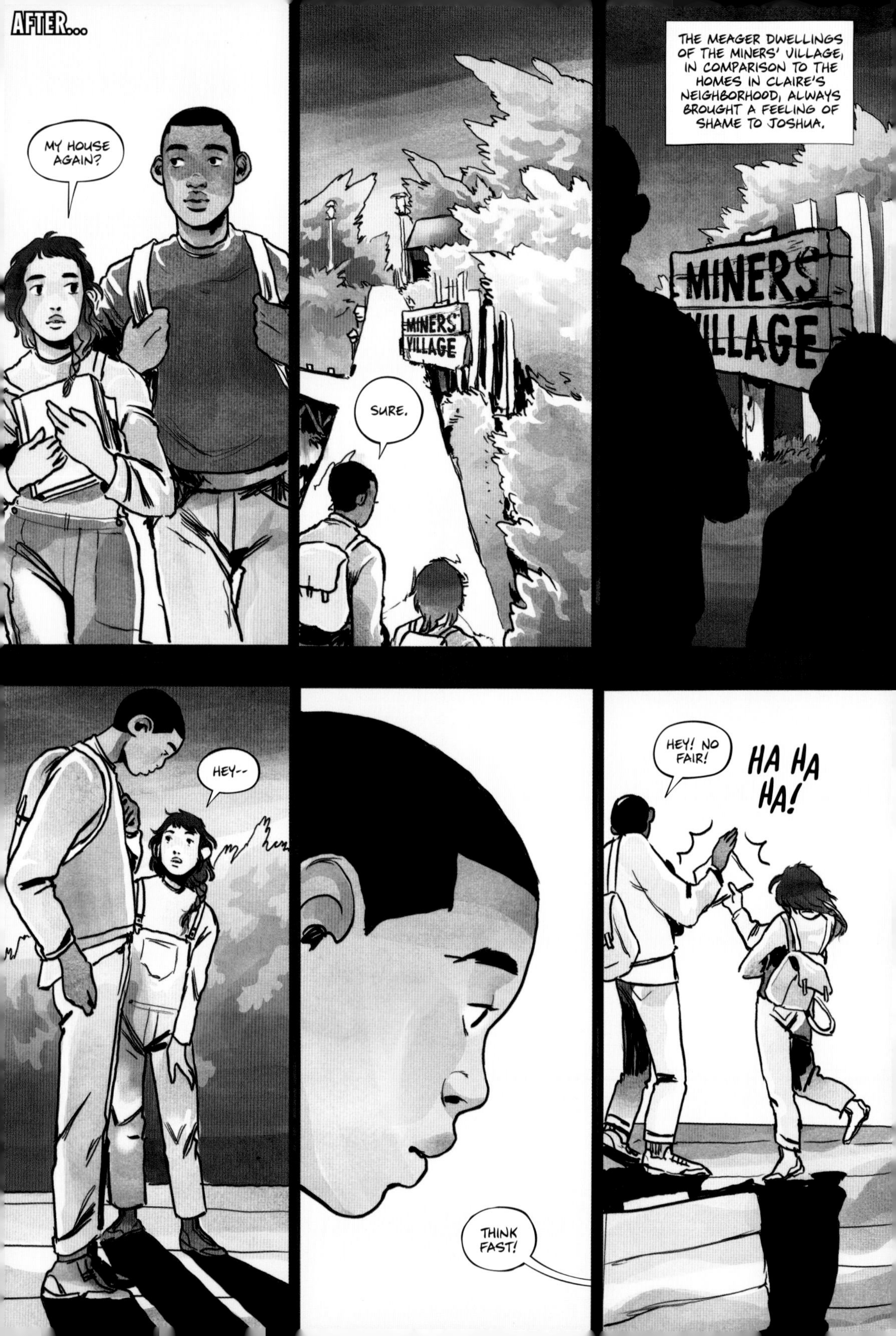
AFTER...
MY HOUSE AGAIN?
SURE.
MINERS' VILLAGE
THE MEAGER DWELLINGS OF THE MINERS' VILLAGE, IN COMPARISON TO THE HOMES IN CLAIRE'S NEIGHBORHOOD, ALWAYS BROUGHT A FEELING OF SHAME TO JOSHUA.
MINERS VILLAGE
HEY--
THINK FAST!
HEY! NO FAIR!
HA HA HA!

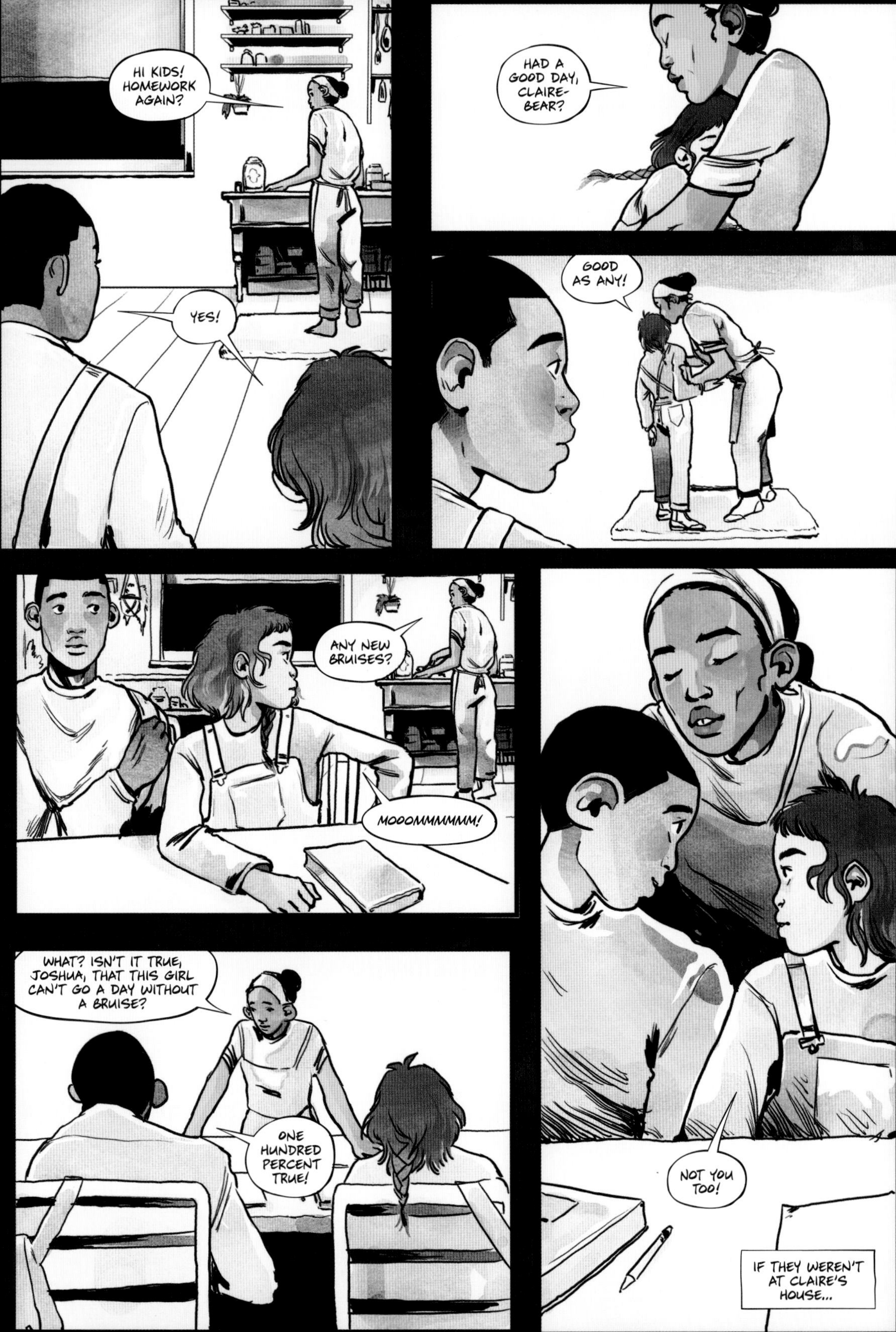
HI KIDS! HOMEWORK AGAIN?
YES!
HAD A GOOD DAY, CLAIRE-BEAR?
GOOD AS ANY!
ANY NEW BRUISES?
MOOOMMMMMM!
WHAT? ISN'T IT TRUE, JOSHUA, THAT THIS GIRL CAN'T GO A DAY WITHOUT A BRUISE?
ONE HUNDRED PERCENT TRUE!
NOT YOU TOO!
IF THEY WEREN'T AT CLAIRE'S HOUSE...

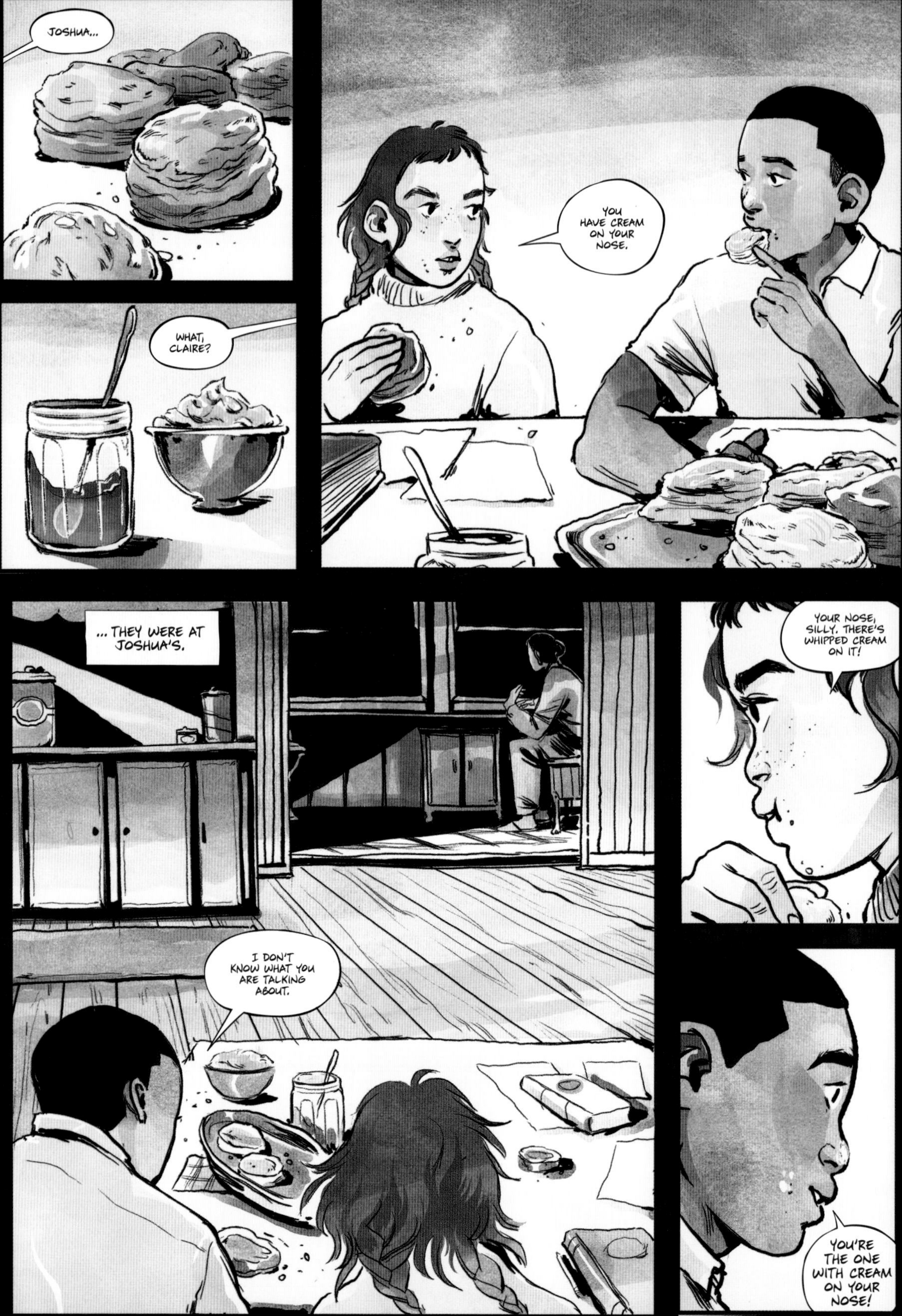
JOSHUA...
WHAT, CLAIRE?
YOU HAVE CREAM ON YOUR NOSE.
... THEY WERE AT JOSHUA'S.
I DON'T KNOW WHAT YOU ARE TALKING ABOUT.
YOUR NOSE, SILLY. THERE'S WHIPPED CREAM ON IT!
YOU'RE THE ONE WITH CREAM ON YOUR NOSE!

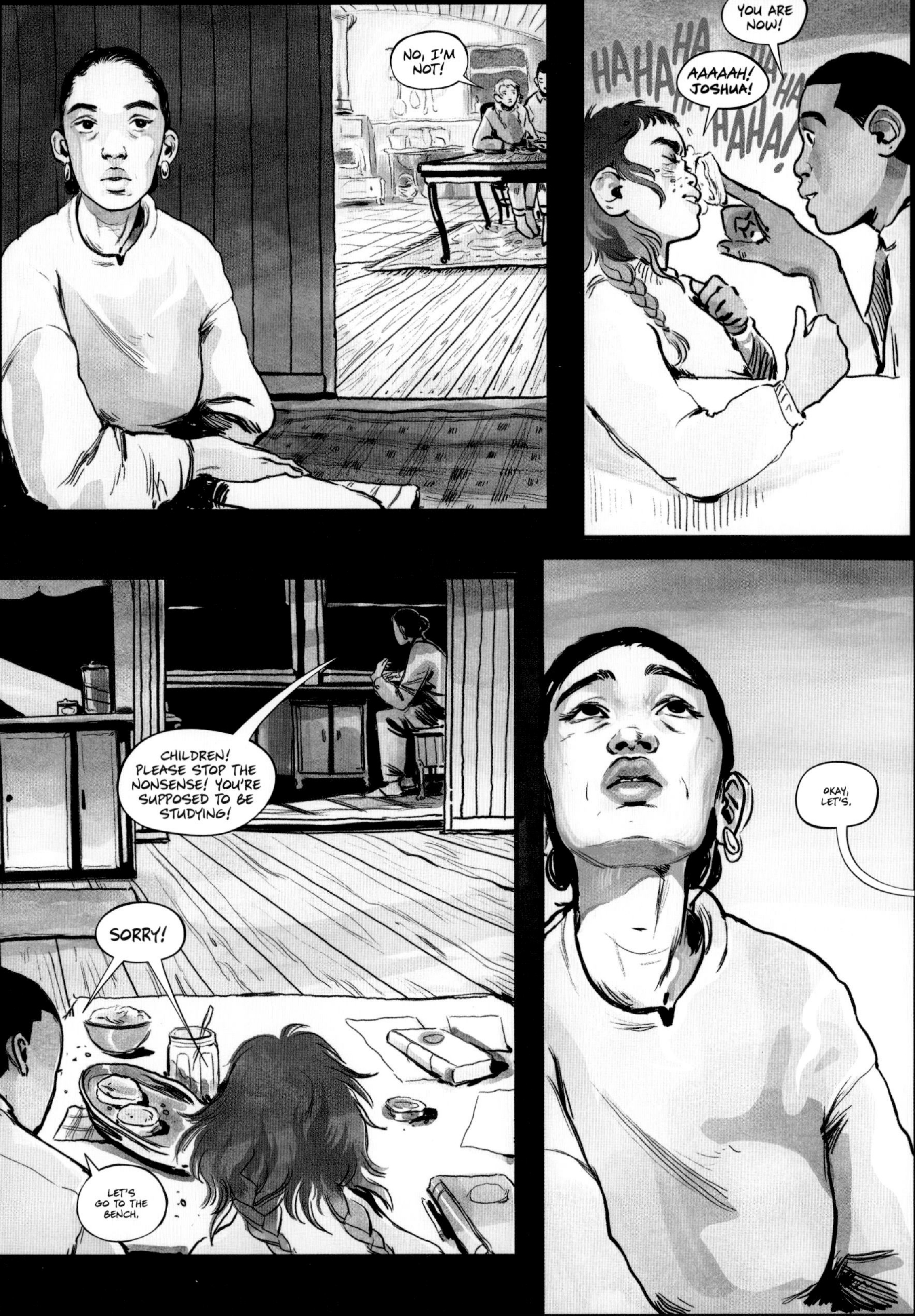
NO, I'M NOT!
YOU ARE NOW!
HAHAHAHAHAHAHAHA!
AAAAAH! JOSHUA!
CHILDREN! PLEASE STOP THE NONSENSE! YOU'RE SUPPOSED TO BE STUDYING!
SORRY!
LET'S GO TO THE BENCH.
OKAY, LET'S.

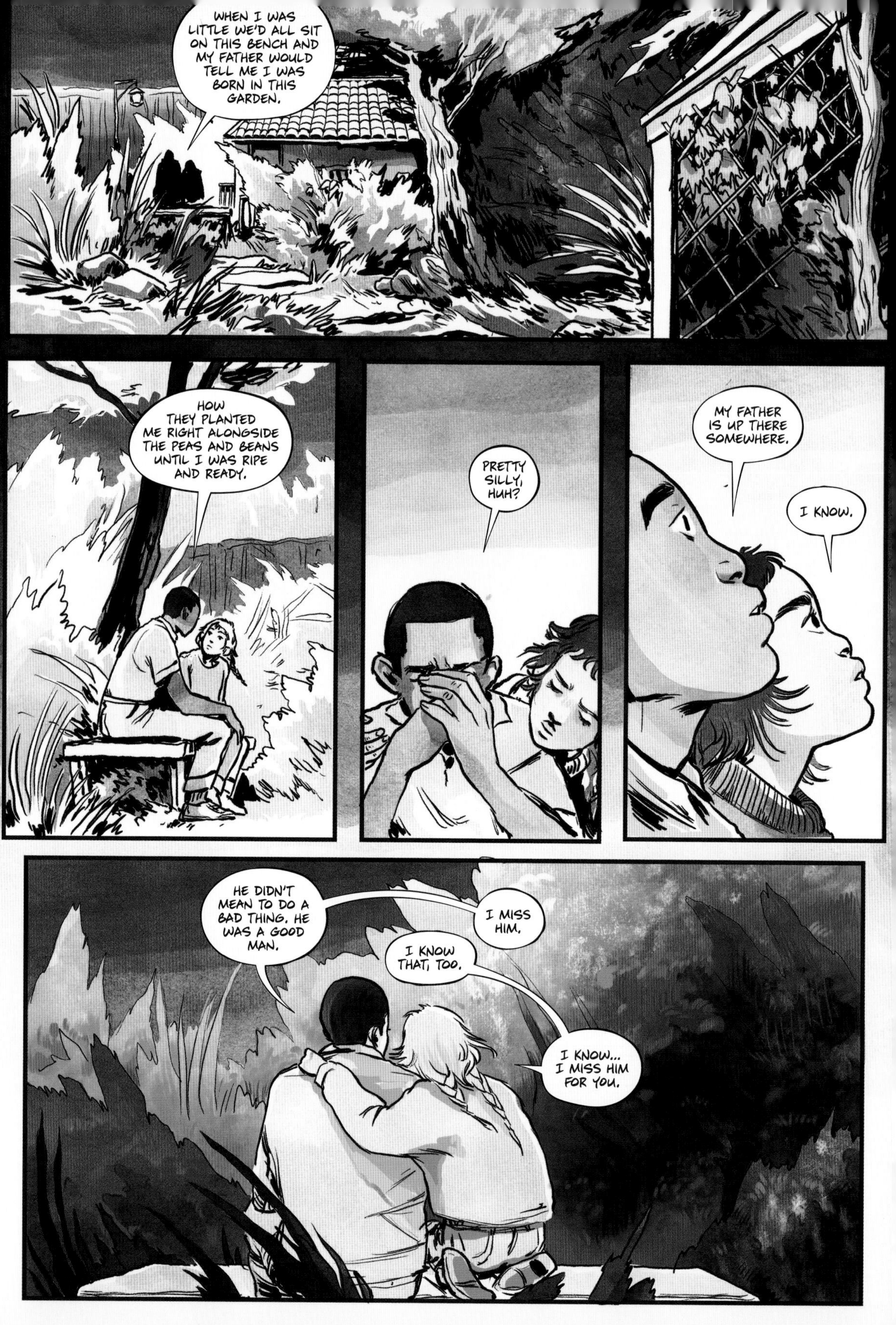
WHEN I WAS LITTLE WE'D ALL SIT ON THIS BENCH AND MY FATHER WOULD TELL ME I WAS BORN IN THIS GARDEN.
HOW THEY PLANTED ME RIGHT ALONGSIDE THE PEAS AND BEANS UNTIL I WAS RIPE AND READY.
PRETTY SILLY, HUH?
MY FATHER IS UP THERE SOMEWHERE.
I KNOW.
HE DIDN'T MEAN TO DO A BAD THING. HE WAS A GOOD MAN.
I MISS HIM.
I KNOW THAT, TOO.
I KNOW... I MISS HIM FOR YOU.

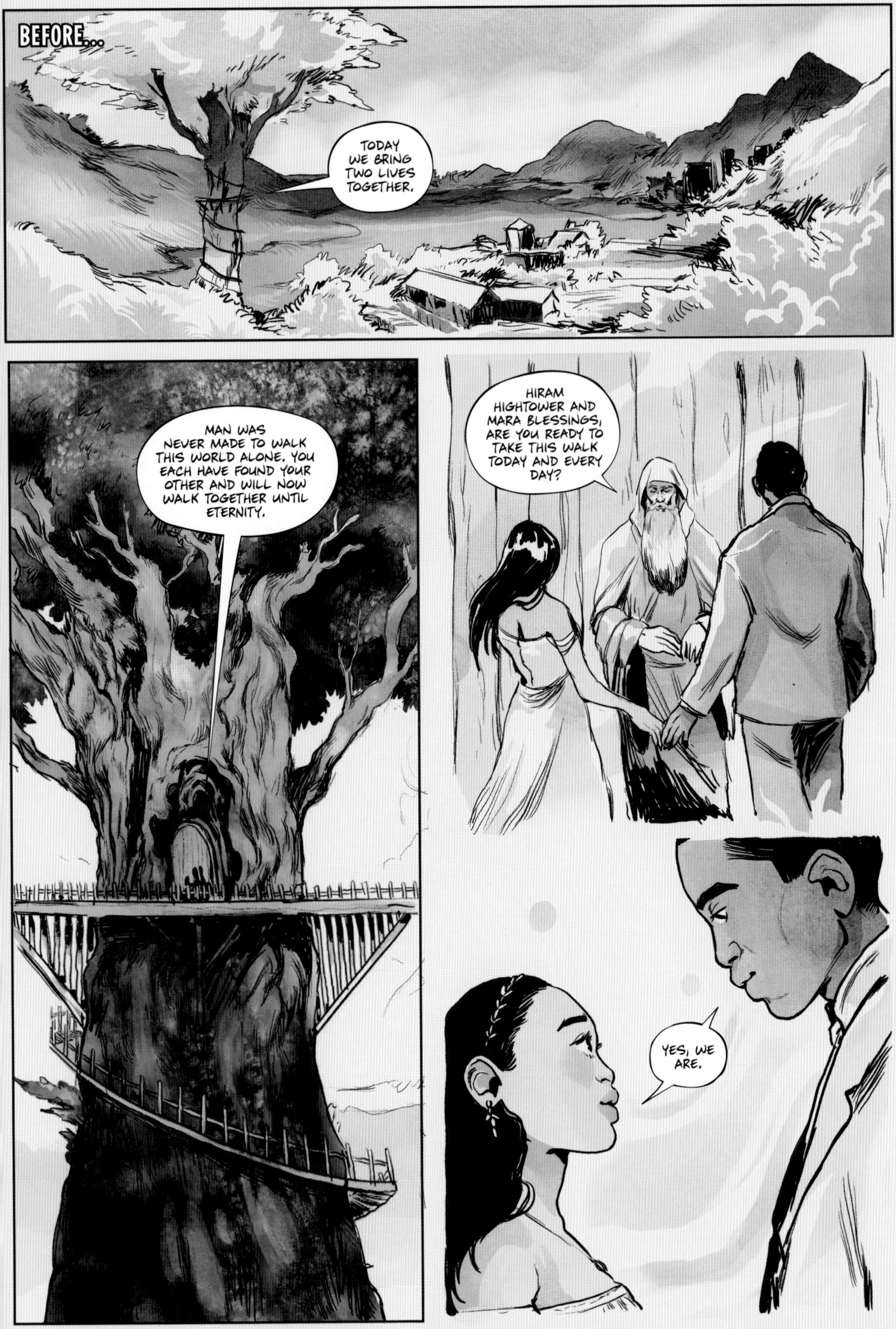
BEFORE...
TODAY WE BRING TWO LIVES TOGETHER.
MAN WAS NEVER MADE TO WALK THIS WORLD ALONE. YOU EACH HAVE FOUND YOUR OTHER AND WILL NOW WALK TOGETHER UNTIL ETERNITY.
HIRAM HIGHTOWER AND MARA BLESSINGS, ARE YOU READY TO TAKE THIS WALK TODAY AND EVERY DAY?
YES, WE ARE.

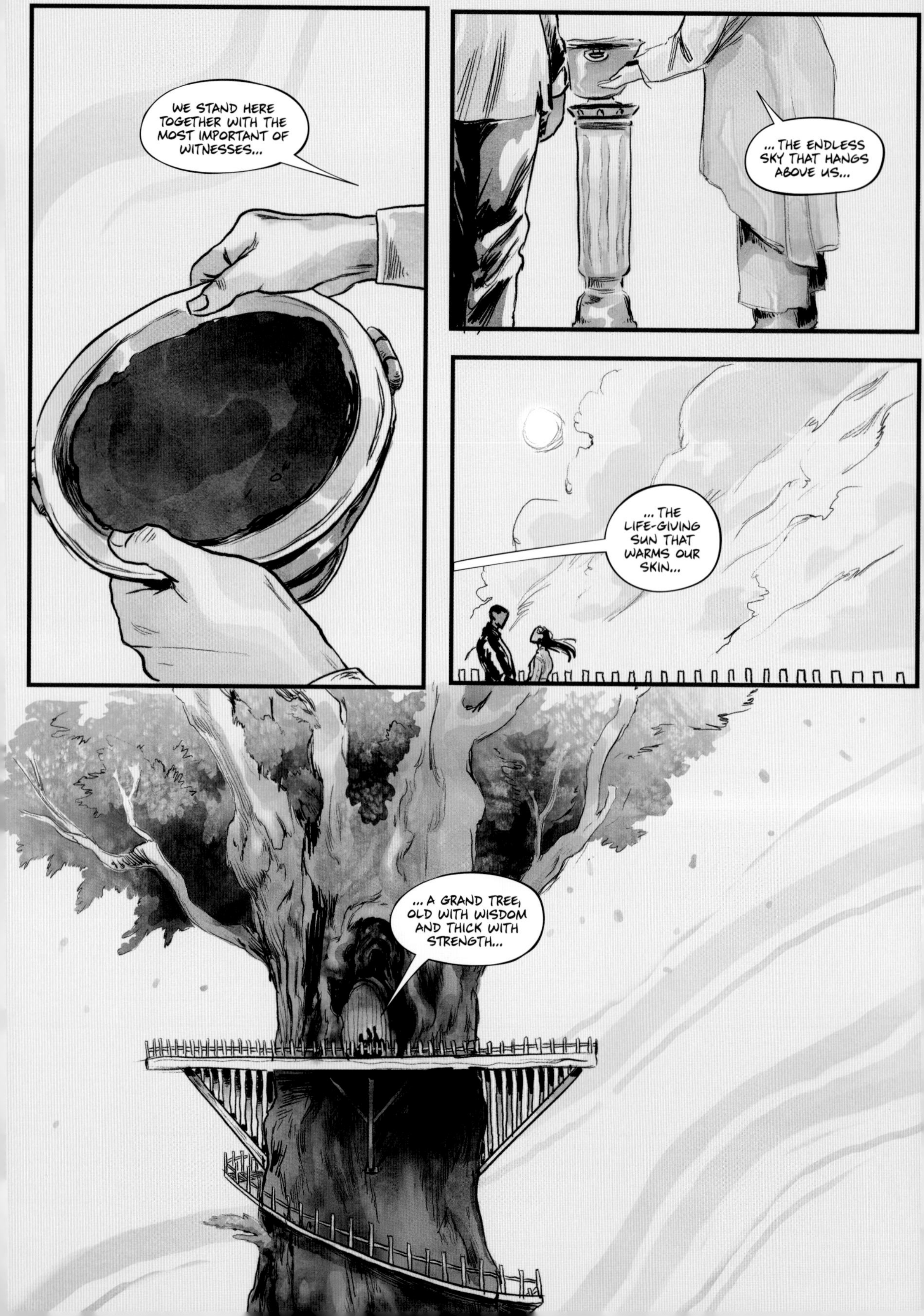
WE STAND HERE TOGETHER WITH THE MOST IMPORTANT OF WITNESSES...
...THE ENDLESS SKY THAT HANGS ABOVE US...
...THE LIFE-GIVING SUN THAT WARMS OUR SKIN...
...A GRAND TREE, OLD WITH WISDOM AND THICK WITH STRENGTH...

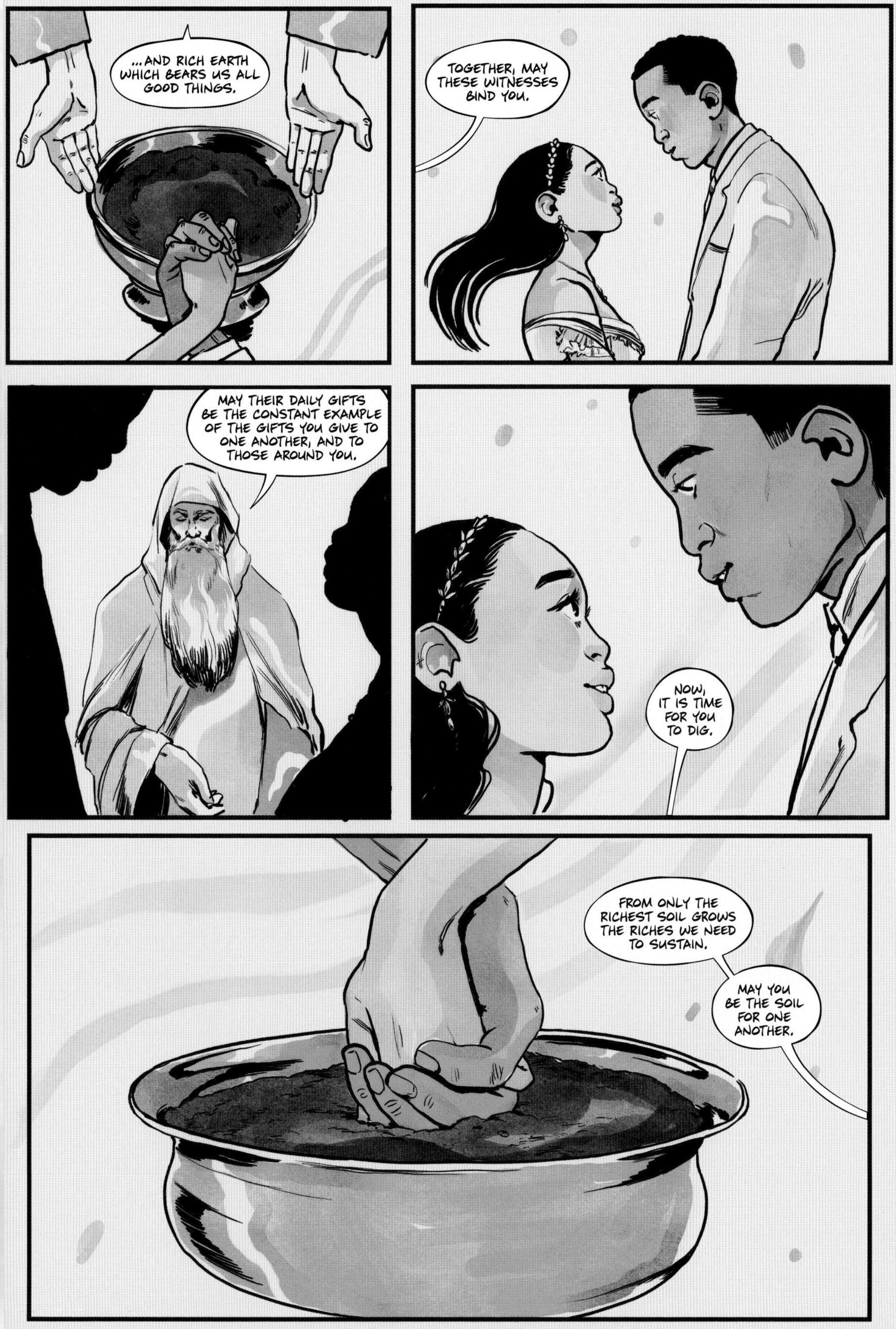
...AND RICH EARTH WHICH BEARS US ALL GOOD THINGS.
TOGETHER, MAY THESE WITNESSES BIND YOU.
MAY THEIR DAILY GIFTS BE THE CONSTANT EXAMPLE OF THE GIFTS YOU GIVE TO ONE ANOTHER, AND TO THOSE AROUND YOU.
NOW, IT IS TIME FOR YOU TO DIG.
FROM ONLY THE RICHEST SOIL GROWS THE RICHES WE NEED TO SUSTAIN.
MAY YOU BE THE SOIL FOR ONE ANOTHER.

HOW YOU FOUND EACH OTHER, NOW YOU FIND THESE RINGS.

AS YOU SOUGHT EACH OTHER, SO YOU SEEK THESE RINGS.

NOW, PLACE THE RINGS ON ONE ANOTHER'S FINGERS.

YOU WEAR THESE RINGS AS A SYMBOL OF THE COVENANT YOU ENTER INTO TODAY.

YOU WEAR THESE RINGS AS AN ETERNAL PROMISE TO LOVE AND CHERISH.

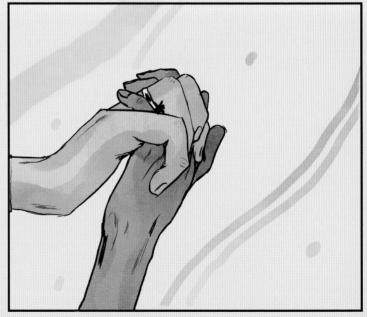

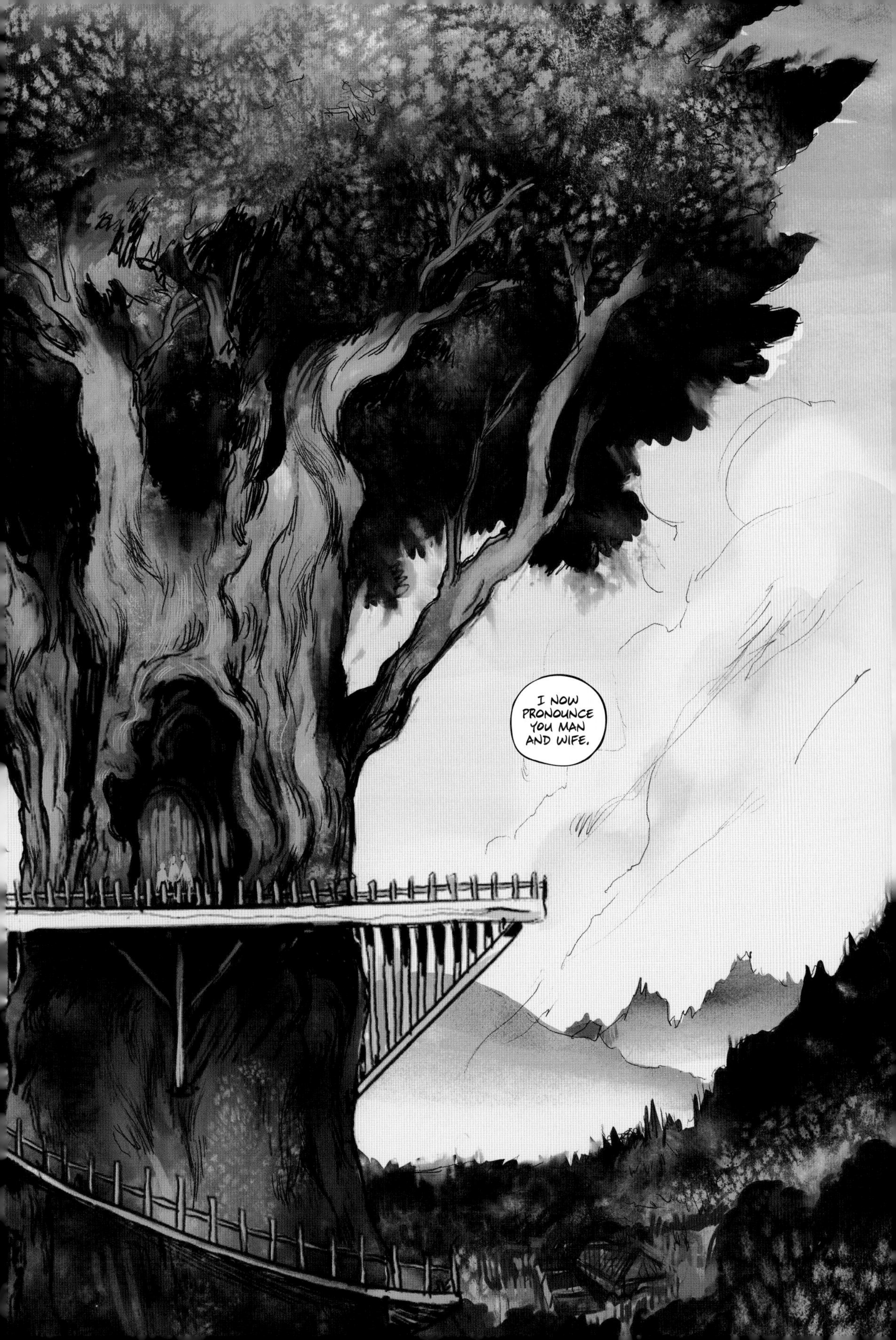
I NOW PRONOUNCE YOU MAN AND WIFE.

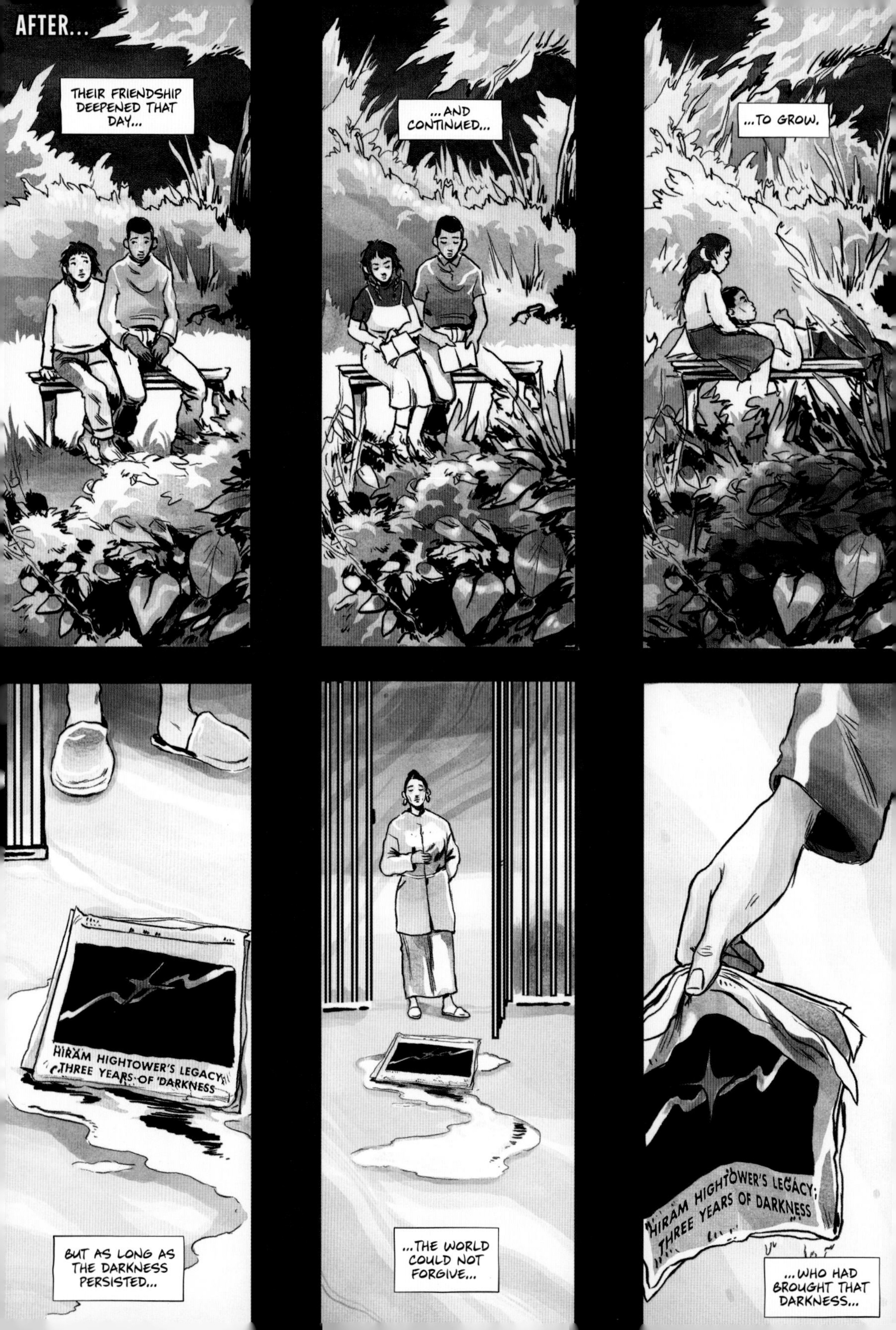
AFTER...
THEIR FRIENDSHIP DEEPENED THAT DAY...
...AND CONTINUED...
...TO GROW.
HIRAM HIGHTOWER'S LEGACY: THREE YEARS OF DARKNESS
BUT AS LONG AS THE DARKNESS PERSISTED...
...THE WORLD COULD NOT FORGIVE...
HIRAM HIGHTOWER'S LEGACY: THREE YEARS OF DARKNESS
...WHO HAD BROUGHT THAT DARKNESS...

...AND THEY WOULDN'T LET ANYONE FORGET.

HOW YA LIKE THAT, HIGHTOWER?

BANG BANG BANG

LET ME OUT!

SHOULD WE KEEP HIM IN THERE FOR THREE YEARS, BOYS?

YEAH! THREE YEARS OF DARKNESS FOR THE THREE YEARS OF DARKNESS YOUR DAD GAVE US!

PUSHED HIM IN AND...

...DIDN'T LET HIM OUT!

OH, YOU TWO!

JUST DESSERTS.

HIRAM
THREE YEA

"On today, the third anni... the day H... Hightower fle... his air machine into the sun, t... world still li... in cold dar... ness."

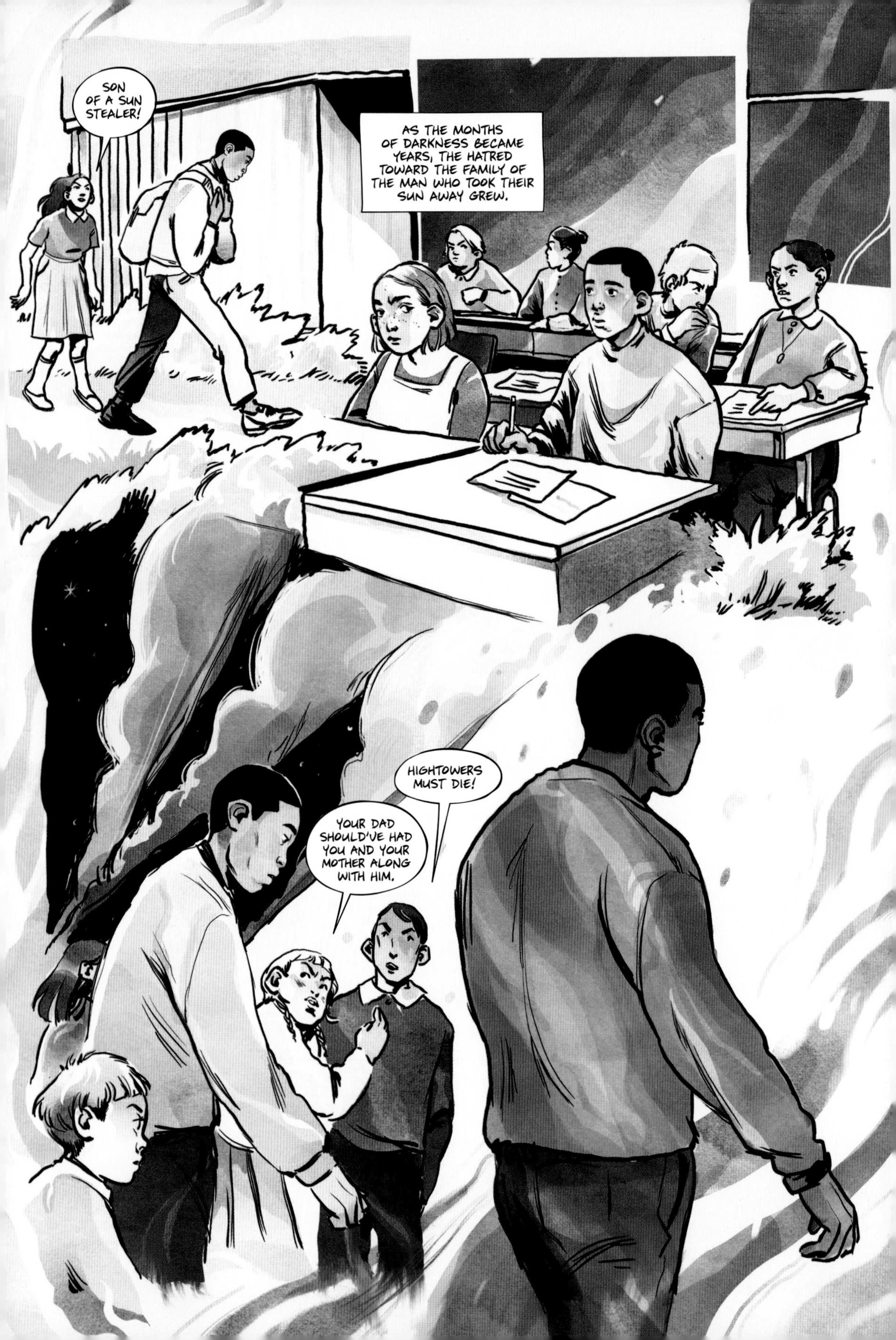
SON OF A SUN STEALER!
AS THE MONTHS OF DARKNESS BECAME YEARS, THE HATRED TOWARD THE FAMILY OF THE MAN WHO TOOK THEIR SUN AWAY GREW.
YOUR DAD SHOULD'VE HAD YOU AND YOUR MOTHER ALONG WITH HIM.
HIGHTOWERS MUST DIE!

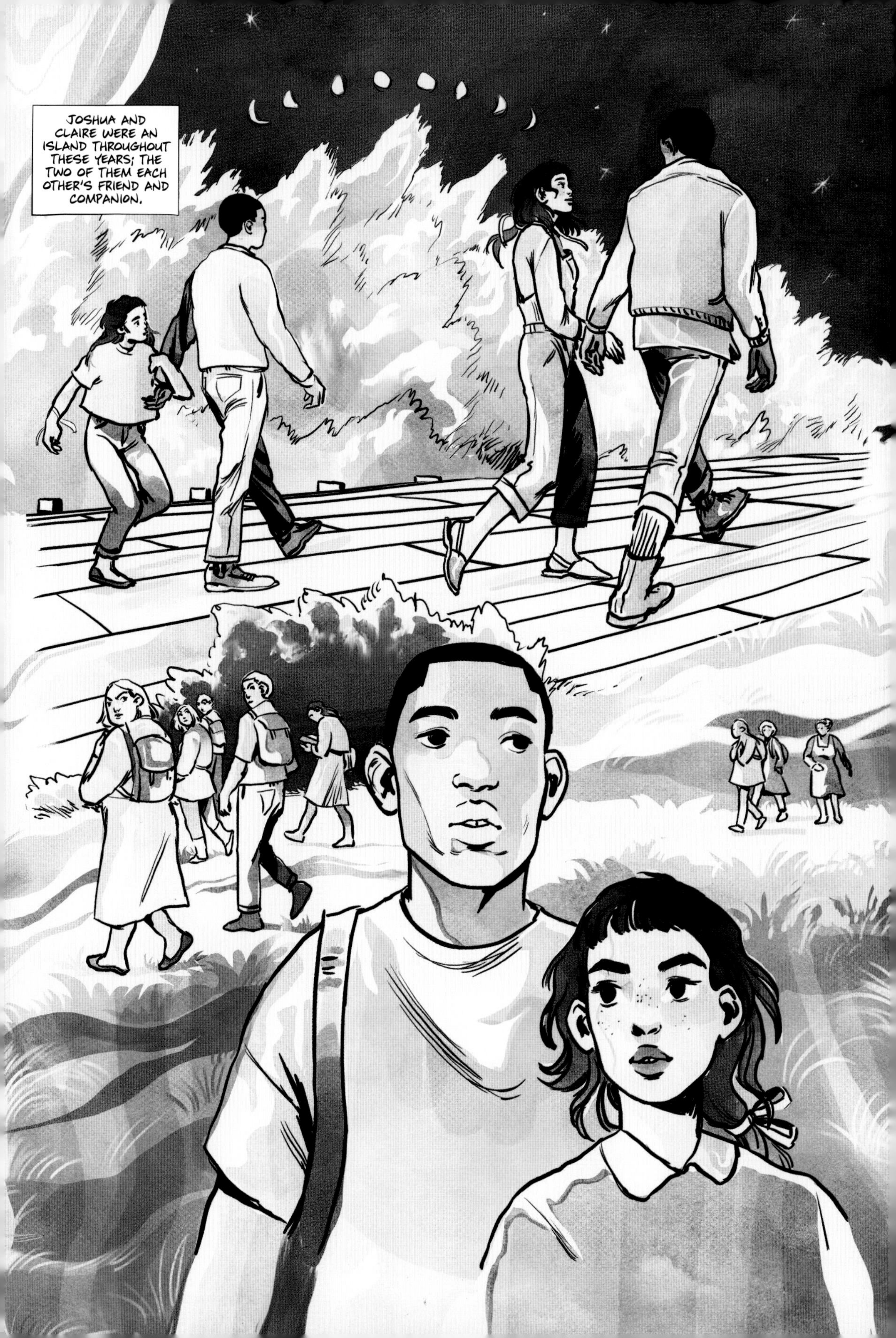
JOSHUA AND CLAIRE WERE AN ISLAND THROUGHOUT THESE YEARS; THE TWO OF THEM EACH OTHER'S FRIEND AND COMPANION.

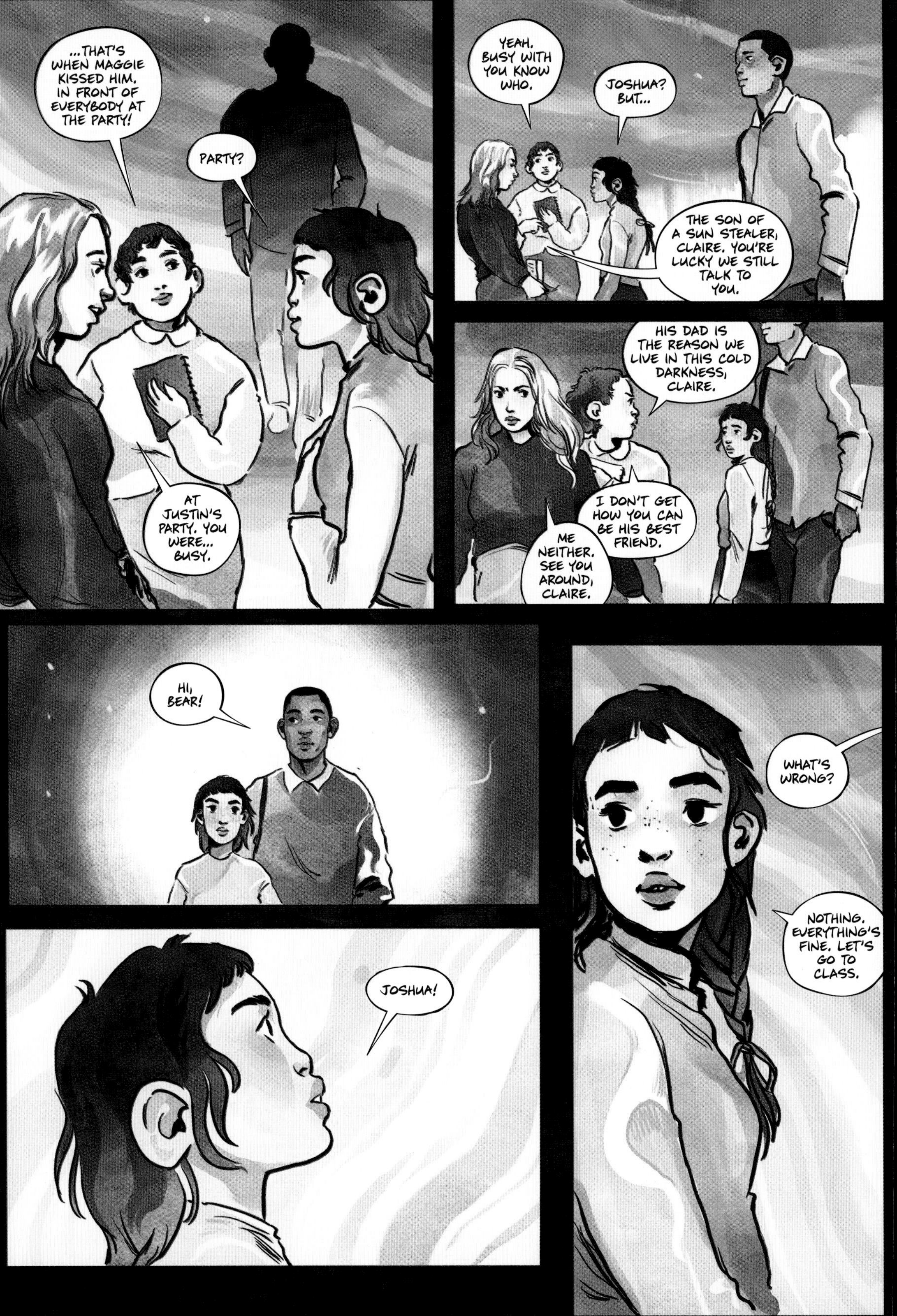
...THAT'S WHEN MAGGIE KISSED HIM, IN FRONT OF EVERYBODY AT THE PARTY!
PARTY?
AT JUSTIN'S PARTY. YOU WERE... BUSY.
YEAH. BUSY WITH YOU KNOW WHO.
JOSHUA? BUT...
THE SON OF A SUN STEALER, CLAIRE. YOU'RE LUCKY WE STILL TALK TO YOU.
HIS DAD IS THE REASON WE LIVE IN THIS COLD DARKNESS, CLAIRE.
I DON'T GET HOW YOU CAN BE HIS BEST FRIEND.
ME NEITHER. SEE YOU AROUND, CLAIRE.
HI, BEAR!
JOSHUA!
WHAT'S WRONG?
NOTHING. EVERYTHING'S FINE. LET'S GO TO CLASS.

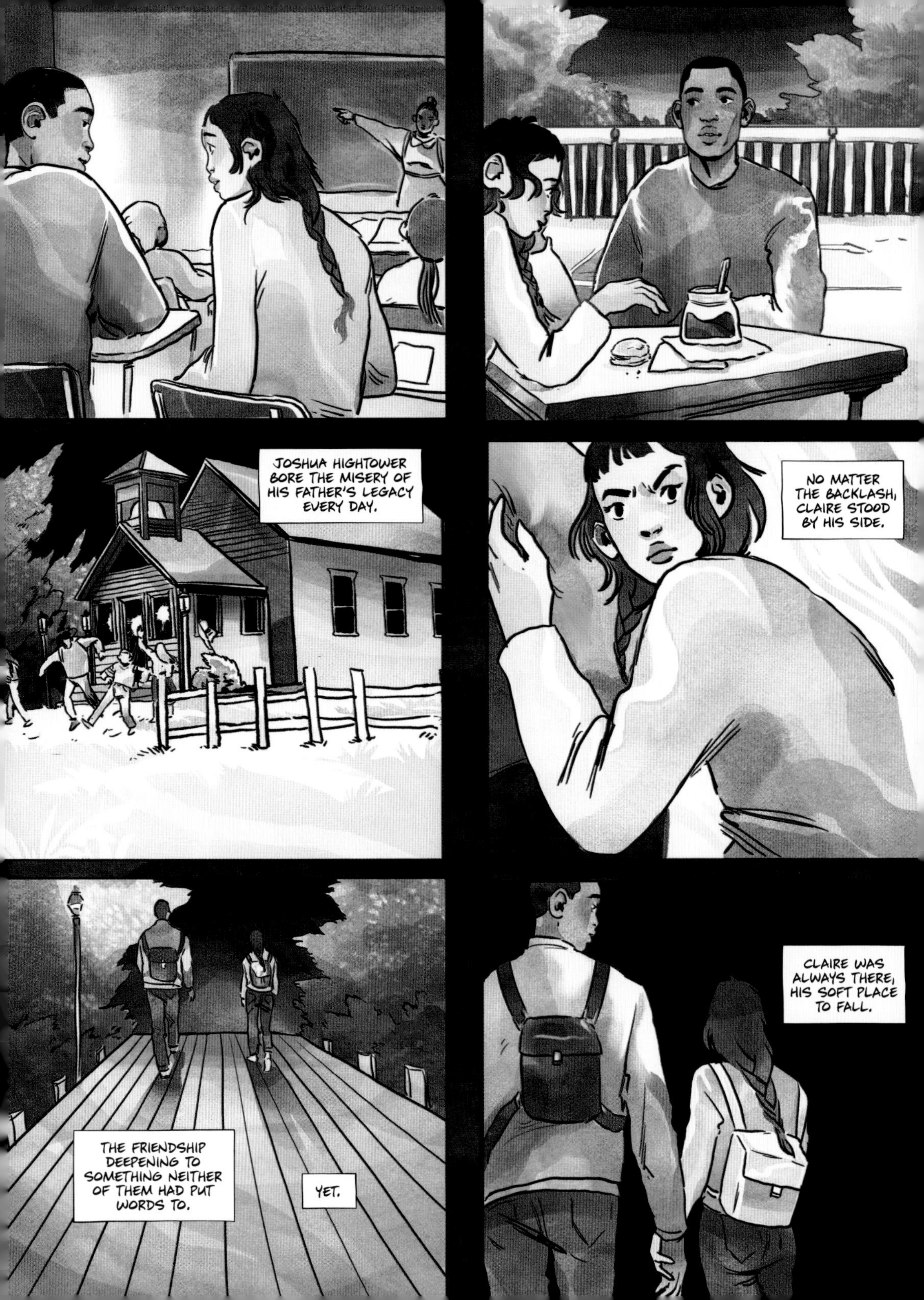
JOSHUA HIGHTOWER BORE THE MISERY OF HIS FATHER'S LEGACY EVERY DAY.
NO MATTER THE BACKLASH, CLAIRE STOOD BY HIS SIDE.
THE FRIENDSHIP DEEPENING TO SOMETHING NEITHER OF THEM HAD PUT WORDS TO.
YET.
CLAIRE WAS ALWAYS THERE, HIS SOFT PLACE TO FALL.

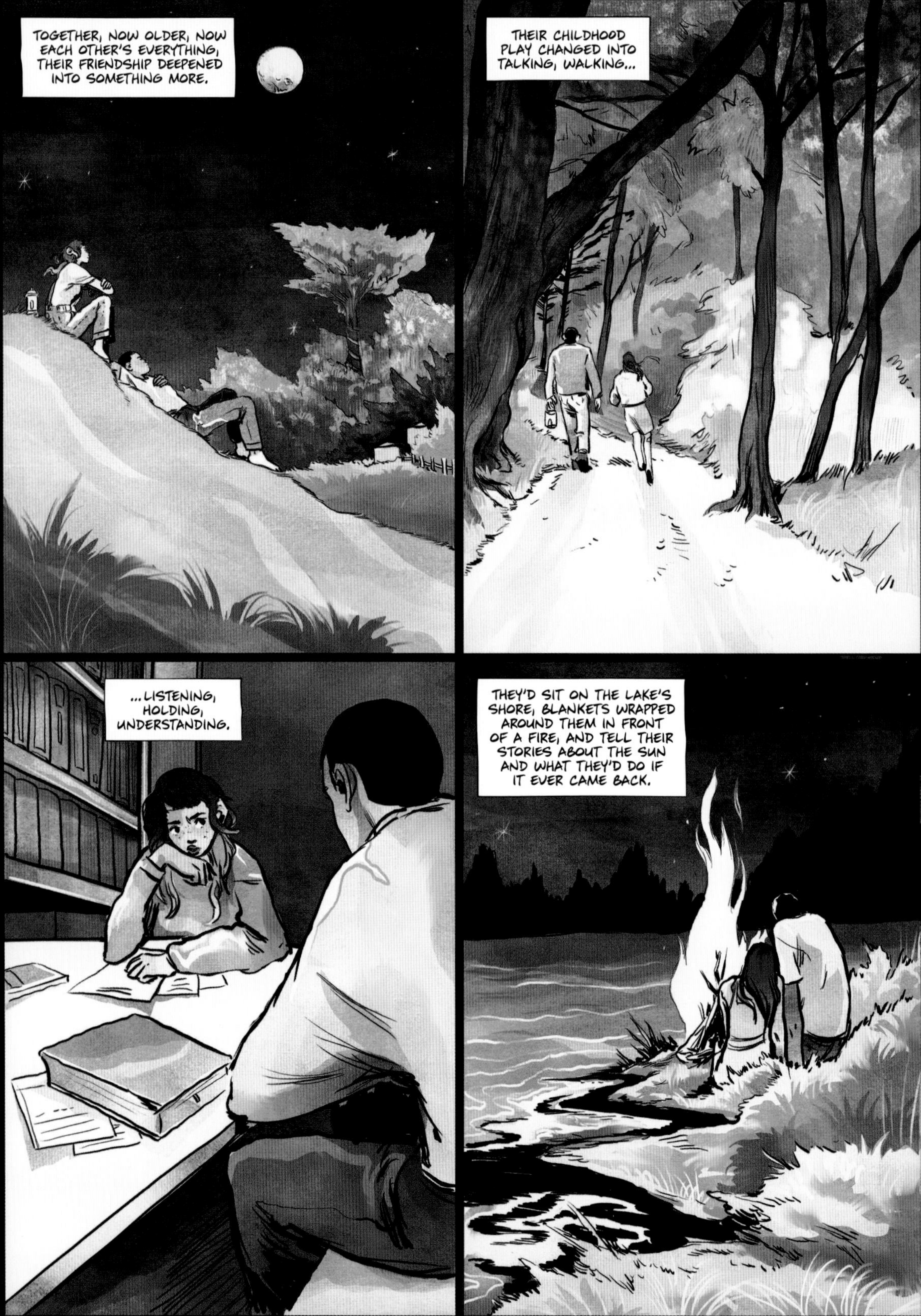
TOGETHER, NOW OLDER, NOW EACH OTHER'S EVERYTHING, THEIR FRIENDSHIP DEEPENED INTO SOMETHING MORE.
THEIR CHILDHOOD PLAY CHANGED INTO TALKING, WALKING...
...LISTENING, HOLDING, UNDERSTANDING.
THEY'D SIT ON THE LAKE'S SHORE, BLANKETS WRAPPED AROUND THEM IN FRONT OF A FIRE, AND TELL THEIR STORIES ABOUT THE SUN AND WHAT THEY'D DO IF IT EVER CAME BACK.

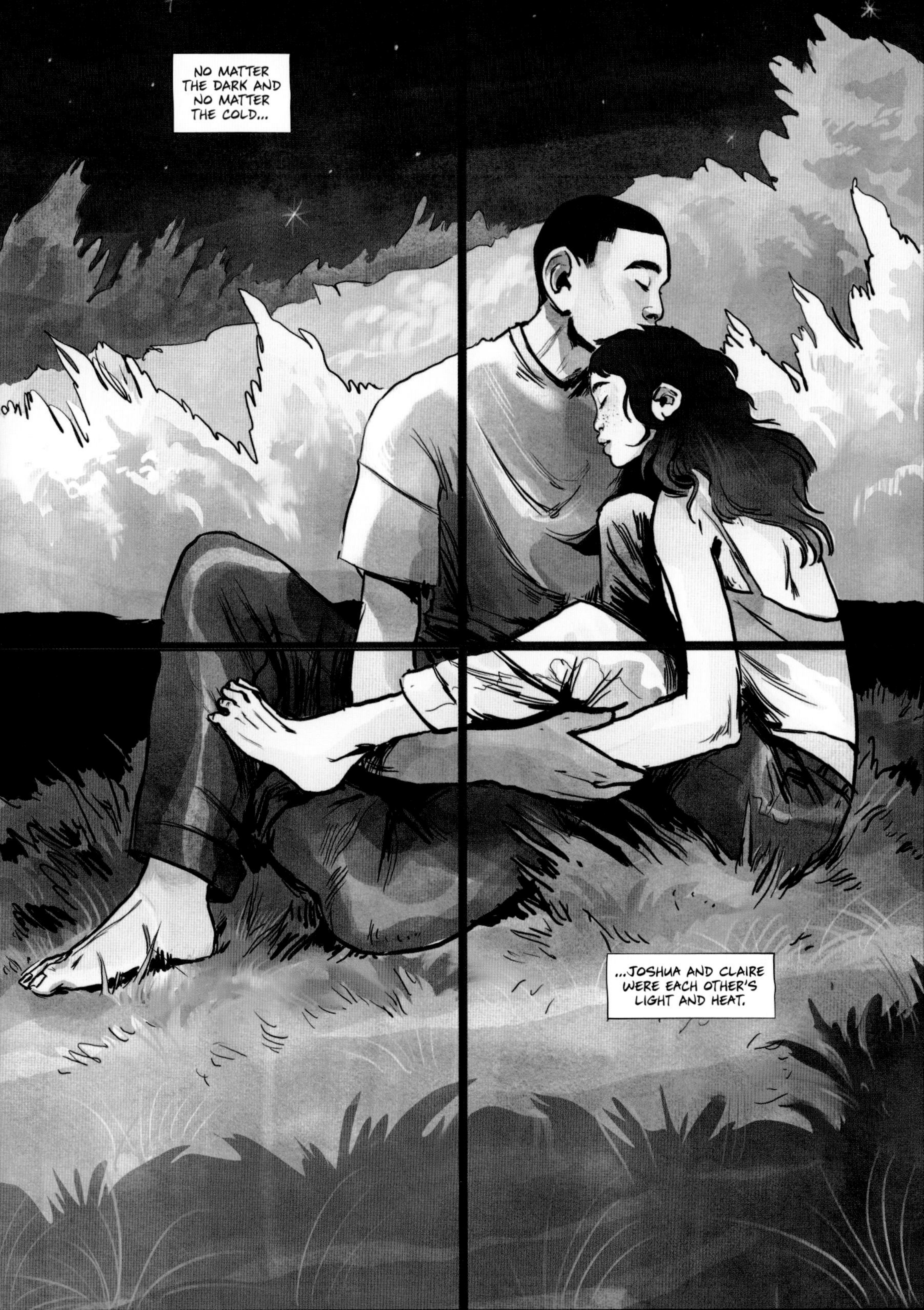
NO MATTER THE DARK AND NO MATTER THE COLD...
...JOSHUA AND CLAIRE WERE EACH OTHER'S LIGHT AND HEAT.

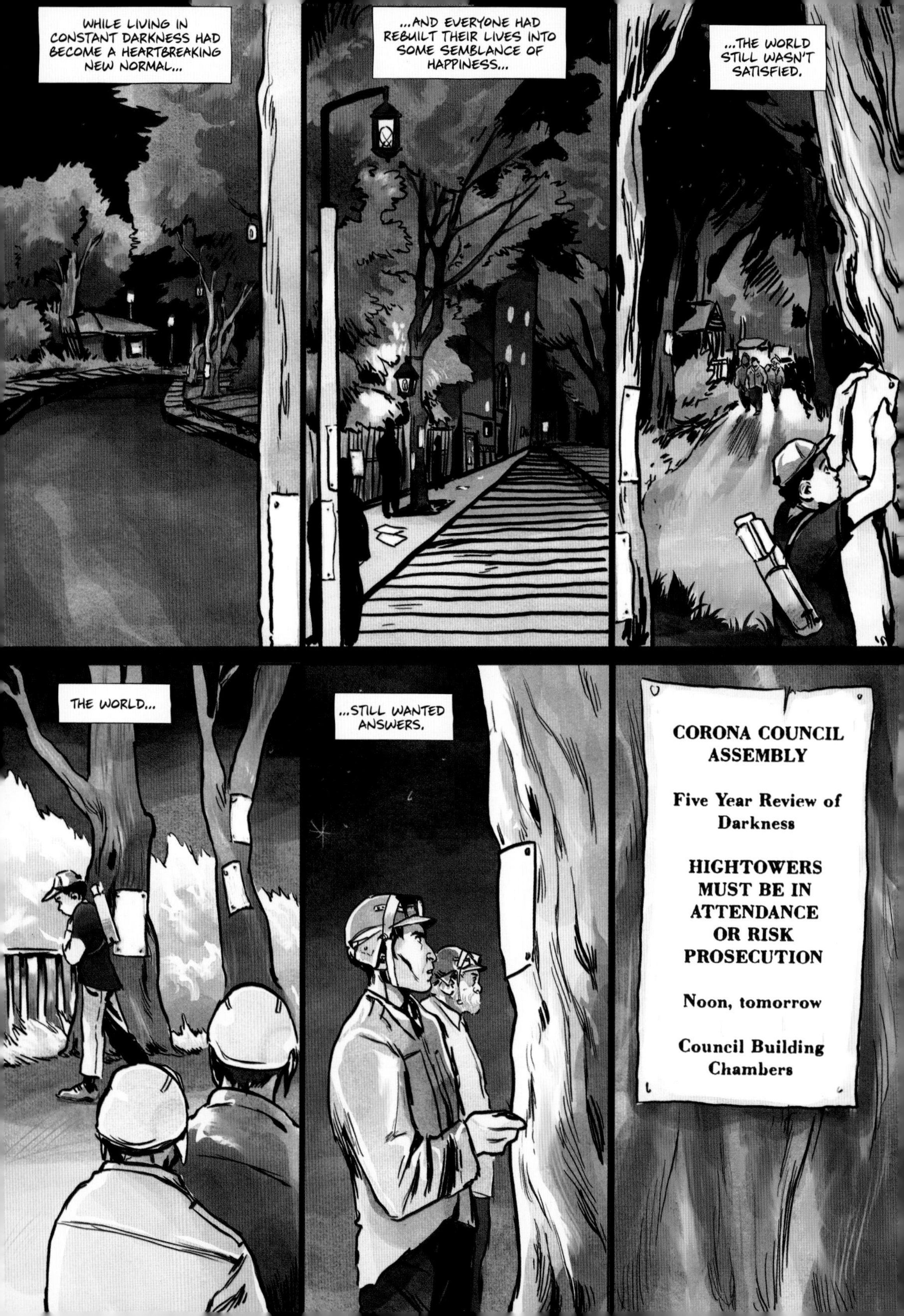
WHILE LIVING IN CONSTANT DARKNESS HAD BECOME A HEARTBREAKING NEW NORMAL...
...AND EVERYONE HAD REBUILT THEIR LIVES INTO SOME SEMBLANCE OF HAPPINESS...
...THE WORLD STILL WASN'T SATISFIED.
THE WORLD...
...STILL WANTED ANSWERS.
CORONA COUNCIL ASSEMBLY
Five Year Review of Darkness
HIGHTOWERS MUST BE IN ATTENDANCE OR RISK PROSECUTION
Noon, tomorrow
Council Building Chambers

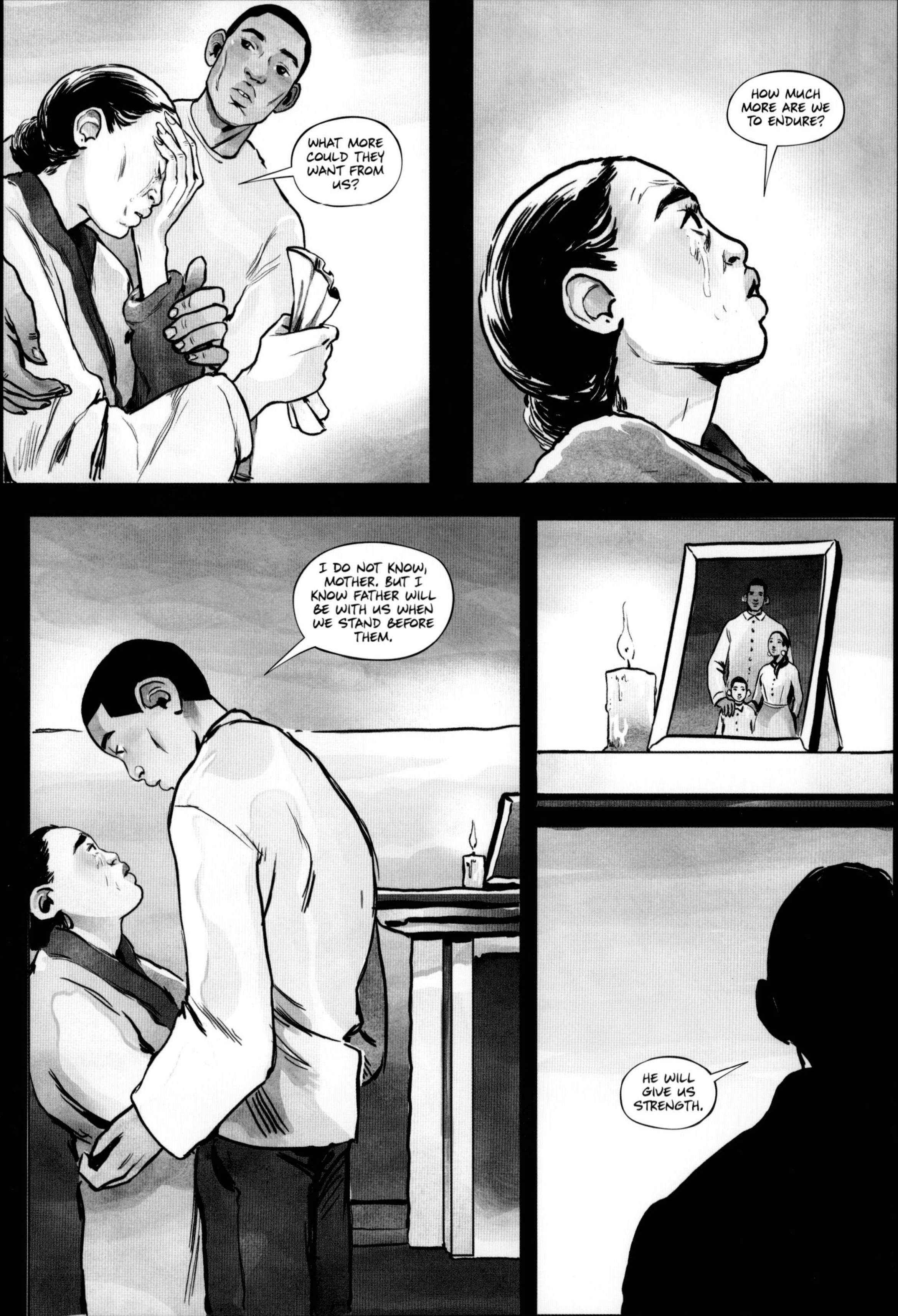
WHAT MORE COULD THEY WANT FROM US?
HOW MUCH MORE ARE WE TO ENDURE?
I DO NOT KNOW, MOTHER. BUT I KNOW FATHER WILL BE WITH US WHEN WE STAND BEFORE THEM.
HE WILL GIVE US STRENGTH.

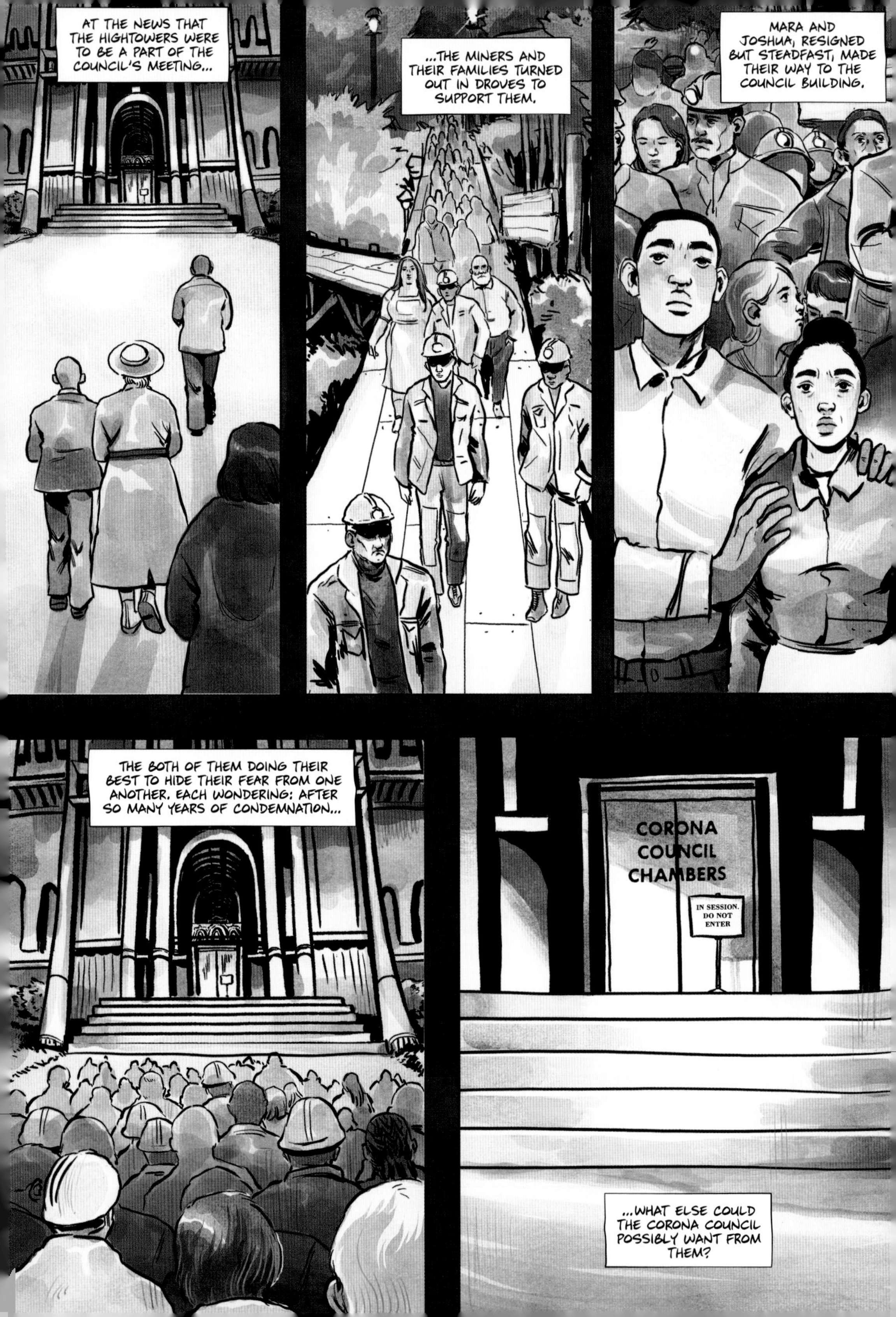
AT THE NEWS THAT THE HIGHTOWERS WERE TO BE A PART OF THE COUNCIL'S MEETING...
...THE MINERS AND THEIR FAMILIES TURNED OUT IN DROVES TO SUPPORT THEM.
MARA AND JOSHUA, RESIGNED BUT STEADFAST, MADE THEIR WAY TO THE COUNCIL BUILDING.
THE BOTH OF THEM DOING THEIR BEST TO HIDE THEIR FEAR FROM ONE ANOTHER. EACH WONDERING: AFTER SO MANY YEARS OF CONDEMNATION...
CORONA COUNCIL CHAMBERS
IN SESSION. DO NOT ENTER
...WHAT ELSE COULD THE CORONA COUNCIL POSSIBLY WANT FROM THEM?

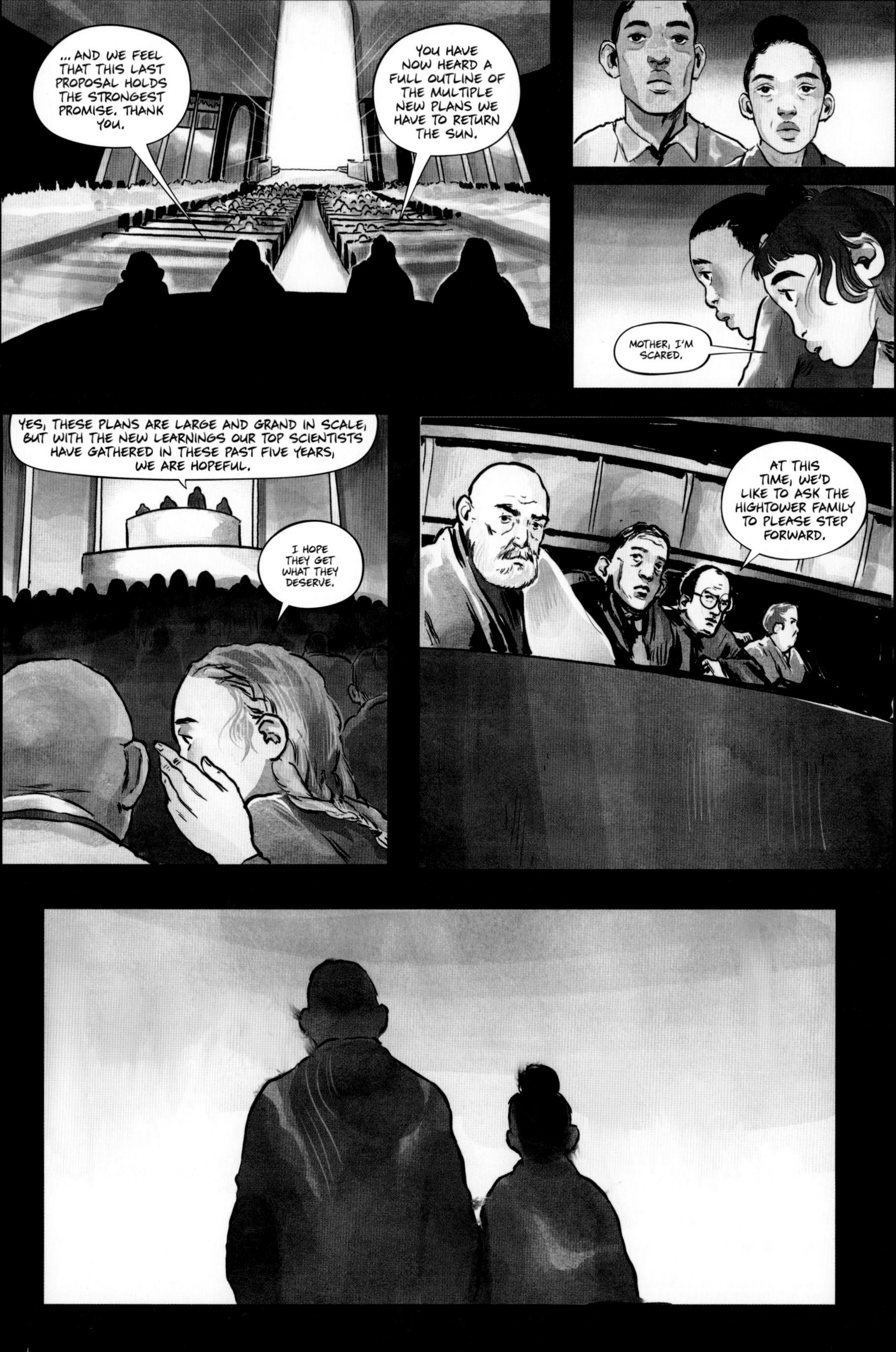
...AND WE FEEL THAT THIS LAST PROPOSAL HOLDS THE STRONGEST PROMISE. THANK YOU.
YOU HAVE NOW HEARD A FULL OUTLINE OF THE MULTIPLE NEW PLANS WE HAVE TO RETURN THE SUN.
MOTHER, I'M SCARED.
YES, THESE PLANS ARE LARGE AND GRAND IN SCALE, BUT WITH THE NEW LEARNINGS OUR TOP SCIENTISTS HAVE GATHERED IN THESE PAST FIVE YEARS, WE ARE HOPEFUL.
I HOPE THEY GET WHAT THEY DESERVE.
AT THIS TIME, WE'D LIKE TO ASK THE HIGHTOWER FAMILY TO PLEASE STEP FORWARD.

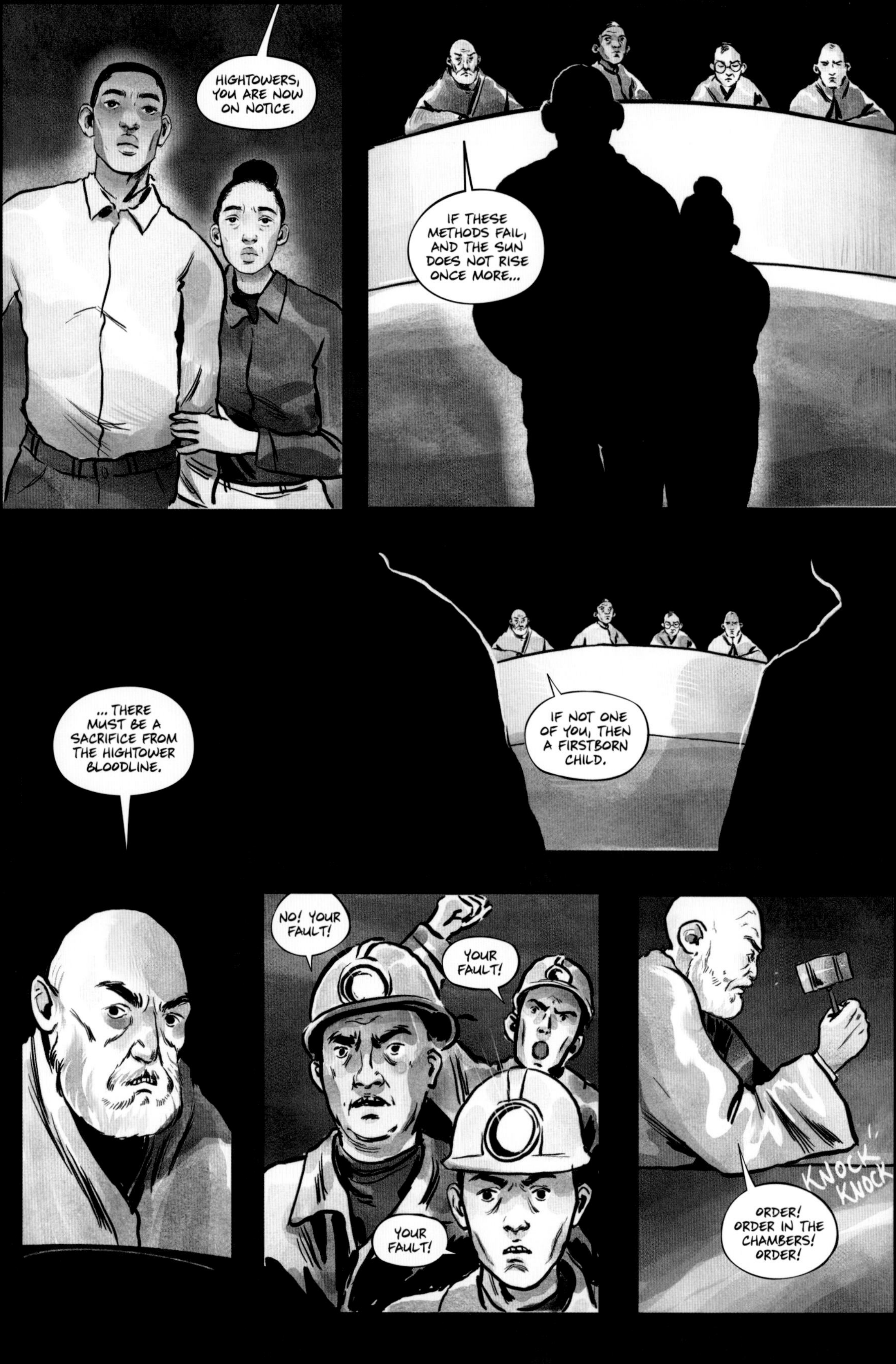
HIGHTOWERS, YOU ARE NOW ON NOTICE.
IF THESE METHODS FAIL, AND THE SUN DOES NOT RISE ONCE MORE...
...THERE MUST BE A SACRIFICE FROM THE HIGHTOWER BLOODLINE.
IF NOT ONE OF YOU, THEN A FIRSTBORN CHILD.
NO! YOUR FAULT!
YOUR FAULT!
YOUR FAULT!
KNOCK KNOCK
ORDER! ORDER IN THE CHAMBERS! ORDER!

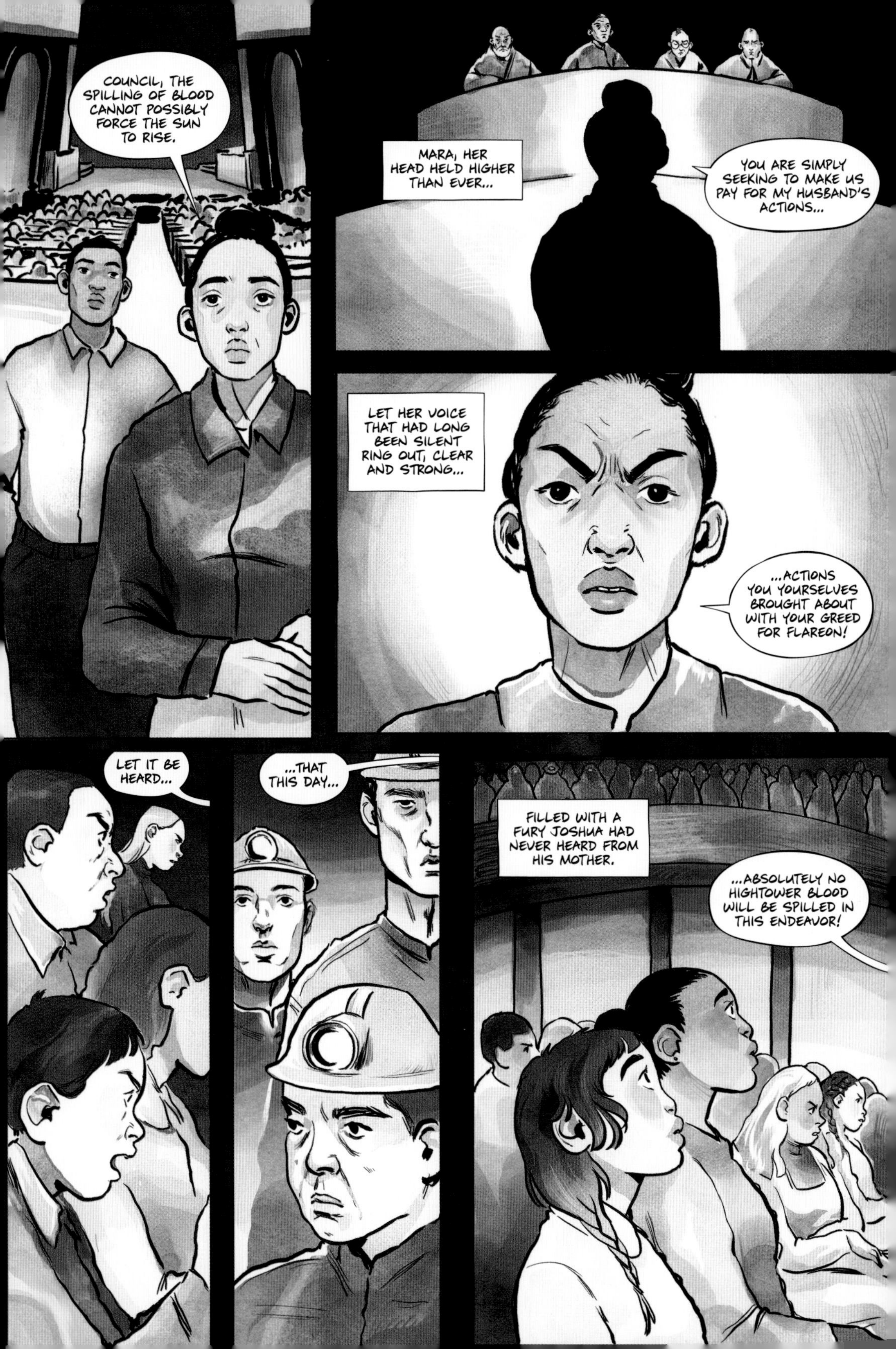
COUNCIL, THE SPILLING OF BLOOD CANNOT POSSIBLY FORCE THE SUN TO RISE.
MARA, HER HEAD HELD HIGHER THAN EVER...
YOU ARE SIMPLY SEEKING TO MAKE US PAY FOR MY HUSBAND'S ACTIONS...
LET HER VOICE THAT HAD LONG BEEN SILENT RING OUT, CLEAR AND STRONG...
...ACTIONS YOU YOURSELVES BROUGHT ABOUT WITH YOUR GREED FOR FLAREON!
LET IT BE HEARD...
...THAT THIS DAY...
FILLED WITH A FURY JOSHUA HAD NEVER HEARD FROM HIS MOTHER.
...ABSOLUTELY NO HIGHTOWER BLOOD WILL BE SPILLED IN THIS ENDEAVOR!

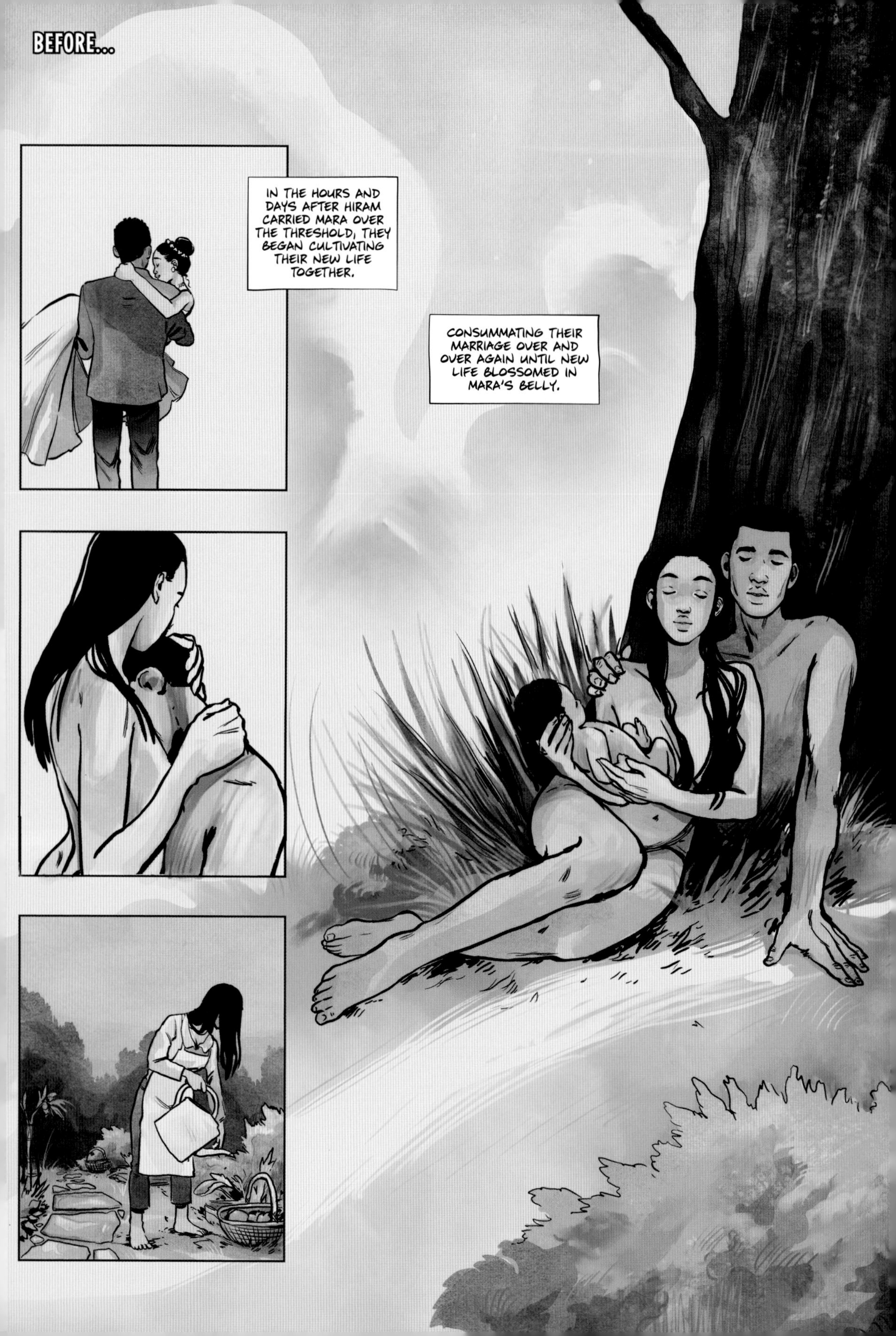
BEFORE...
IN THE HOURS AND DAYS AFTER HIRAM CARRIED MARA OVER THE THRESHOLD, THEY BEGAN CULTIVATING THEIR NEW LIFE TOGETHER.
CONSUMMATING THEIR MARRIAGE OVER AND OVER AGAIN UNTIL NEW LIFE BLOSSOMED IN MARA'S BELLY.

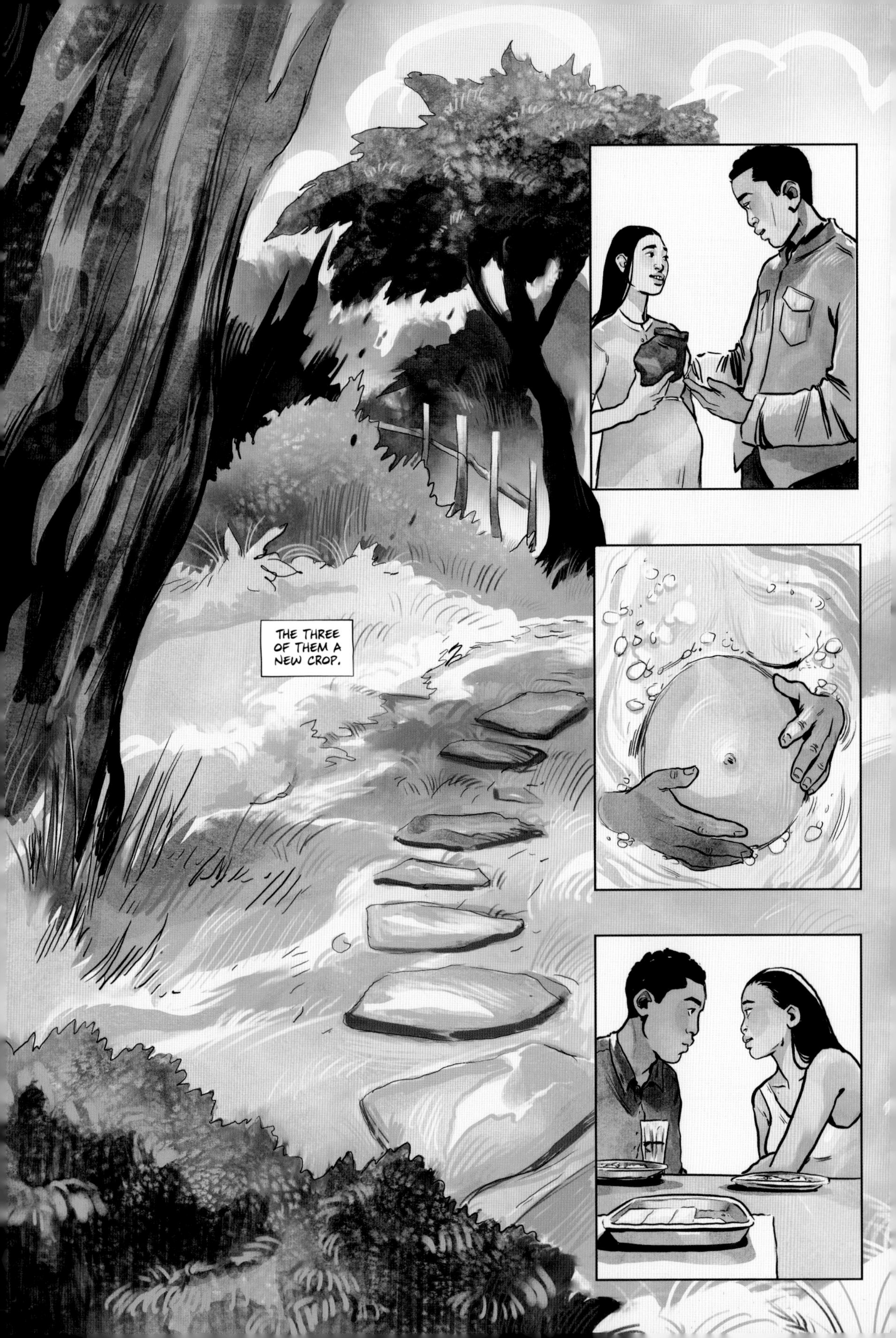
THE THREE OF THEM A NEW CROP.

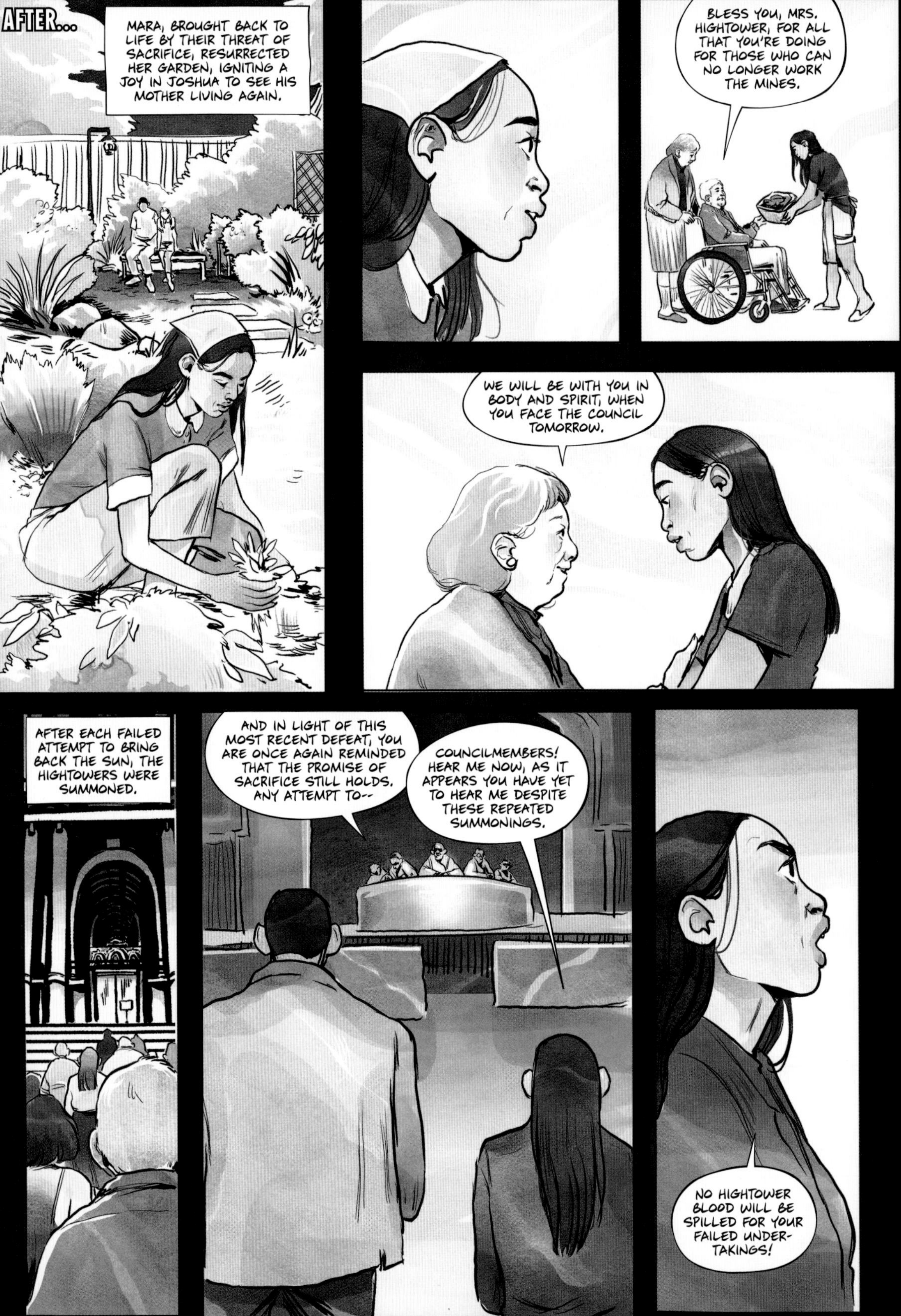
AFTER...
MARA, BROUGHT BACK TO LIFE BY THEIR THREAT OF SACRIFICE, RESURRECTED HER GARDEN, IGNITING A JOY IN JOSHUA TO SEE HIS MOTHER LIVING AGAIN.
BLESS YOU, MRS. HIGHTOWER, FOR ALL THAT YOU'RE DOING FOR THOSE WHO CAN NO LONGER WORK THE MINES.
WE WILL BE WITH YOU IN BODY AND SPIRIT, WHEN YOU FACE THE COUNCIL TOMORROW.
AFTER EACH FAILED ATTEMPT TO BRING BACK THE SUN, THE HIGHTOWERS WERE SUMMONED.
AND IN LIGHT OF THIS MOST RECENT DEFEAT, YOU ARE ONCE AGAIN REMINDED THAT THE PROMISE OF SACRIFICE STILL HOLDS. ANY ATTEMPT TO--
COUNCILMEMBERS! HEAR ME NOW, AS IT APPEARS YOU HAVE YET TO HEAR ME DESPITE THESE REPEATED SUMMONINGS.
NO HIGHTOWER BLOOD WILL BE SPILLED FOR YOUR FAILED UNDER-TAKINGS!

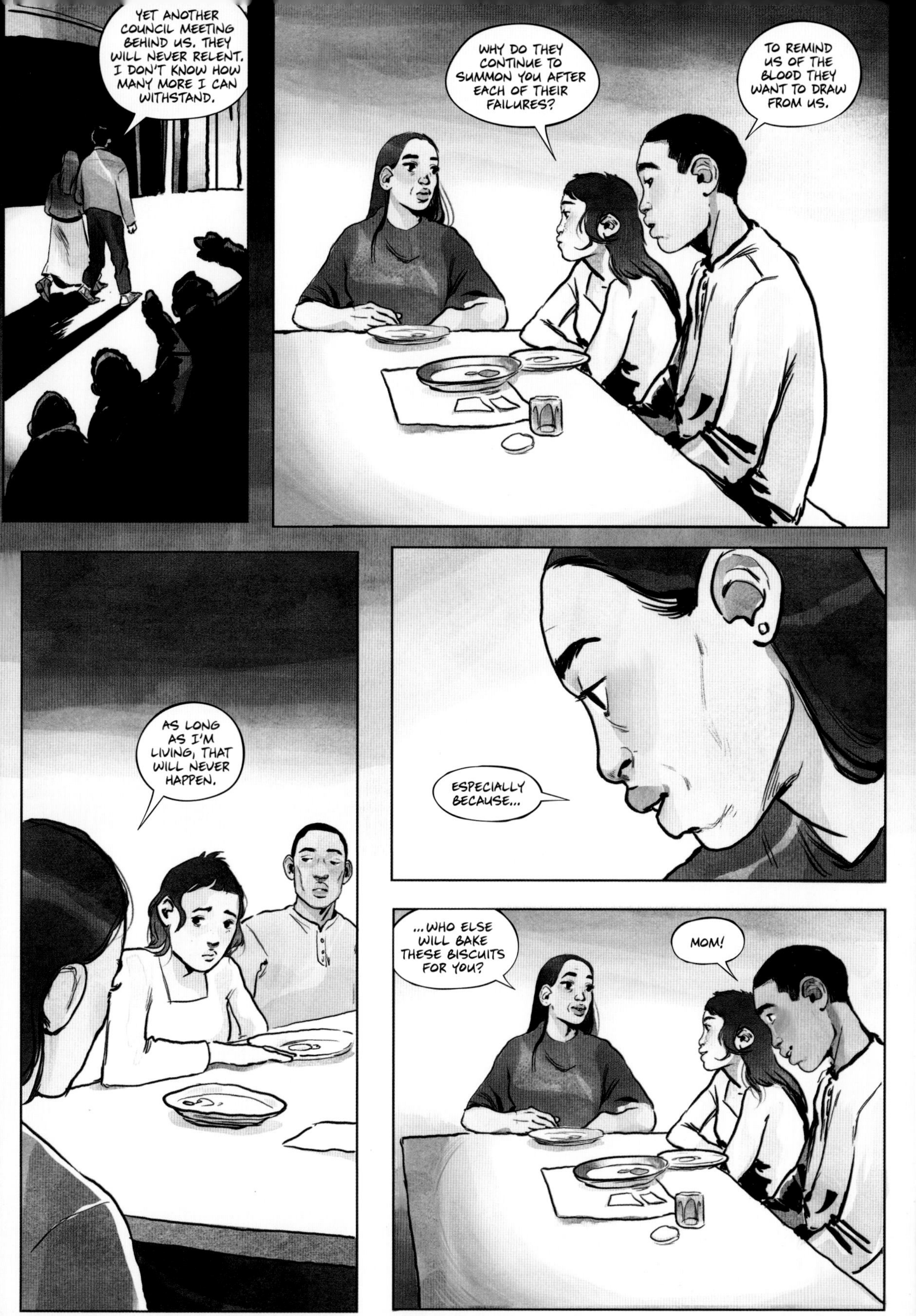
YET ANOTHER COUNCIL MEETING BEHIND US. THEY WILL NEVER RELENT. I DON'T KNOW HOW MANY MORE I CAN WITHSTAND.
WHY DO THEY CONTINUE TO SUMMON YOU AFTER EACH OF THEIR FAILURES?
TO REMIND US OF THE BLOOD THEY WANT TO DRAW FROM US.
AS LONG AS I'M LIVING, THAT WILL NEVER HAPPEN.
ESPECIALLY BECAUSE...
...WHO ELSE WILL BAKE THESE BISCUITS FOR YOU?
MOM!

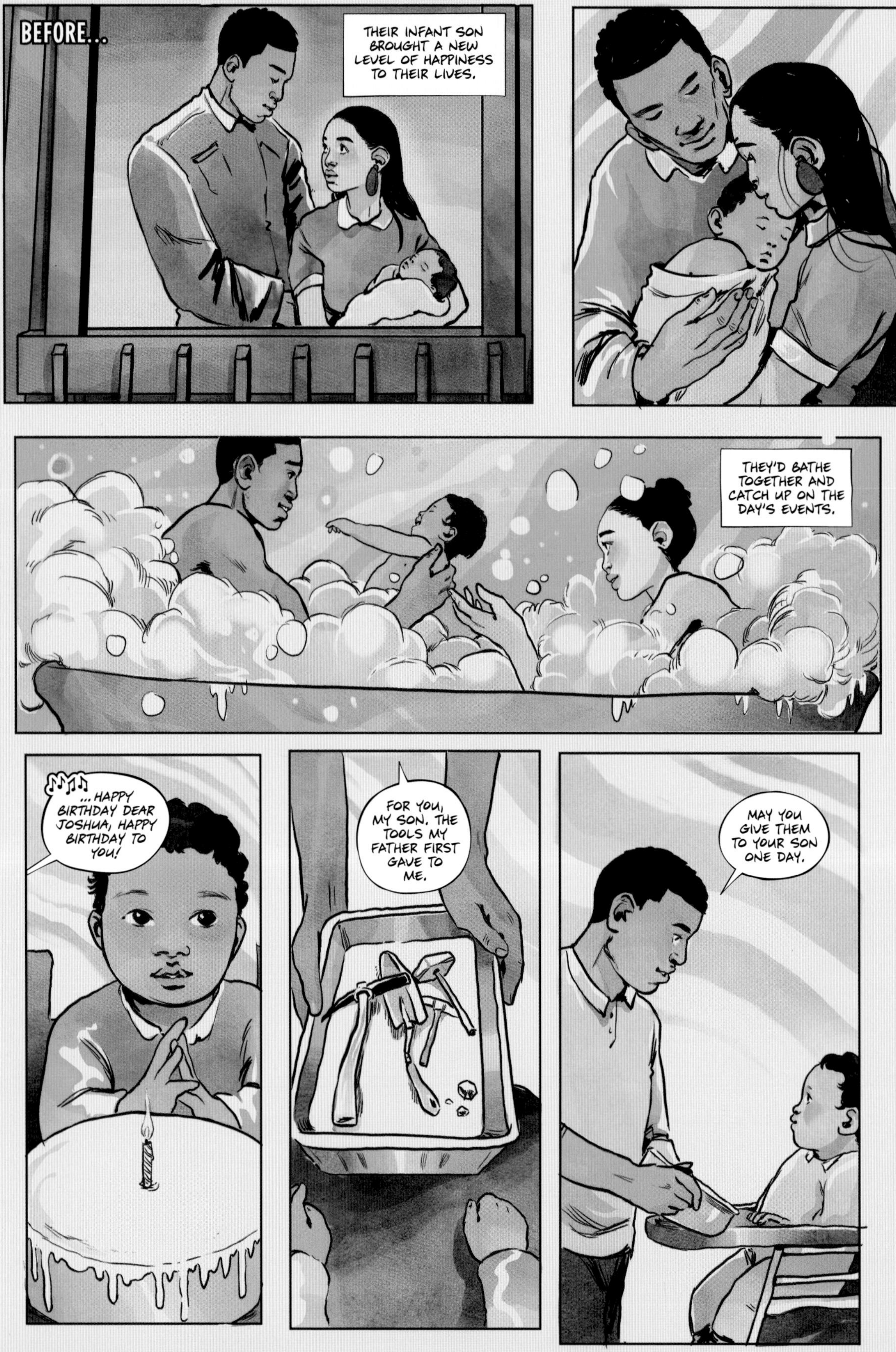
BEFORE...
THEIR INFANT SON BROUGHT A NEW LEVEL OF HAPPINESS TO THEIR LIVES.
THEY'D BATHE TOGETHER AND CATCH UP ON THE DAY'S EVENTS.
...HAPPY BIRTHDAY DEAR JOSHUA, HAPPY BIRTHDAY TO YOU!
FOR YOU, MY SON. THE TOOLS MY FATHER FIRST GAVE TO ME.
MAY YOU GIVE THEM TO YOUR SON ONE DAY.

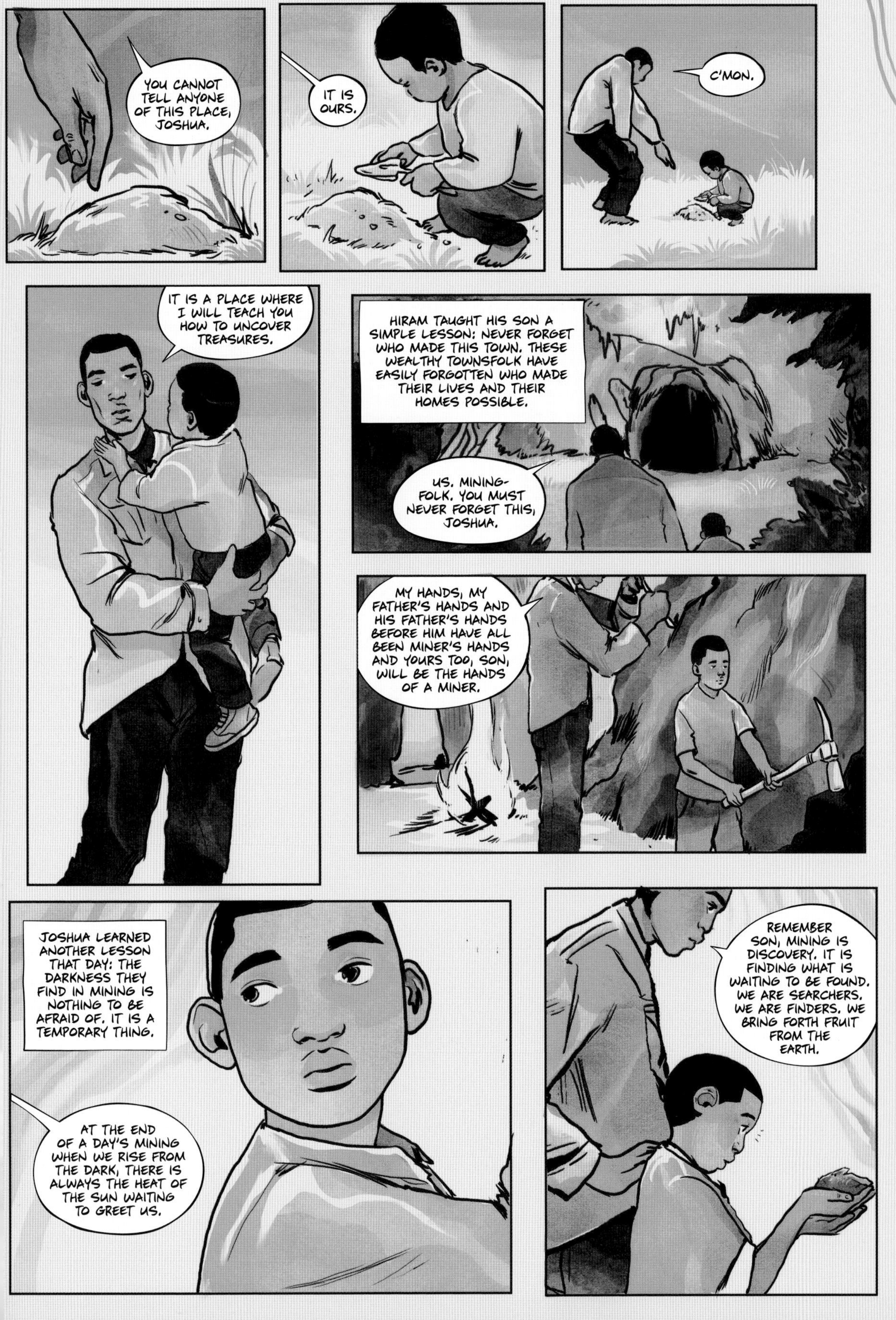
YOU CANNOT TELL ANYONE OF THIS PLACE, JOSHUA.
IT IS OURS.
C'MON.
IT IS A PLACE WHERE I WILL TEACH YOU HOW TO UNCOVER TREASURES.
HIRAM TAUGHT HIS SON A SIMPLE LESSON: NEVER FORGET WHO MADE THIS TOWN. THESE WEALTHY TOWNSFOLK HAVE EASILY FORGOTTEN WHO MADE THEIR LIVES AND THEIR HOMES POSSIBLE.
US. MINING-FOLK. YOU MUST NEVER FORGET THIS, JOSHUA.
MY HANDS, MY FATHER'S HANDS AND HIS FATHER'S HANDS BEFORE HIM HAVE ALL BEEN MINER'S HANDS AND YOURS TOO, SON, WILL BE THE HANDS OF A MINER.
JOSHUA LEARNED ANOTHER LESSON THAT DAY: THE DARKNESS THEY FIND IN MINING IS NOTHING TO BE AFRAID OF. IT IS A TEMPORARY THING.
AT THE END OF A DAY'S MINING WHEN WE RISE FROM THE DARK, THERE IS ALWAYS THE HEAT OF THE SUN WAITING TO GREET US.
REMEMBER SON, MINING IS DISCOVERY. IT IS FINDING WHAT IS WAITING TO BE FOUND. WE ARE SEARCHERS. WE ARE FINDERS. WE BRING FORTH FRUIT FROM THE EARTH.

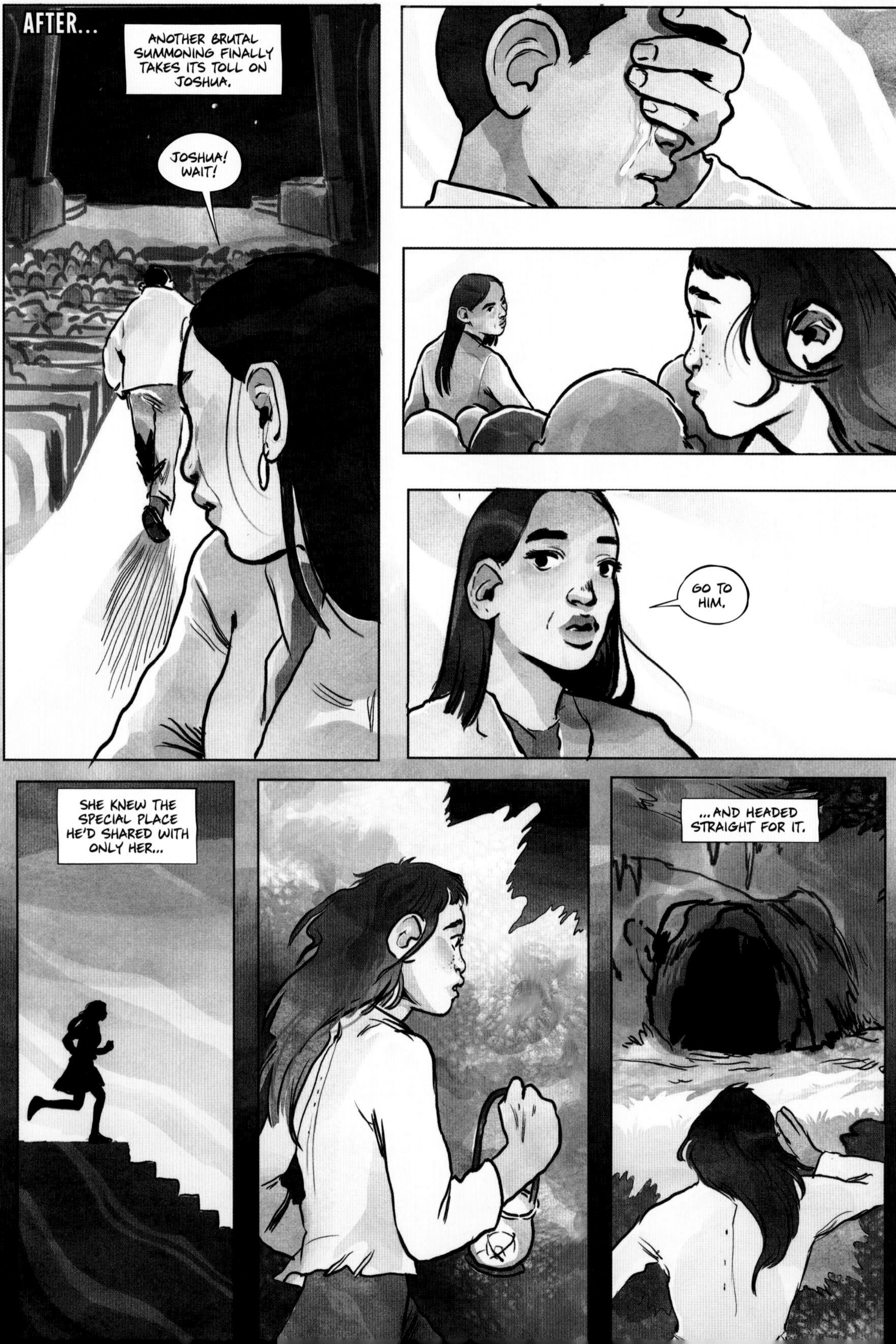
AFTER...
ANOTHER BRUTAL SUMMONING FINALLY TAKES ITS TOLL ON JOSHUA.
JOSHUA! WAIT!
GO TO HIM.
SHE KNEW THE SPECIAL PLACE HE'D SHARED WITH ONLY HER...
...AND HEADED STRAIGHT FOR IT.

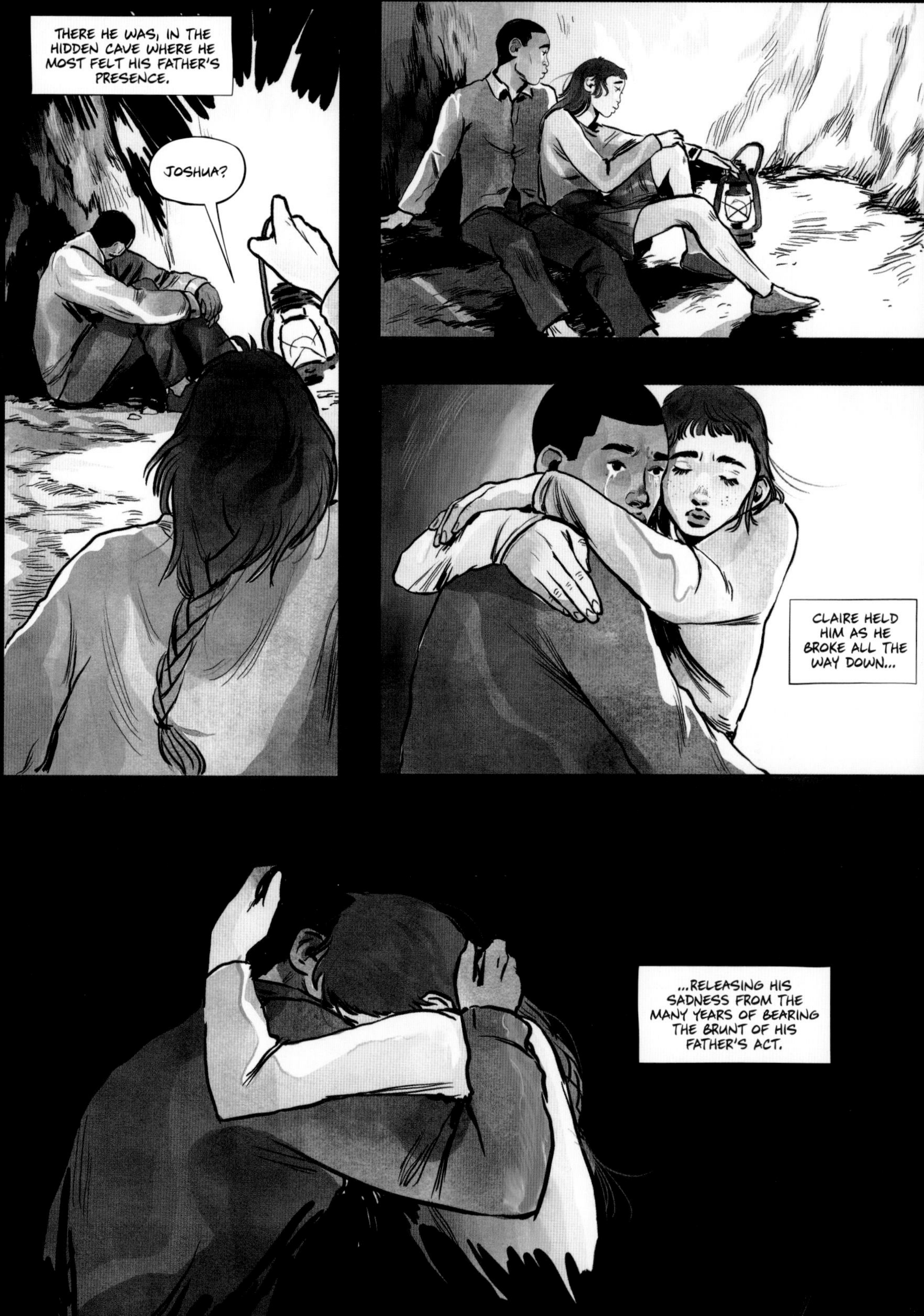
THERE HE WAS, IN THE HIDDEN CAVE WHERE HE MOST FELT HIS FATHER'S PRESENCE.
JOSHUA?
CLAIRE HELD HIM AS HE BROKE ALL THE WAY DOWN...
...RELEASING HIS SADNESS FROM THE MANY YEARS OF BEARING THE BRUNT OF HIS FATHER'S ACT.

JOSHUA HIGHTOWER...

...I WILL NEVER LET THEM HURT YOU.

YOU OR ANYTHING WE MAY PLANT TOGETHER IN THE GARDEN.

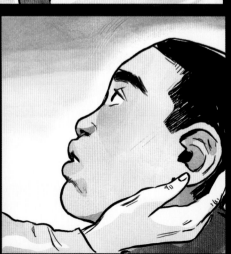

ONE YEAR LATER THE CORONA COUNCIL SUMMONED THE HIGHTOWERS AGAIN.

PLEASE.

THE CRUELTY AND CONDEMNATION HAMMERED UPON THEM LIKE NEVER BEFORE.

HIGHTOWERS SHOULD DIE!

YOU RUINED OUR LIVES!

...YOUR HUSBAND'S SELFISH ACT!

BRING BACK THE SUN OR DIE!

SACRIFICE!

HE TOOK OUR WORLD AWAY!

SACRIFICE!

SACRIFICE! SACRIFICE!

SACRIFICE!

SACRIFICE!

SACRIFICE!

SACRIFICE!

SACRIFICE! SACRIFICE! RIFICE! SACRIFICE! SACRIFICE! SAC SACRIFICE!

STOP!

SACRIFICE!

ENOUGH! I OFFER MY LIFE!

AND LIKE HIS FATHER BEFORE HIM...

...JOSHUA COULD NOT TAKE IT ANYMORE.

LET THIS CEASE.

DON'T YOU DO THIS, JOSHUA HIGHTOWER!

NOBODY SPEAKS UNLESS CALLED UPON! I DEMAND SILENCE! YOU'VE ALL BEEN WARNED!

STOP THIS. NOW. THE SPILLING OF HIGHTOWER BLOOD WILL NOT BRING BACK THE SUN AND IT IS ABSURD THAT ANYONE IN THIS TOWN THINKS IT MIGHT.

CLAIRE'S VOICE RANG OUT IN THE CHAMBER FOR THE TWO PEOPLE WHO HAD BECOME A SECOND FAMILY TO HER.

NEVER CALL US BACK HERE AGAIN.

ENOUGH. LEAVE THESE CHAMBERS. NOW.

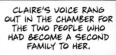

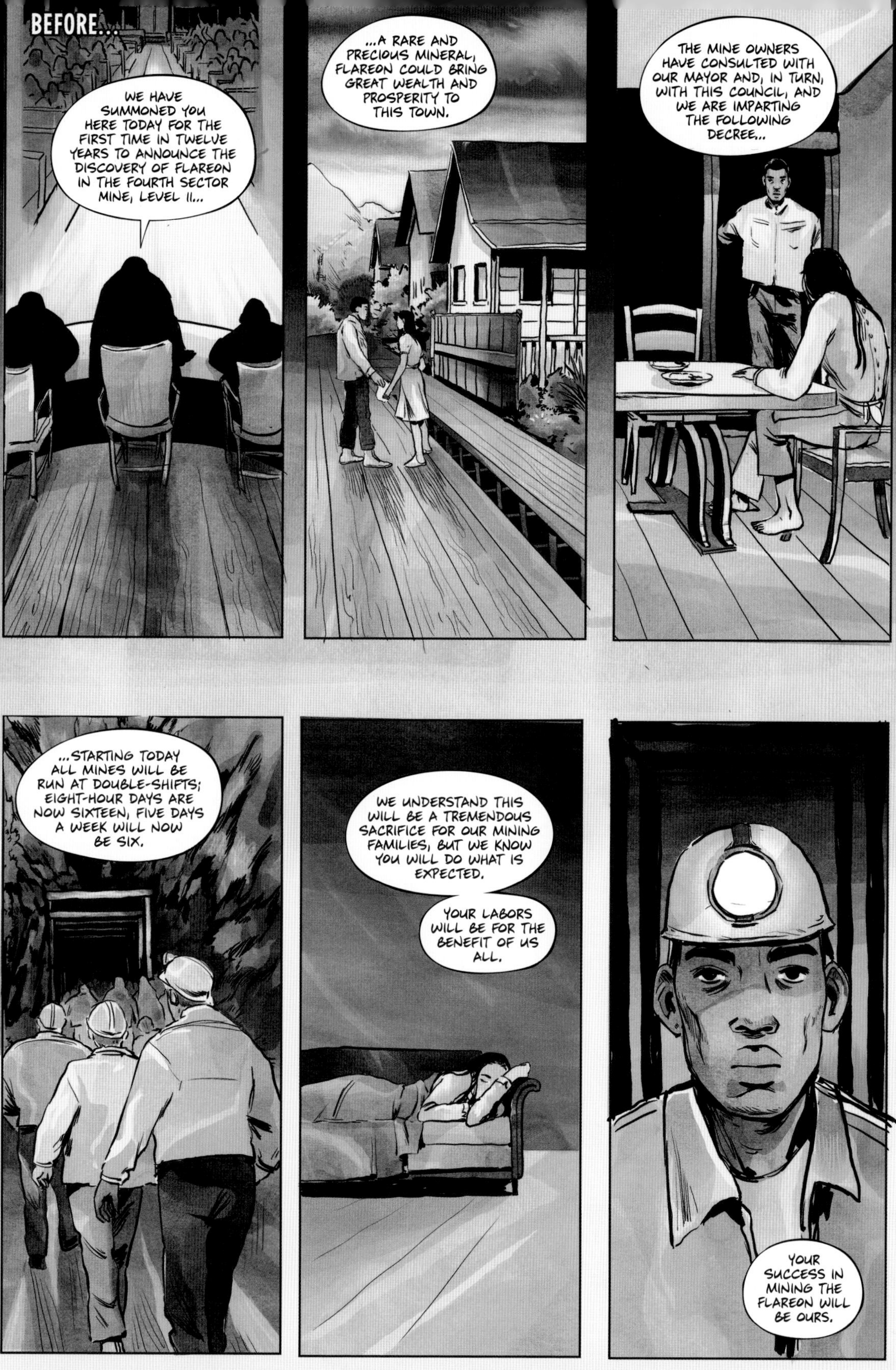
BEFORE...
WE HAVE SUMMONED YOU HERE TODAY FOR THE FIRST TIME IN TWELVE YEARS TO ANNOUNCE THE DISCOVERY OF FLAREON IN THE FOURTH SECTOR MINE, LEVEL 11...
...A RARE AND PRECIOUS MINERAL, FLAREON COULD BRING GREAT WEALTH AND PROSPERITY TO THIS TOWN.
THE MINE OWNERS HAVE CONSULTED WITH OUR MAYOR AND, IN TURN, WITH THIS COUNCIL, AND WE ARE IMPARTING THE FOLLOWING DECREE...
...STARTING TODAY ALL MINES WILL BE RUN AT DOUBLE-SHIFTS; EIGHT-HOUR DAYS ARE NOW SIXTEEN, FIVE DAYS A WEEK WILL NOW BE SIX.
WE UNDERSTAND THIS WILL BE A TREMENDOUS SACRIFICE FOR OUR MINING FAMILIES, BUT WE KNOW YOU WILL DO WHAT IS EXPECTED.
YOUR LABORS WILL BE FOR THE BENEFIT OF US ALL.
YOUR SUCCESS IN MINING THE FLAREON WILL BE OURS.

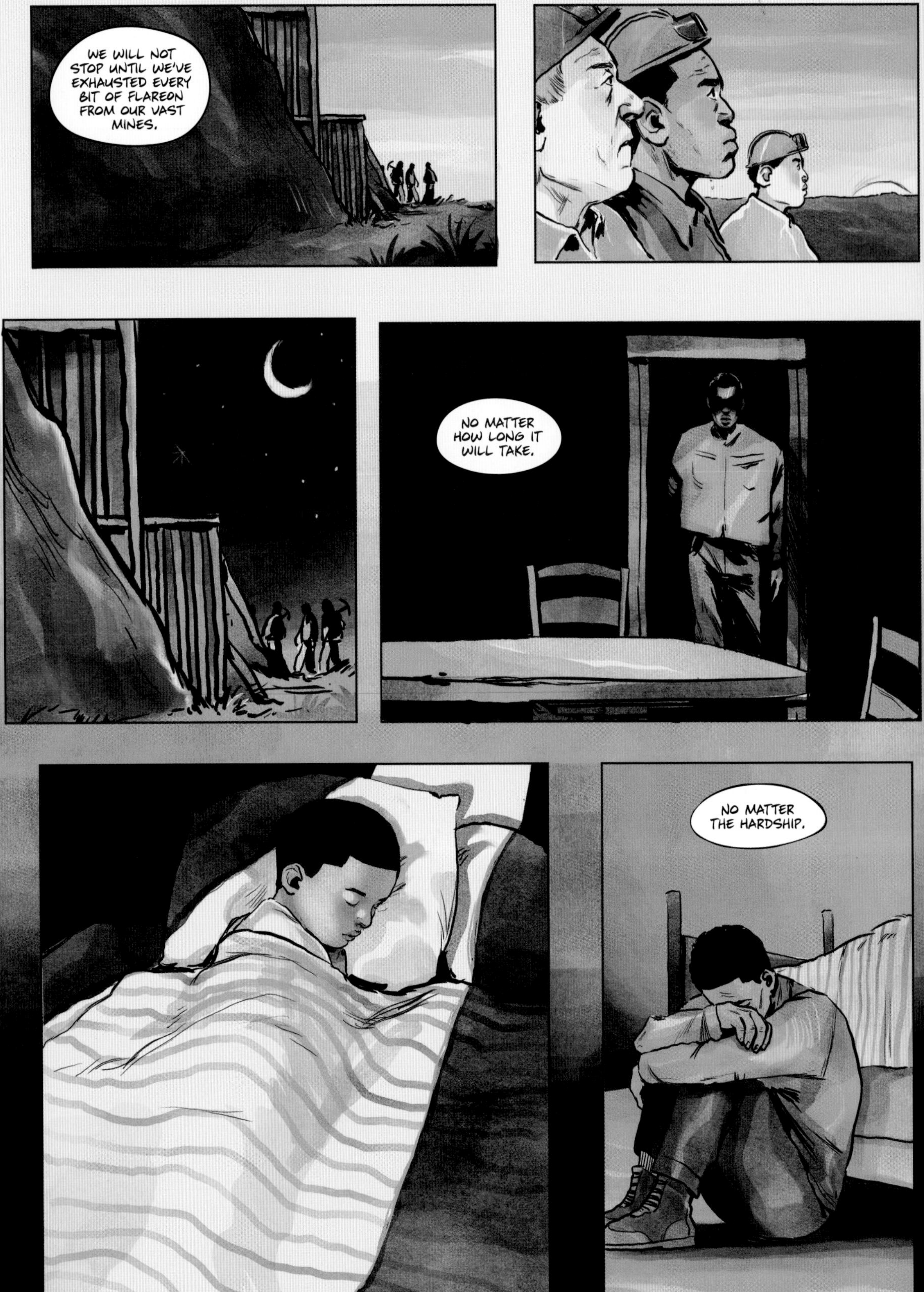
WE WILL NOT STOP UNTIL WE'VE EXHAUSTED EVERY BIT OF FLAREON FROM OUR VAST MINES.
NO MATTER HOW LONG IT WILL TAKE.
NO MATTER THE HARDSHIP.

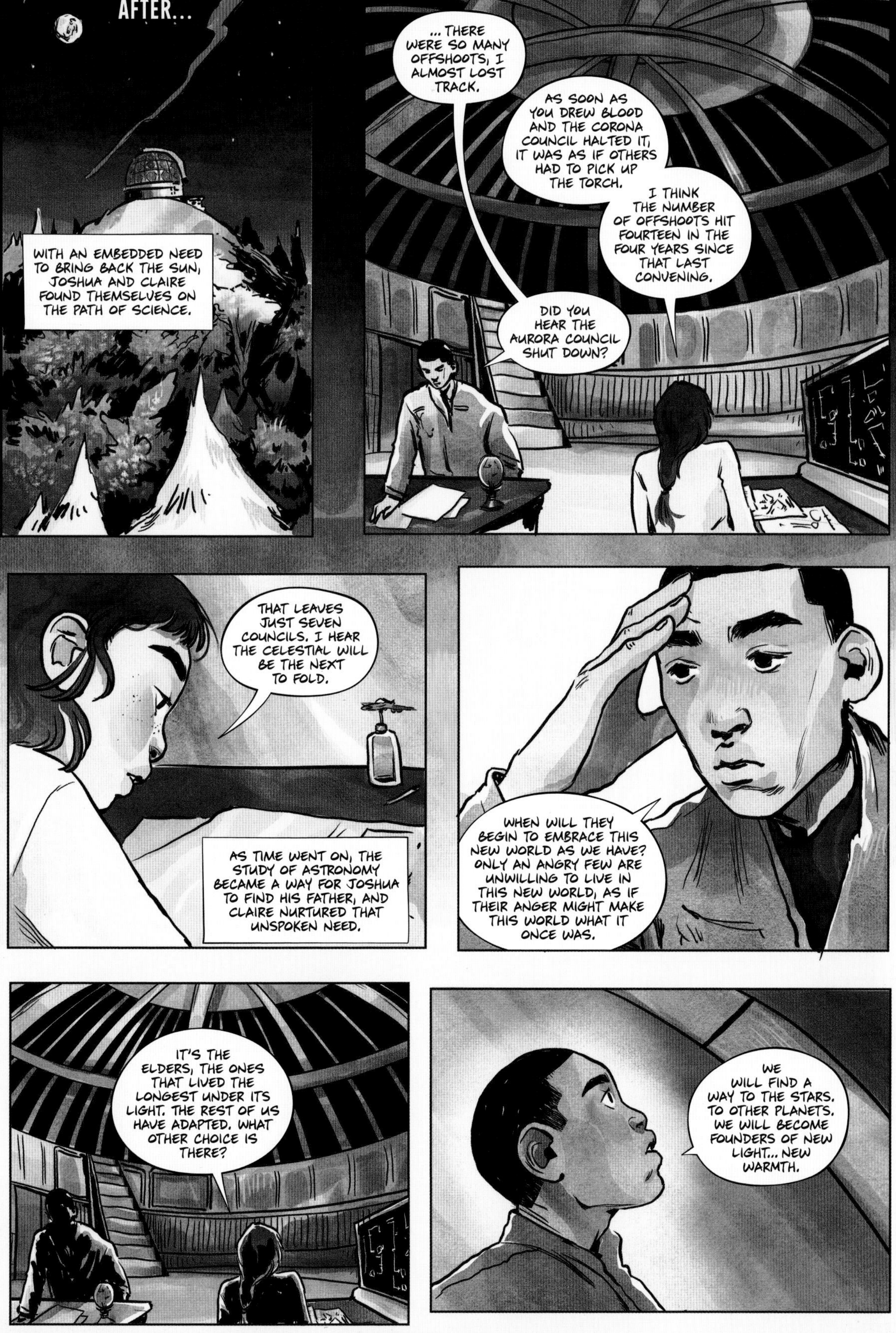
AFTER...
WITH AN EMBEDDED NEED TO BRING BACK THE SUN, JOSHUA AND CLAIRE FOUND THEMSELVES ON THE PATH OF SCIENCE.
DID YOU HEAR THE AURORA COUNCIL SHUT DOWN?
... THERE WERE SO MANY OFFSHOOTS, I ALMOST LOST TRACK.
AS SOON AS YOU DREW BLOOD AND THE CORONA COUNCIL HALTED IT, IT WAS AS IF OTHERS HAD TO PICK UP THE TORCH.
I THINK THE NUMBER OF OFFSHOOTS HIT FOURTEEN IN THE FOUR YEARS SINCE THAT LAST CONVENING.
THAT LEAVES JUST SEVEN COUNCILS. I HEAR THE CELESTIAL WILL BE THE NEXT TO FOLD.
AS TIME WENT ON, THE STUDY OF ASTRONOMY BECAME A WAY FOR JOSHUA TO FIND HIS FATHER, AND CLAIRE NURTURED THAT UNSPOKEN NEED.
WHEN WILL THEY BEGIN TO EMBRACE THIS NEW WORLD AS WE HAVE? ONLY AN ANGRY FEW ARE UNWILLING TO LIVE IN THIS NEW WORLD, AS IF THEIR ANGER MIGHT MAKE THIS WORLD WHAT IT ONCE WAS.
IT'S THE ELDERS, THE ONES THAT LIVED THE LONGEST UNDER ITS LIGHT. THE REST OF US HAVE ADAPTED. WHAT OTHER CHOICE IS THERE?
WE WILL FIND A WAY TO THE STARS. TO OTHER PLANETS. WE WILL BECOME FOUNDERS OF NEW LIGHT... NEW WARMTH.

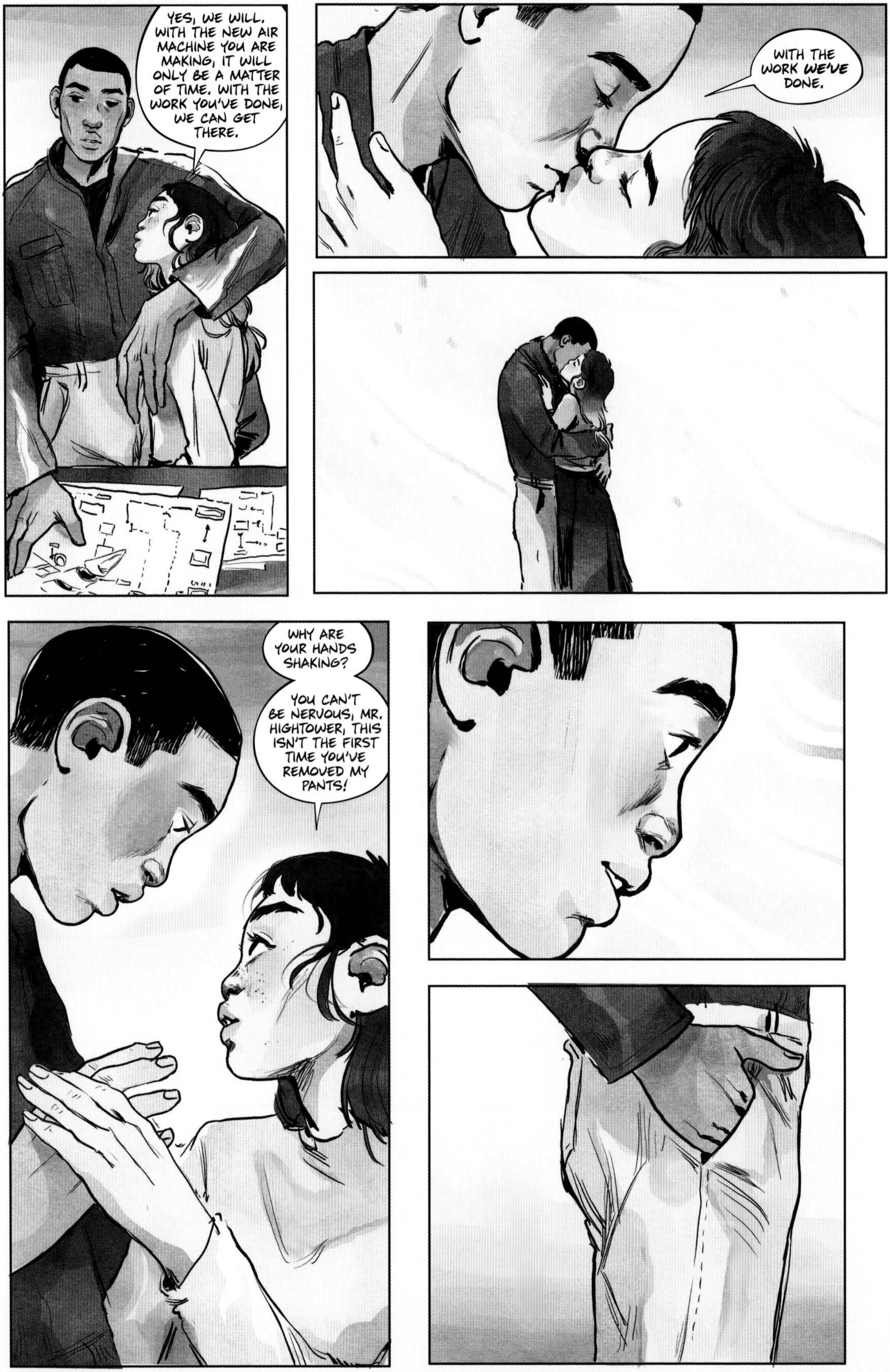
YES, WE WILL. WITH THE NEW AIR MACHINE YOU ARE MAKING, IT WILL ONLY BE A MATTER OF TIME. WITH THE WORK YOU'VE DONE, WE CAN GET THERE.
WITH THE WORK WE'VE DONE.
WHY ARE YOUR HANDS SHAKING?
YOU CAN'T BE NERVOUS, MR. HIGHTOWER, THIS ISN'T THE FIRST TIME YOU'VE REMOVED MY PANTS!

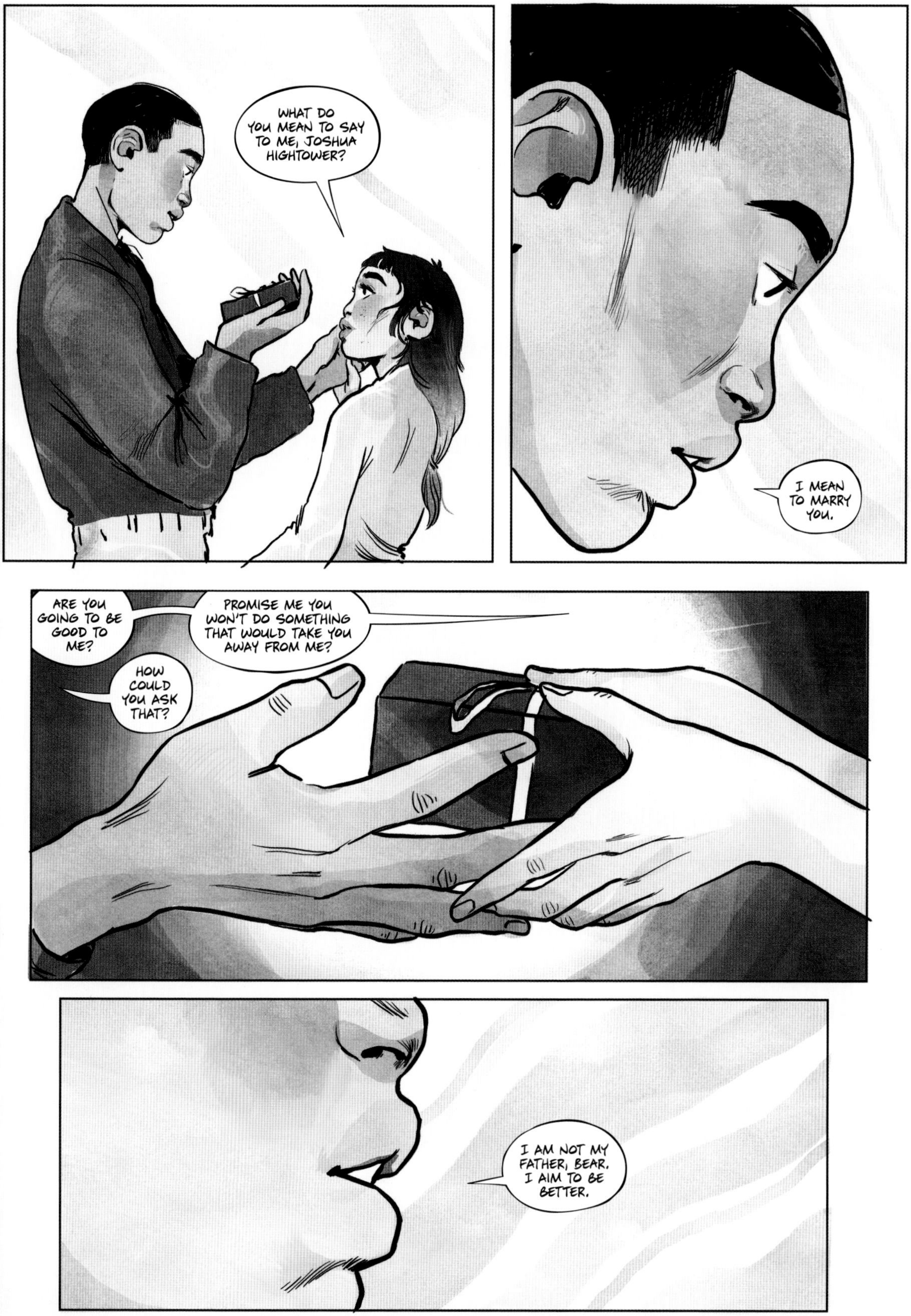
WHAT DO YOU MEAN TO SAY TO ME, JOSHUA HIGHTOWER?
I MEAN TO MARRY YOU.
ARE YOU GOING TO BE GOOD TO ME?
PROMISE ME YOU WON'T DO SOMETHING THAT WOULD TAKE YOU AWAY FROM ME?
HOW COULD YOU ASK THAT?
I AM NOT MY FATHER, BEAR. I AIM TO BE BETTER.

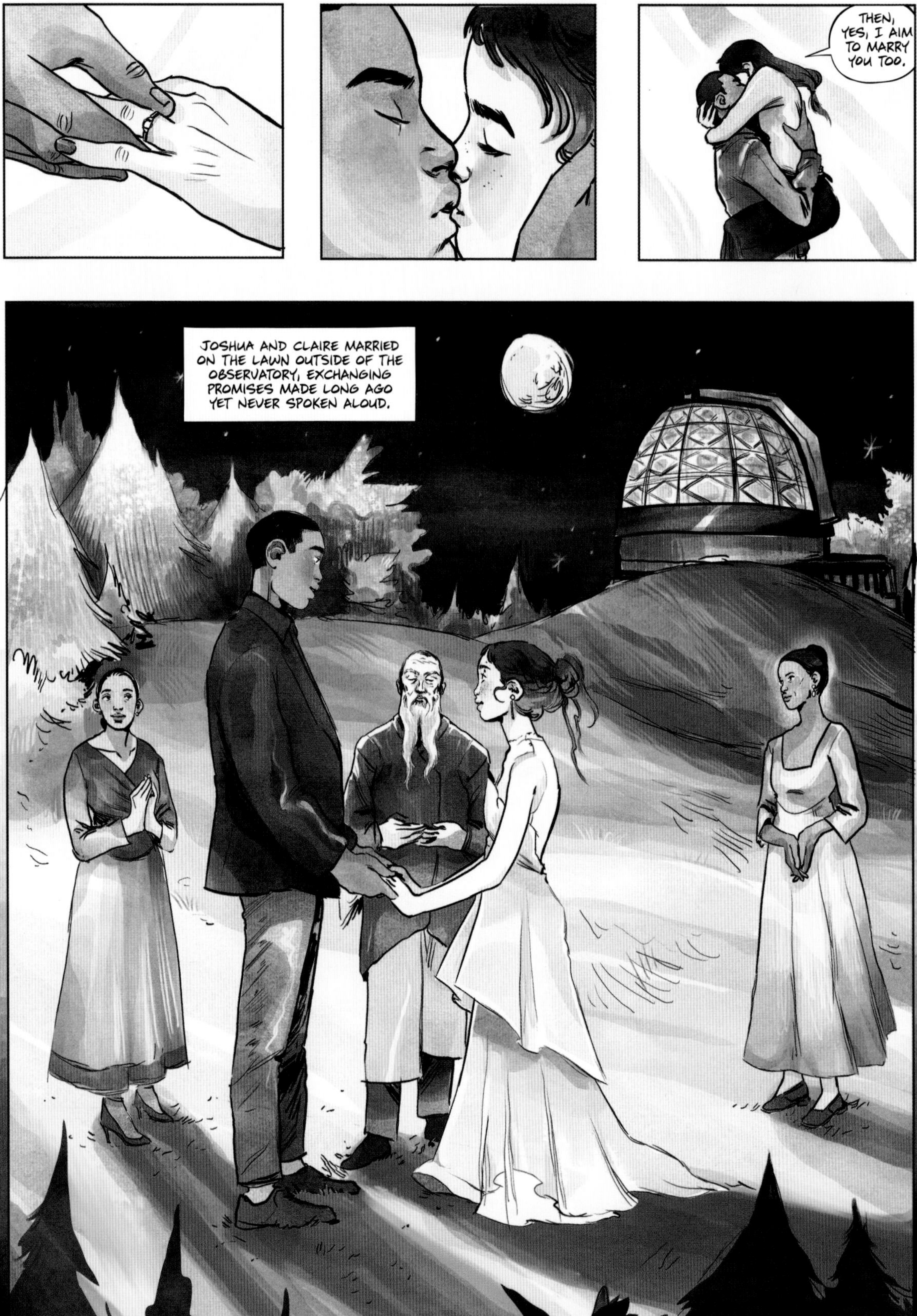
THEN, YES, I AIM TO MARRY YOU TOO.
JOSHUA AND CLAIRE MARRIED ON THE LAWN OUTSIDE OF THE OBSERVATORY, EXCHANGING PROMISES MADE LONG AGO YET NEVER SPOKEN ALOUD.

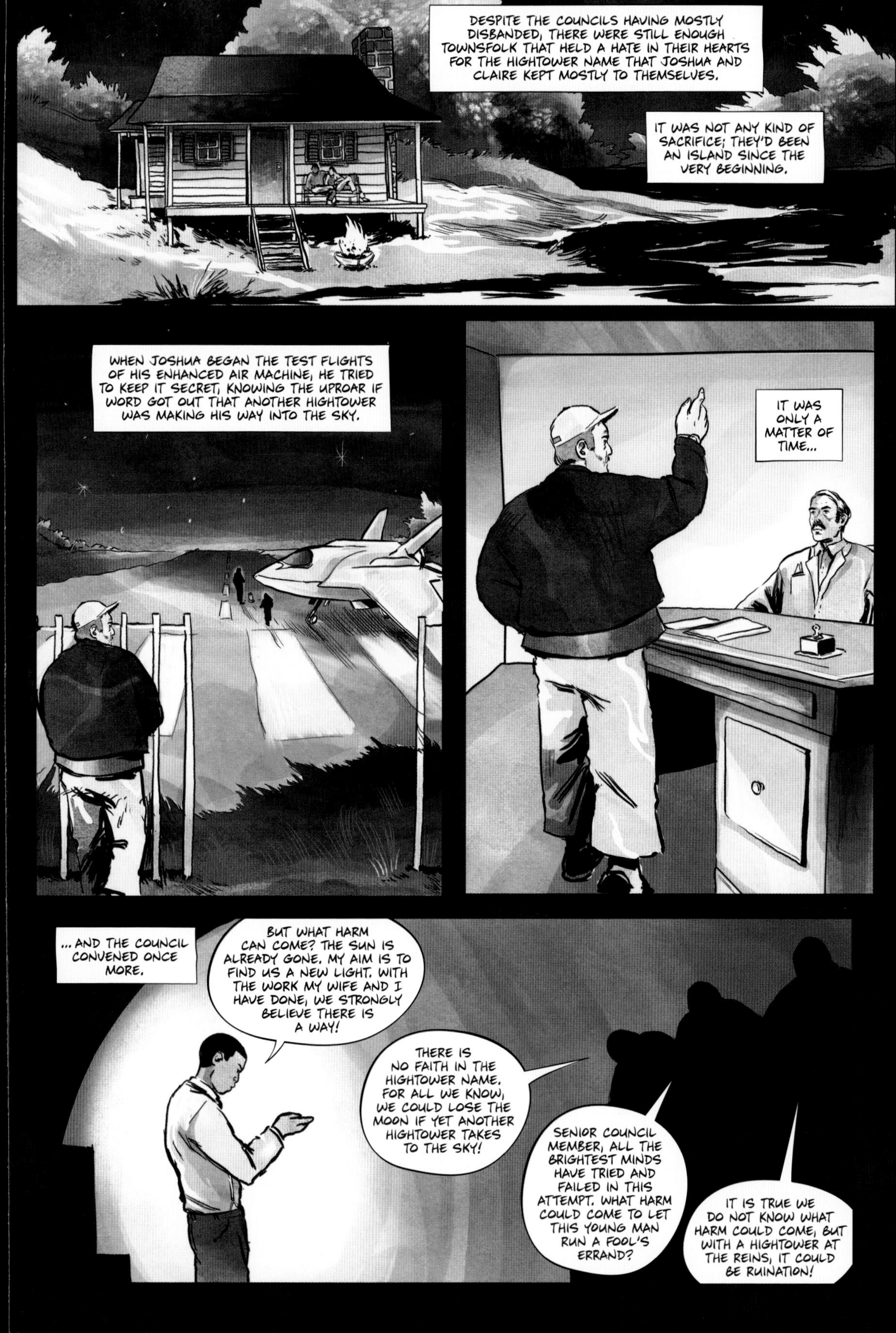

DESPITE THE COUNCILS HAVING MOSTLY DISBANDED, THERE WERE STILL ENOUGH TOWNSFOLK THAT HELD A HATE IN THEIR HEARTS FOR THE HIGHTOWER NAME THAT JOSHUA AND CLAIRE KEPT MOSTLY TO THEMSELVES.
IT WAS NOT ANY KIND OF SACRIFICE; THEY'D BEEN AN ISLAND SINCE THE VERY BEGINNING.
WHEN JOSHUA BEGAN THE TEST FLIGHTS OF HIS ENHANCED AIR MACHINE, HE TRIED TO KEEP IT SECRET, KNOWING THE UPROAR IF WORD GOT OUT THAT ANOTHER HIGHTOWER WAS MAKING HIS WAY INTO THE SKY.
IT WAS ONLY A MATTER OF TIME...
...AND THE COUNCIL CONVENED ONCE MORE.
BUT WHAT HARM CAN COME? THE SUN IS ALREADY GONE. MY AIM IS TO FIND US A NEW LIGHT. WITH THE WORK MY WIFE AND I HAVE DONE, WE STRONGLY BELIEVE THERE IS A WAY!
THERE IS NO FAITH IN THE HIGHTOWER NAME. FOR ALL WE KNOW, WE COULD LOSE THE MOON IF YET ANOTHER HIGHTOWER TAKES TO THE SKY!
SENIOR COUNCIL MEMBER, ALL THE BRIGHTEST MINDS HAVE TRIED AND FAILED IN THIS ATTEMPT. WHAT HARM COULD COME TO LET THIS YOUNG MAN RUN A FOOL'S ERRAND?
IT IS TRUE WE DO NOT KNOW WHAT HARM COULD COME, BUT WITH A HIGHTOWER AT THE REINS, IT COULD BE RUINATION!

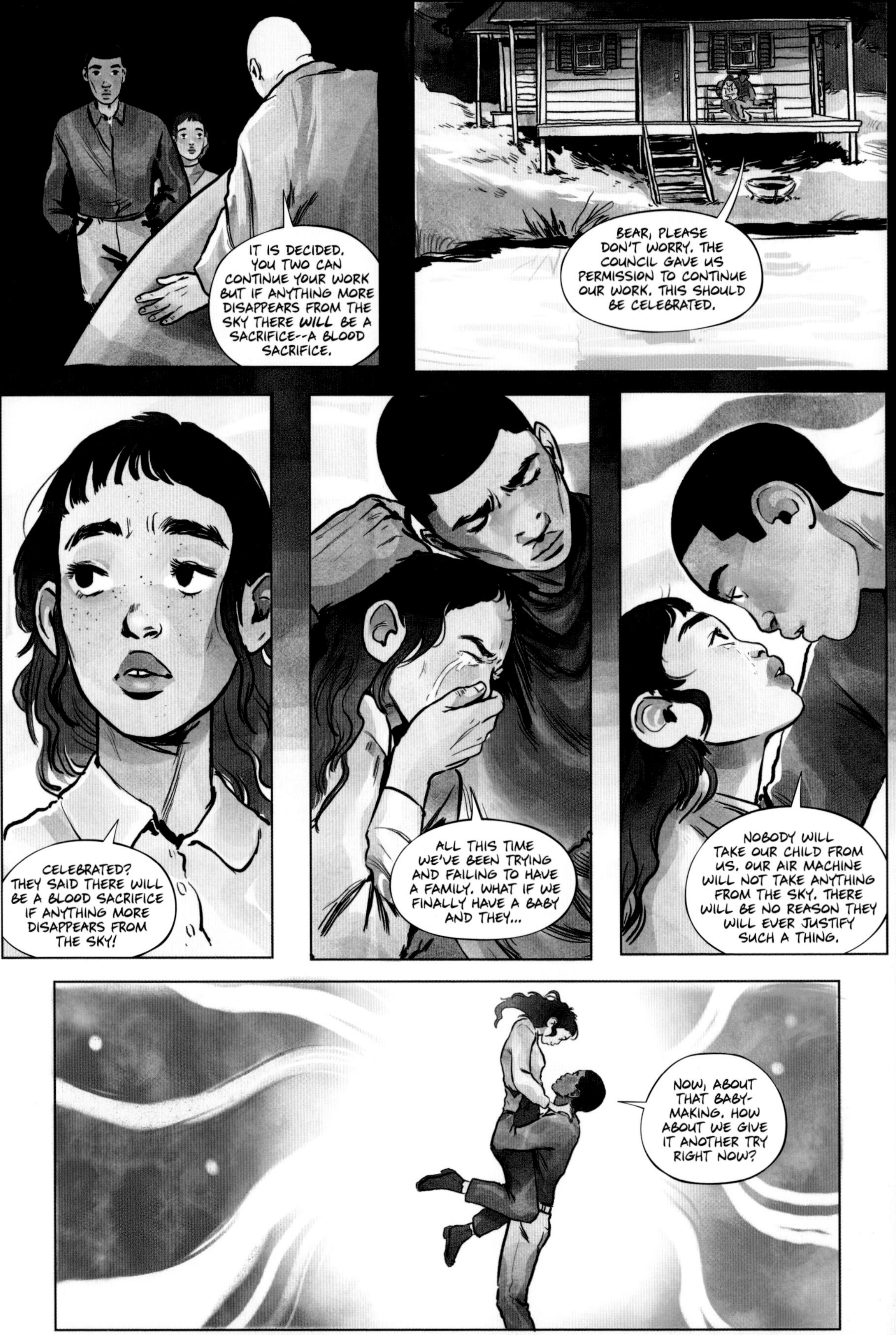
IT IS DECIDED. YOU TWO CAN CONTINUE YOUR WORK BUT IF ANYTHING MORE DISAPPEARS FROM THE SKY THERE *WILL* BE A SACRIFICE--A BLOOD SACRIFICE.
BEAR, PLEASE DON'T WORRY. THE COUNCIL GAVE US PERMISSION TO CONTINUE OUR WORK. THIS SHOULD BE CELEBRATED.
CELEBRATED? THEY SAID THERE WILL BE A BLOOD SACRIFICE IF ANYTHING MORE DISAPPEARS FROM THE SKY!
ALL THIS TIME WE'VE BEEN TRYING AND FAILING TO HAVE A FAMILY. WHAT IF WE FINALLY HAVE A BABY AND THEY...
NOBODY WILL TAKE OUR CHILD FROM US. OUR AIR MACHINE WILL NOT TAKE ANYTHING FROM THE SKY. THERE WILL BE NO REASON THEY WILL EVER JUSTIFY SUCH A THING.
NOW, ABOUT THAT BABY-MAKING. HOW ABOUT WE GIVE IT ANOTHER TRY RIGHT NOW?

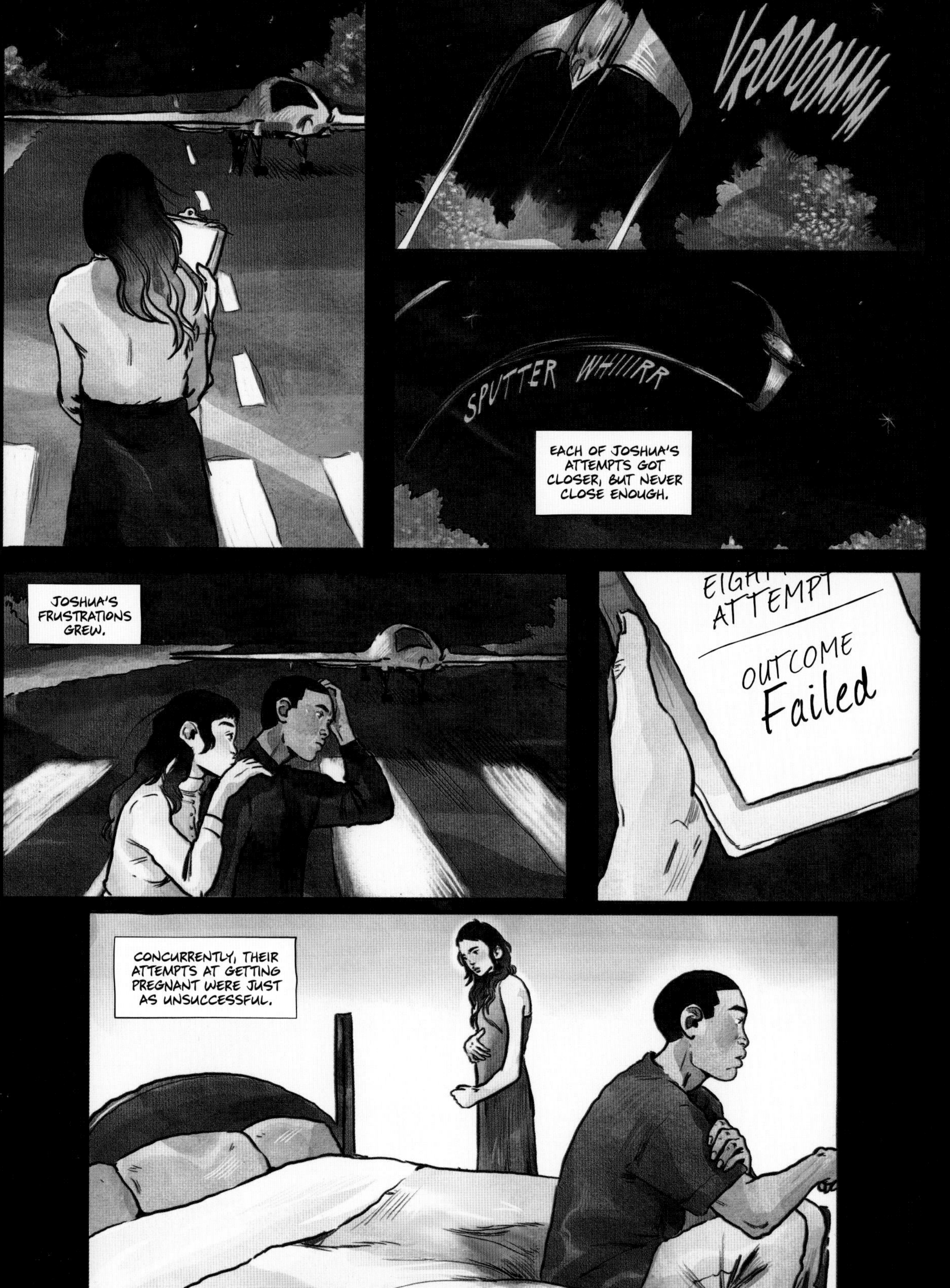
VROOOMMM
SPUTTER WHIIIRR
EACH OF JOSHUA'S ATTEMPTS GOT CLOSER, BUT NEVER CLOSE ENOUGH.
JOSHUA'S FRUSTRATIONS GREW.
ATTEMPT
OUTCOME
Failed
CONCURRENTLY, THEIR ATTEMPTS AT GETTING PREGNANT WERE JUST AS UNSUCCESSFUL.

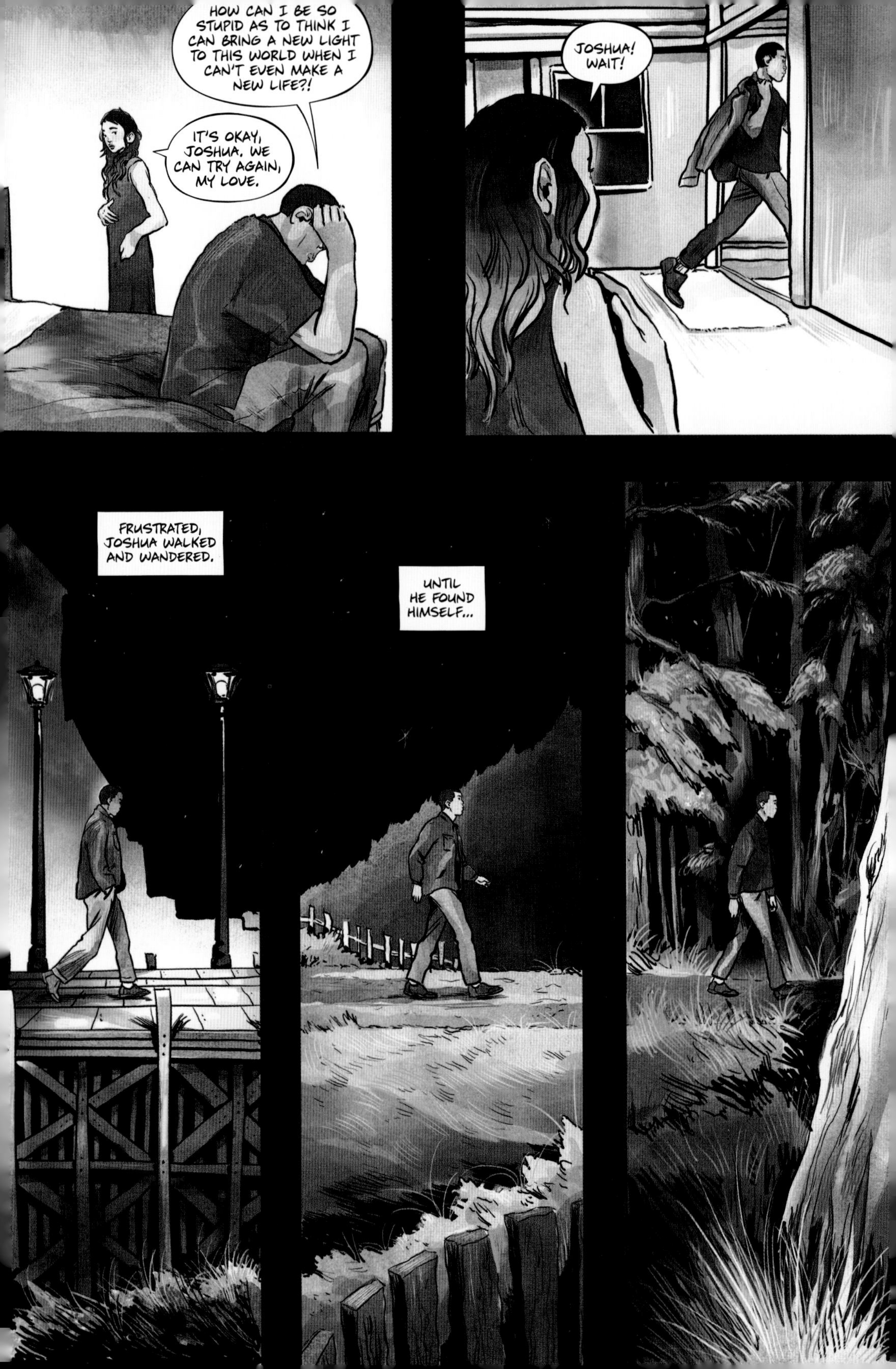
HOW CAN I BE SO STUPID AS TO THINK I CAN BRING A NEW LIGHT TO THIS WORLD WHEN I CAN'T EVEN MAKE A NEW LIFE?!
IT'S OKAY, JOSHUA. WE CAN TRY AGAIN, MY LOVE.
JOSHUA! WAIT!
FRUSTRATED, JOSHUA WALKED AND WANDERED.
UNTIL HE FOUND HIMSELF...

...AT HIS FATHER'S CAVE.

"MINERS BRING FORTH FRUIT FROM THE EARTH," JOSHUA HEARD HIS FATHER'S WORDS ECHO IN HIS HEAD AND HIS FEELING OF FAILURE EXPLODED.

WHAM

CRACK

BAM

BAM

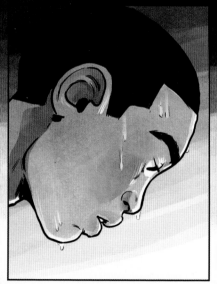

FLAREON?!

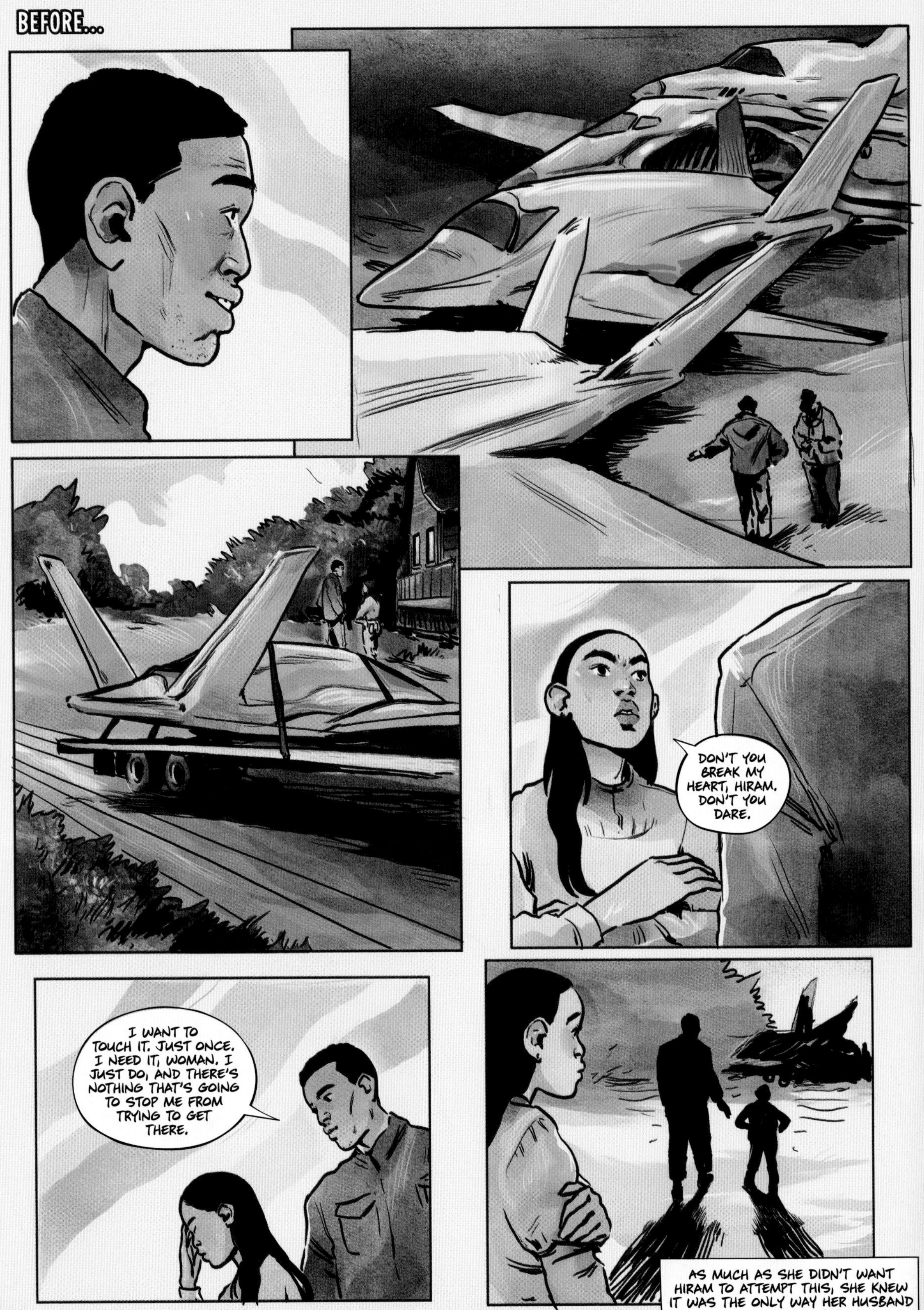
BEFORE...
DON'T YOU BREAK MY HEART, HIRAM. DON'T YOU DARE.
I WANT TO TOUCH IT. JUST ONCE. I NEED IT, WOMAN. I JUST DO, AND THERE'S NOTHING THAT'S GOING TO STOP ME FROM TRYING TO GET THERE.
AS MUCH AS SHE DIDN'T WANT HIRAM TO ATTEMPT THIS, SHE KNEW IT WAS THE ONLY WAY HER HUSBAND COULD COME BACK TO HER.

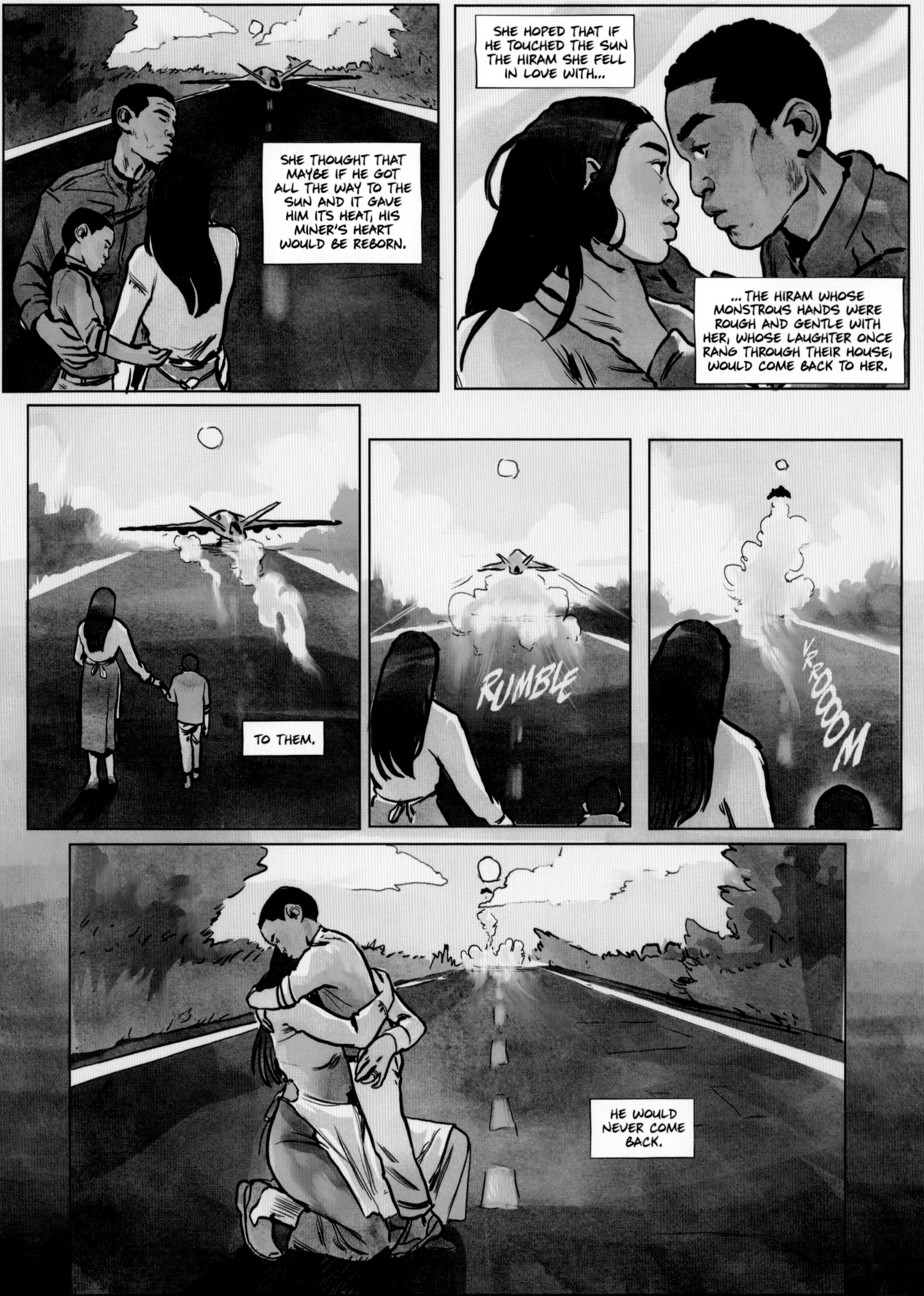
SHE THOUGHT THAT MAYBE IF HE GOT ALL THE WAY TO THE SUN AND IT GAVE HIM ITS HEAT, HIS MINER'S HEART WOULD BE REBORN.
SHE HOPED THAT IF HE TOUCHED THE SUN THE HIRAM SHE FELL IN LOVE WITH...
... THE HIRAM WHOSE MONSTROUS HANDS WERE ROUGH AND GENTLE WITH HER, WHOSE LAUGHTER ONCE RANG THROUGH THEIR HOUSE, WOULD COME BACK TO HER.
TO THEM.
RUMBLE
VROOOOM
HE WOULD NEVER COME BACK.

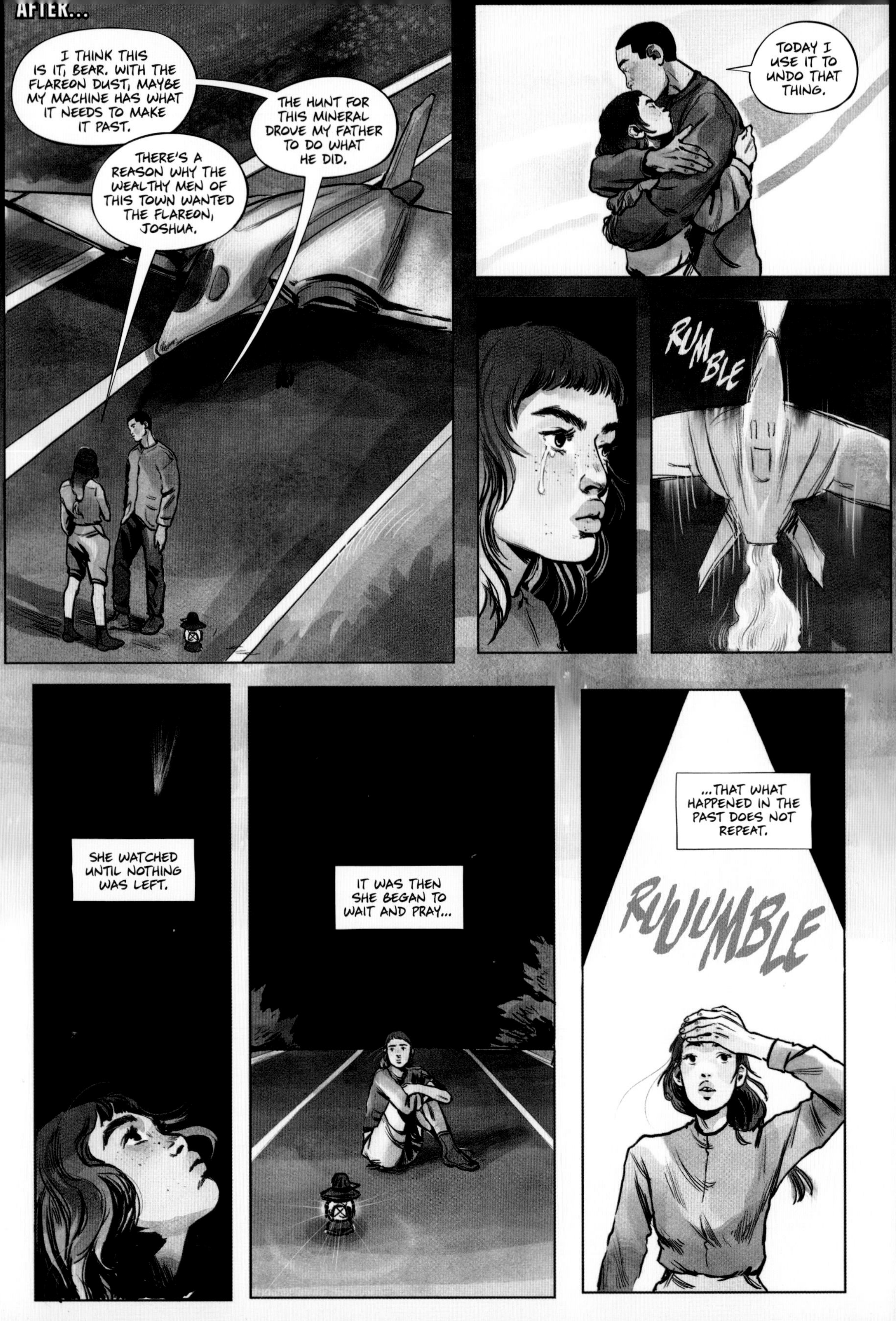
AFTER...
I THINK THIS IS IT, BEAR. WITH THE FLAREON DUST, MAYBE MY MACHINE HAS WHAT IT NEEDS TO MAKE IT PAST.
THERE'S A REASON WHY THE WEALTHY MEN OF THIS TOWN WANTED THE FLAREON, JOSHUA.
THE HUNT FOR THIS MINERAL DROVE MY FATHER TO DO WHAT HE DID.
TODAY I USE IT TO UNDO THAT THING.
RUMBLE
SHE WATCHED UNTIL NOTHING WAS LEFT.
IT WAS THEN SHE BEGAN TO WAIT AND PRAY...
...THAT WHAT HAPPENED IN THE PAST DOES NOT REPEAT.
RUUUMBLE

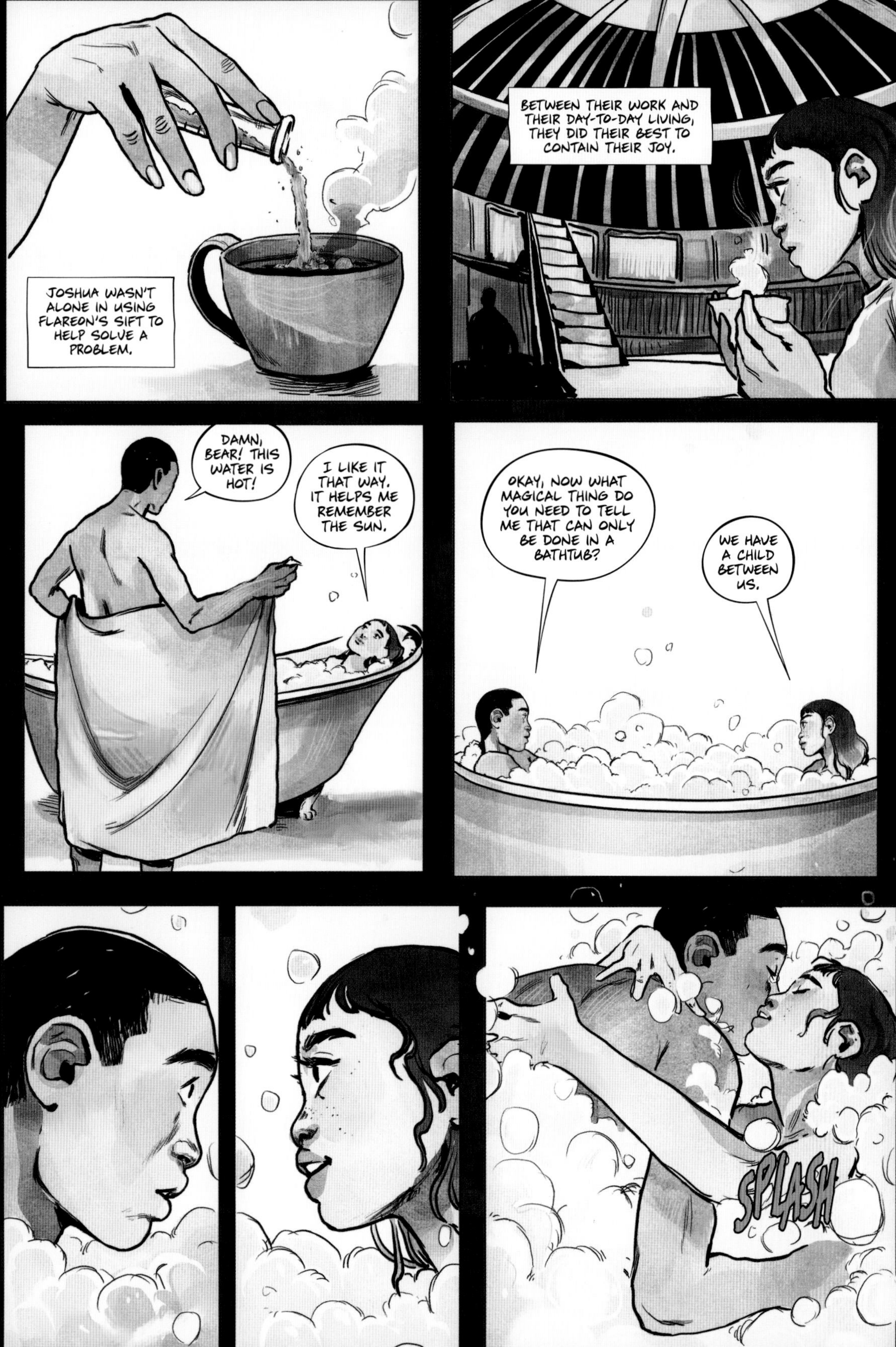
JOSHUA WASN'T ALONE IN USING FLAREON'S SIFT TO HELP SOLVE A PROBLEM.
BETWEEN THEIR WORK AND THEIR DAY-TO-DAY LIVING, THEY DID THEIR BEST TO CONTAIN THEIR JOY.
DAMN, BEAR! THIS WATER IS HOT!
I LIKE IT THAT WAY. IT HELPS ME REMEMBER THE SUN.
OKAY, NOW WHAT MAGICAL THING DO YOU NEED TO TELL ME THAT CAN ONLY BE DONE IN A BATHTUB?
WE HAVE A CHILD BETWEEN US.
SPLASH

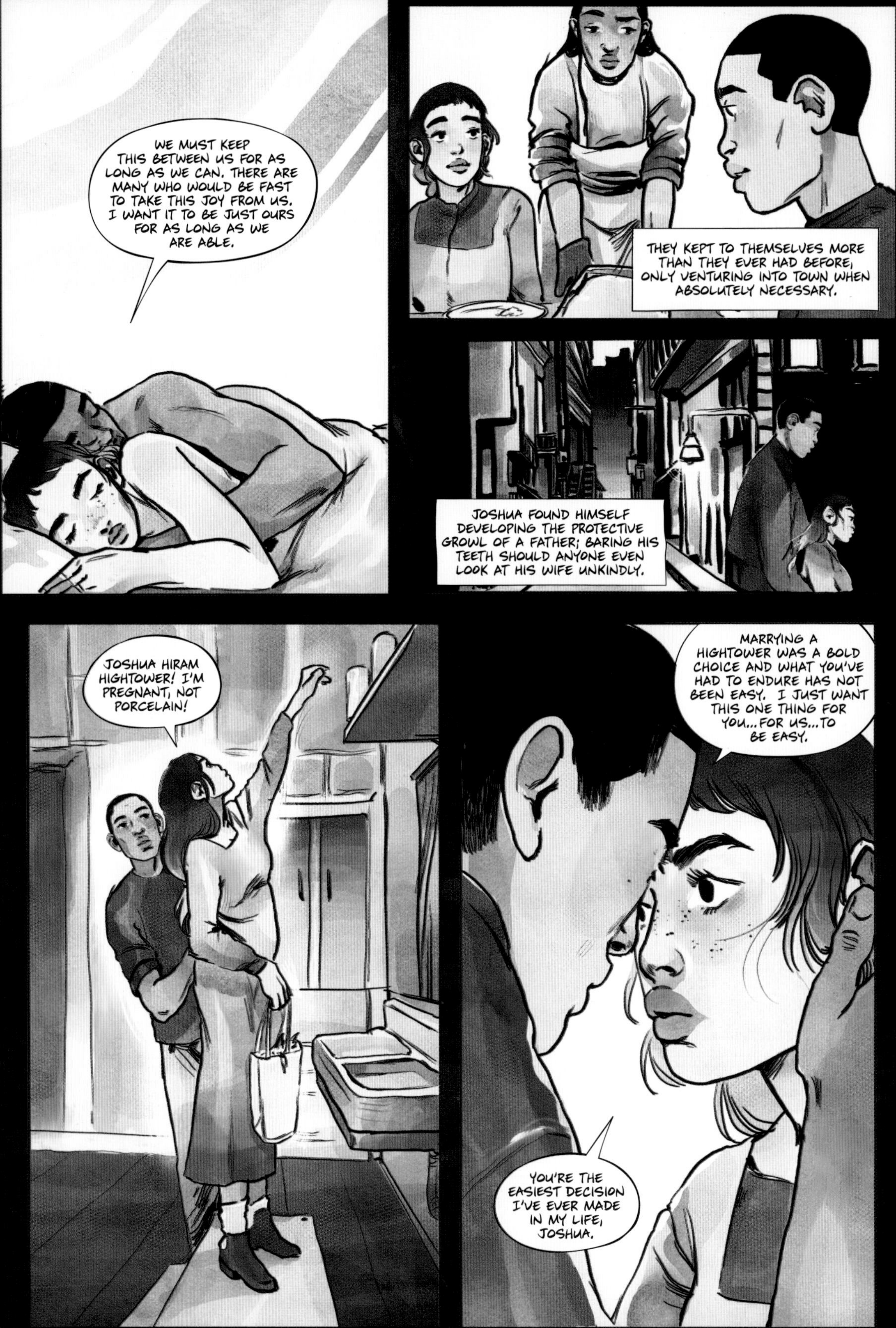
WE MUST KEEP THIS BETWEEN US FOR AS LONG AS WE CAN. THERE ARE MANY WHO WOULD BE FAST TO TAKE THIS JOY FROM US. I WANT IT TO BE JUST OURS FOR AS LONG AS WE ARE ABLE.
THEY KEPT TO THEMSELVES MORE THAN THEY EVER HAD BEFORE, ONLY VENTURING INTO TOWN WHEN ABSOLUTELY NECESSARY.
JOSHUA FOUND HIMSELF DEVELOPING THE PROTECTIVE GROWL OF A FATHER; BARING HIS TEETH SHOULD ANYONE EVEN LOOK AT HIS WIFE UNKINDLY.
JOSHUA HIRAM HIGHTOWER! I'M PREGNANT, NOT PORCELAIN!
MARRYING A HIGHTOWER WAS A BOLD CHOICE AND WHAT YOU'VE HAD TO ENDURE HAS NOT BEEN EASY. I JUST WANT THIS ONE THING FOR YOU...FOR US...TO BE EASY.
YOU'RE THE EASIEST DECISION I'VE EVER MADE IN MY LIFE, JOSHUA.

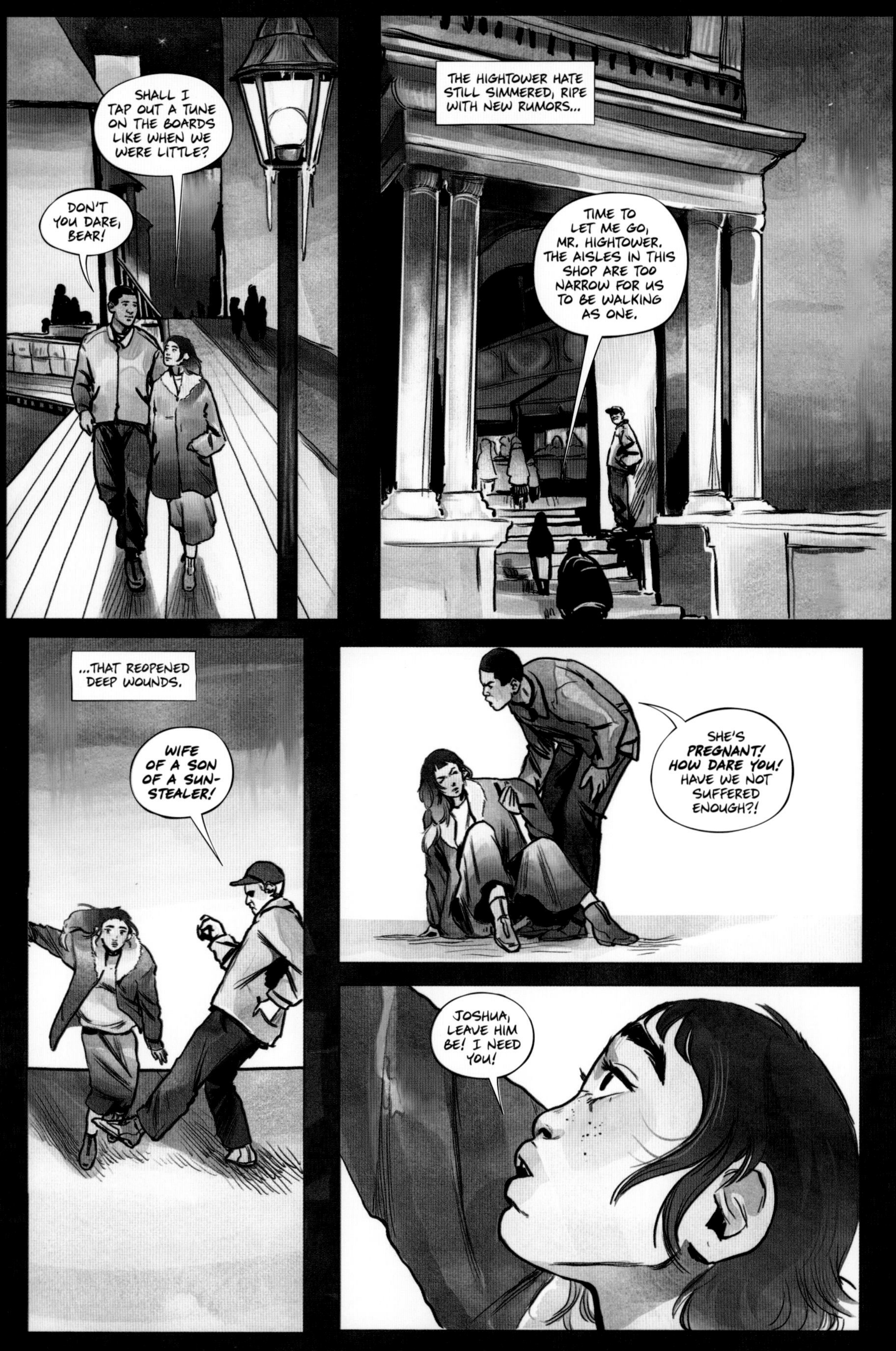
SHALL I TAP OUT A TUNE ON THE BOARDS LIKE WHEN WE WERE LITTLE?
DON'T YOU DARE, BEAR!
THE HIGHTOWER HATE STILL SIMMERED, RIPE WITH NEW RUMORS...
TIME TO LET ME GO, MR. HIGHTOWER. THE AISLES IN THIS SHOP ARE TOO NARROW FOR US TO BE WALKING AS ONE.
...THAT REOPENED DEEP WOUNDS.
WIFE OF A SON OF A SUN-STEALER!
SHE'S PREGNANT! HOW DARE YOU! HAVE WE NOT SUFFERED ENOUGH?!
JOSHUA, LEAVE HIM BE! I NEED YOU!

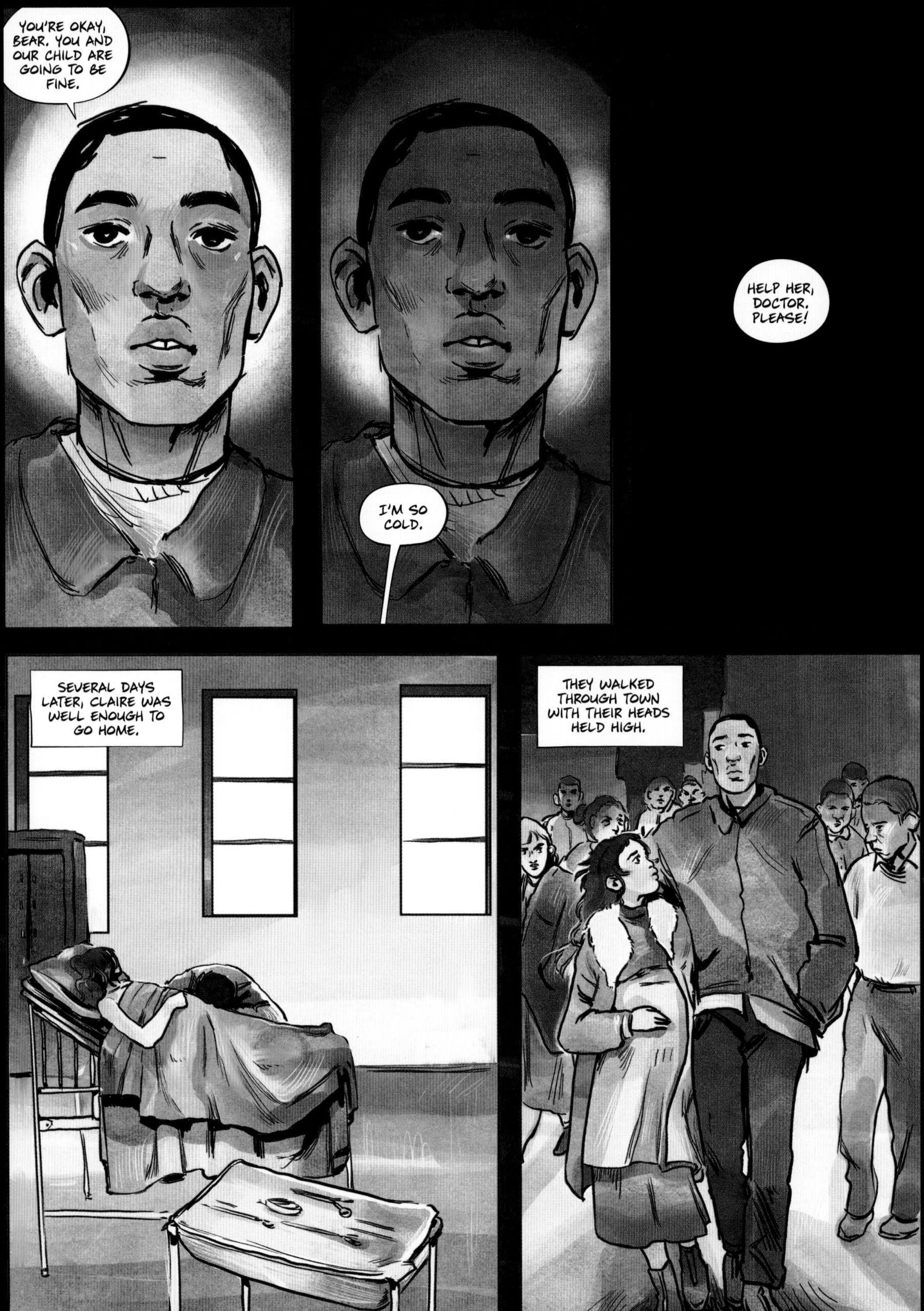
YOU'RE OKAY, BEAR. YOU AND OUR CHILD ARE GOING TO BE FINE.
I'M SO COLD.
HELP HER, DOCTOR. PLEASE!
SEVERAL DAYS LATER, CLAIRE WAS WELL ENOUGH TO GO HOME.
THEY WALKED THROUGH TOWN WITH THEIR HEADS HELD HIGH.

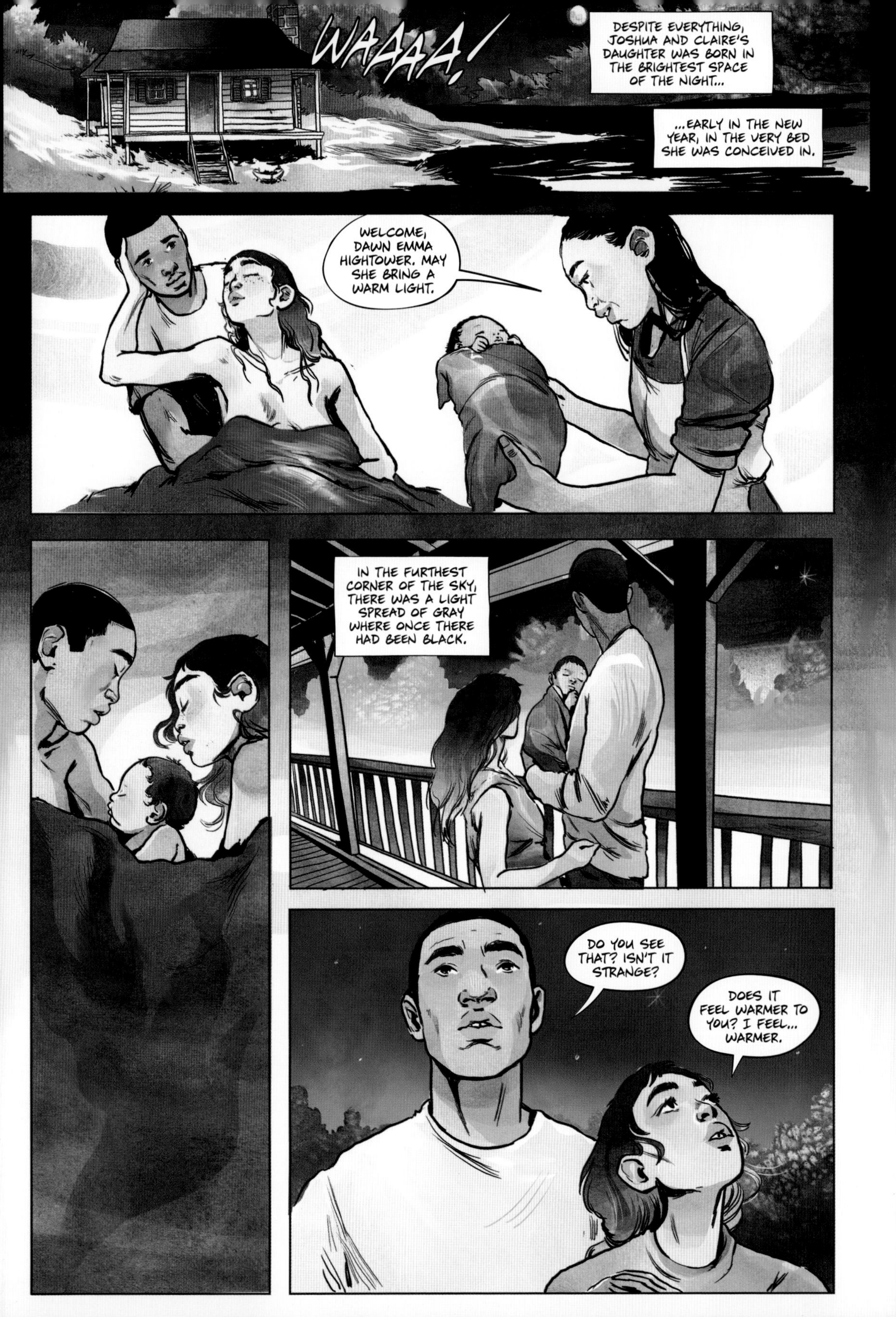

WAAAA!
DESPITE EVERYTHING, JOSHUA AND CLAIRE'S DAUGHTER WAS BORN IN THE BRIGHTEST SPACE OF THE NIGHT...
...EARLY IN THE NEW YEAR, IN THE VERY BED SHE WAS CONCEIVED IN.
WELCOME, DAWN EMMA HIGHTOWER. MAY SHE BRING A WARM LIGHT.
IN THE FURTHEST CORNER OF THE SKY, THERE WAS A LIGHT SPREAD OF GRAY WHERE ONCE THERE HAD BEEN BLACK.
DO YOU SEE THAT? ISN'T IT STRANGE?
DOES IT FEEL WARMER TO YOU? I FEEL... WARMER.

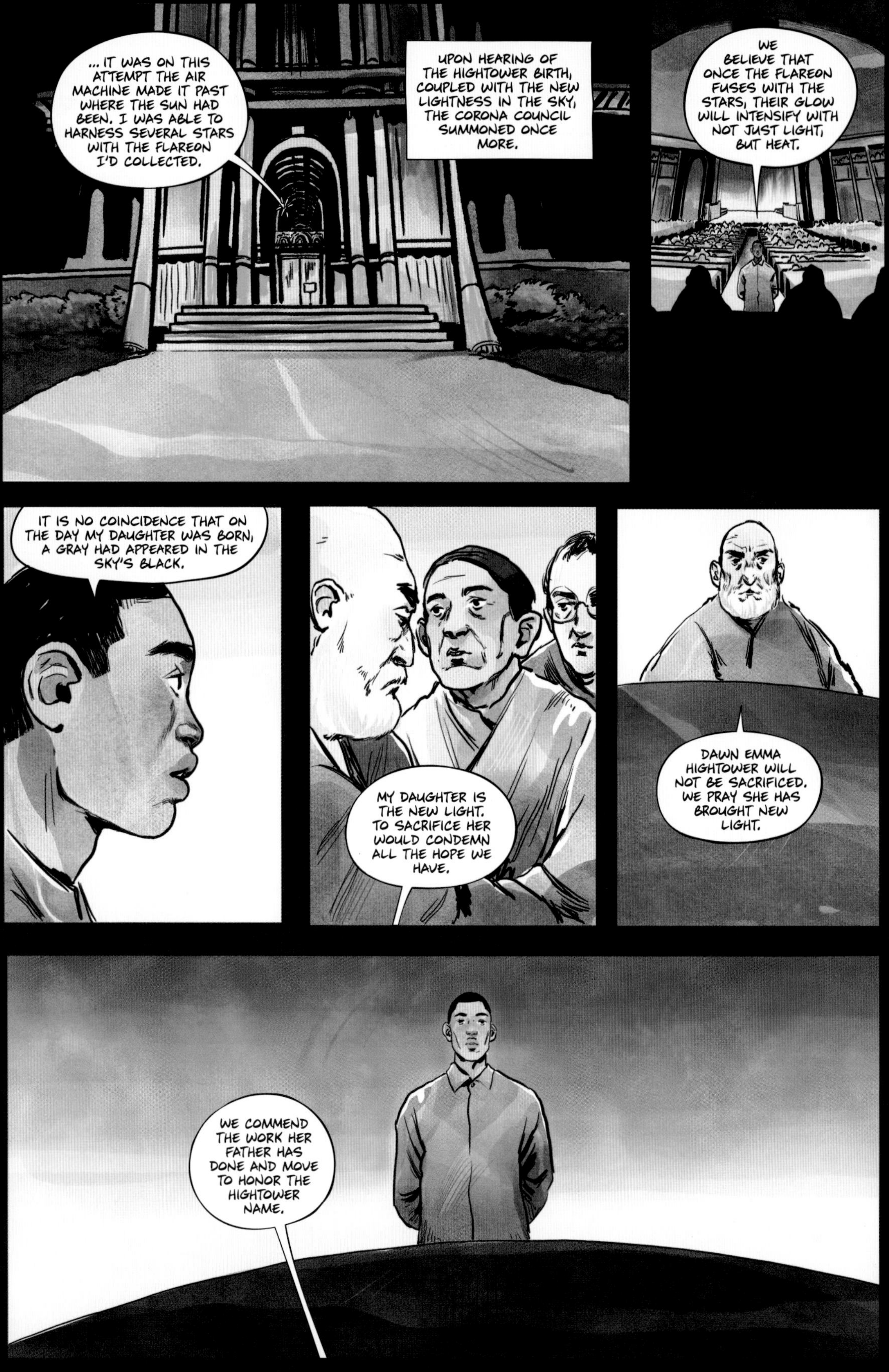
... IT WAS ON THIS ATTEMPT THE AIR MACHINE MADE IT PAST WHERE THE SUN HAD BEEN. I WAS ABLE TO HARNESS SEVERAL STARS WITH THE FLAREON I'D COLLECTED.
UPON HEARING OF THE HIGHTOWER BIRTH, COUPLED WITH THE NEW LIGHTNESS IN THE SKY, THE CORONA COUNCIL SUMMONED ONCE MORE.
WE BELIEVE THAT ONCE THE FLAREON FUSES WITH THE STARS, THEIR GLOW WILL INTENSIFY WITH NOT JUST LIGHT, BUT HEAT.
IT IS NO COINCIDENCE THAT ON THE DAY MY DAUGHTER WAS BORN, A GRAY HAD APPEARED IN THE SKY'S BLACK.
MY DAUGHTER IS THE NEW LIGHT. TO SACRIFICE HER WOULD CONDEMN ALL THE HOPE WE HAVE.
DAWN EMMA HIGHTOWER WILL NOT BE SACRIFICED. WE PRAY SHE HAS BROUGHT NEW LIGHT.
WE COMMEND THE WORK HER FATHER HAS DONE AND MOVE TO HONOR THE HIGHTOWER NAME.

I'LL PUT HER DOWN AND TIDY UP BEFORE I LEAVE. YOU TWO GO ON UP AND DO YOUR STARGAZING.

THANKS, MOM. I LOVE YOU.

I LOVE YOU TOO, SON.

MANY NIGHTS AFTER DAWN WAS PUT TO BED, JOSHUA AND CLAIRE WOULD CLIMB UP ONTO THEIR ROOF AND TALK ABOUT WHAT THEY BELIEVED WAS THE REAL REASON THE SKY HAD LIGHTENED.

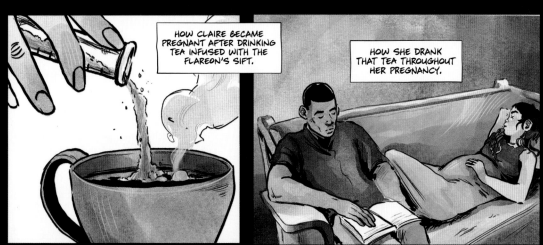

HOW CLAIRE BECAME PREGNANT AFTER DRINKING TEA INFUSED WITH THE FLAREON'S SIFT.

HOW SHE DRANK THAT TEA THROUGHOUT HER PREGNANCY.

HOW WHEN THEY MAKE THEIR DAUGHTER LAUGH, HER EYES RIM WITH AMBER LIGHT.

HOW, WHEN SHE TOSSES IN HER SLEEP, HER SKIN BRIGHTENS WITH GLOW, A NIGHTLIGHT.

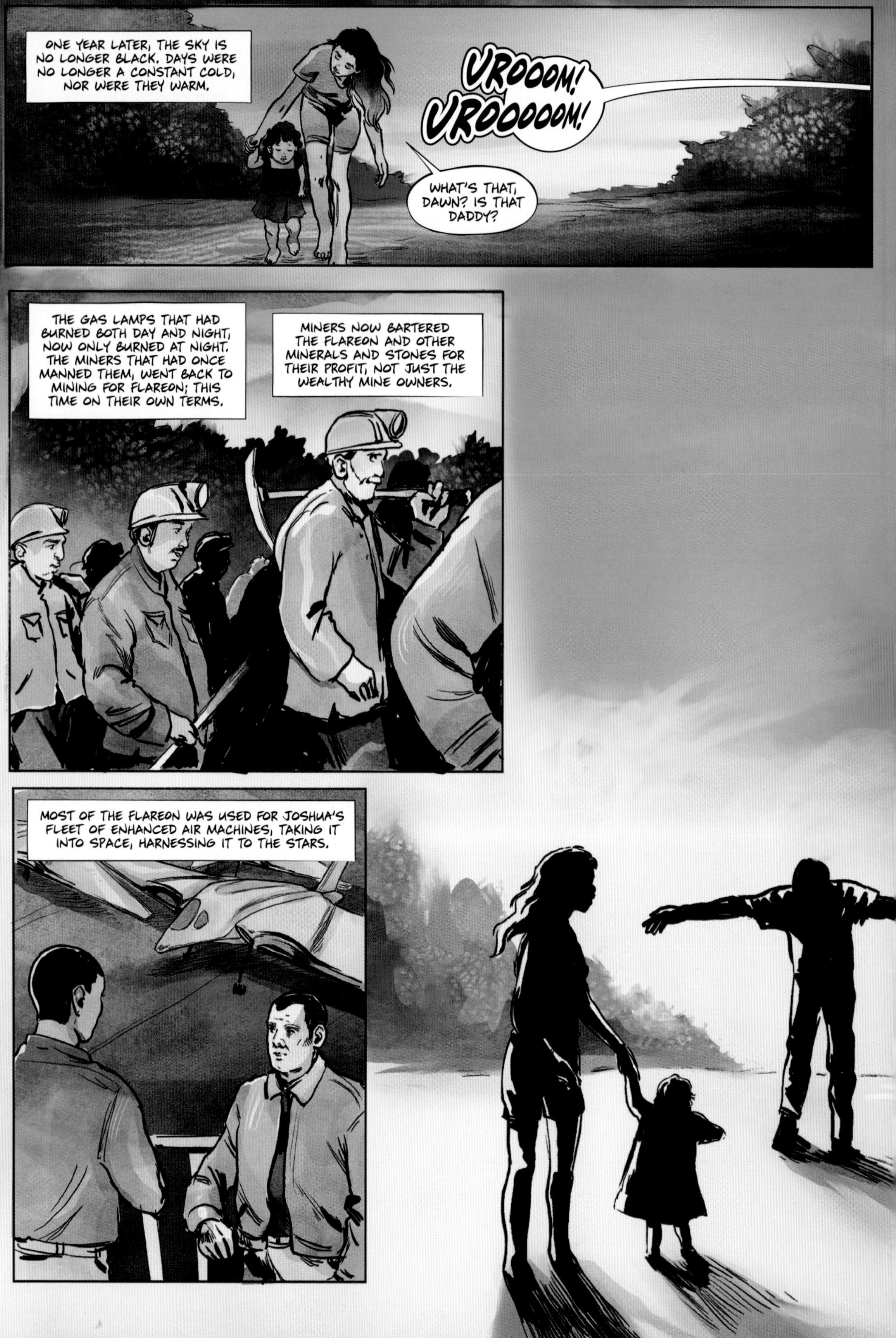
ONE YEAR LATER, THE SKY IS NO LONGER BLACK. DAYS WERE NO LONGER A CONSTANT COLD, NOR WERE THEY WARM.
UROOOM! UROOOOOM!
WHAT'S THAT, DAWN? IS THAT DADDY?
THE GAS LAMPS THAT HAD BURNED BOTH DAY AND NIGHT, NOW ONLY BURNED AT NIGHT. THE MINERS THAT HAD ONCE MANNED THEM, WENT BACK TO MINING FOR FLAREON; THIS TIME ON THEIR OWN TERMS.
MINERS NOW BARTERED THE FLAREON AND OTHER MINERALS AND STONES FOR THEIR PROFIT, NOT JUST THE WEALTHY MINE OWNERS.
MOST OF THE FLAREON WAS USED FOR JOSHUA'S FLEET OF ENHANCED AIR MACHINES, TAKING IT INTO SPACE, HARNESSING IT TO THE STARS.

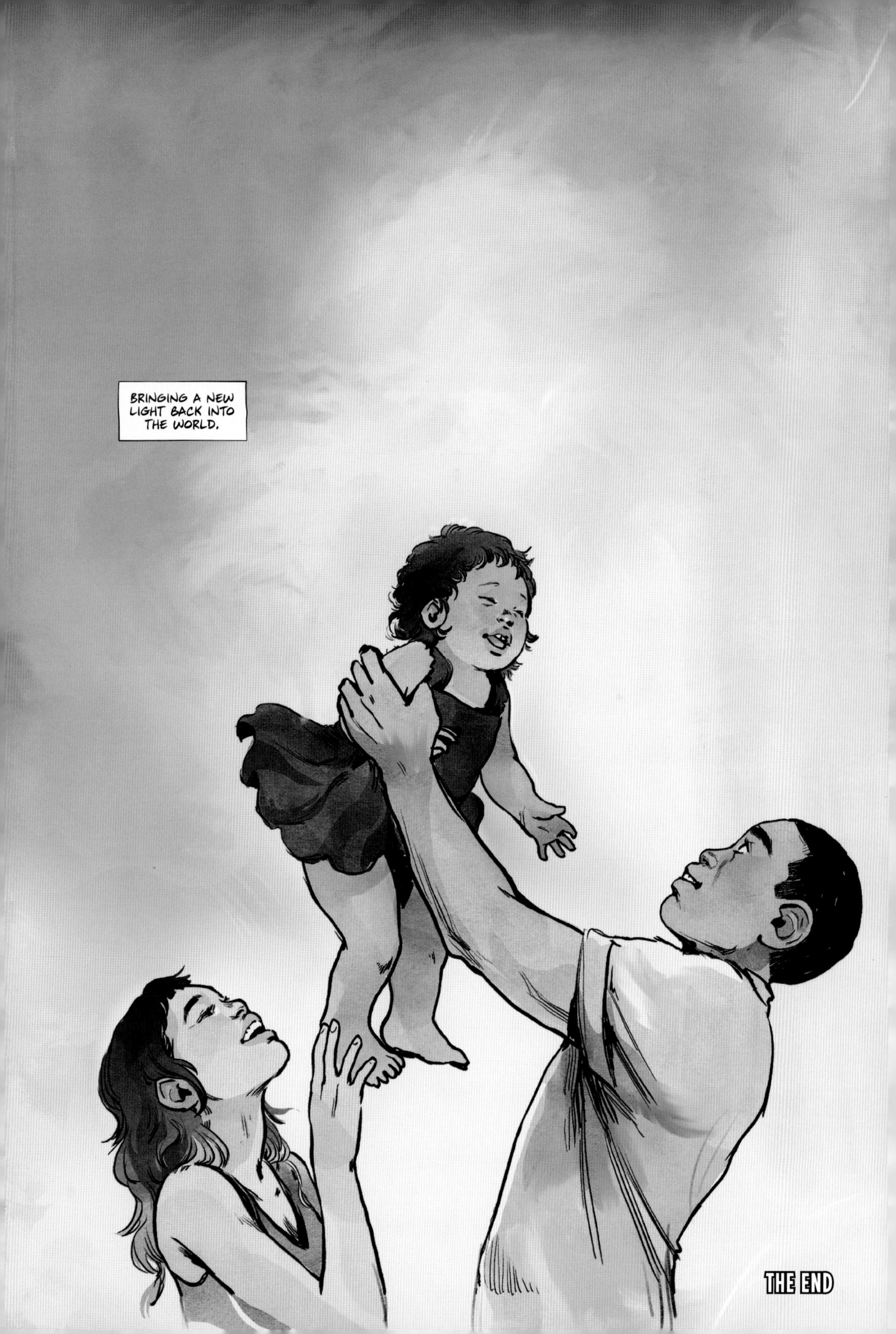
BRINGING A NEW LIGHT BACK INTO THE WORLD.
THE END

ABOUT THE AUTHORS

Roxane Gay's writing appears in *Best American Nonrequired Reading 2018*, *Best American Mystery Stories 2014*, *Best American Short Stories 2012*, *Best Sex Writing 2012*, *Harper's Bazaar*, *A Public Space*, *McSweeney's*, *Tin House*, *Oxford American*, *American Short Fiction*, *Virginia Quarterly Review*, and many others. She is a contributing opinion writer for *The New York Times*. She is the author of the books *Ayiti*, *An Untamed State*, the *New York Times* best-selling *Bad Feminist*, the nationally best-selling *Difficult Women* and *New York Times* bestselling *Hunger: A Memoir of My Body*. She is also the author of *World of Wakanda* for Marvel and the editor of *Best American Short Stories 2018*. She is currently at work on film and television projects, a book of writing advice, an essay collection about television and culture, and a YA novel entitled *The Year I Learned Everything*. In 2018, she won a Guggenheim fellowship.

Tracy Lynne Oliver is a writer based in Los Angeles. She has been published online at a variety of places such as Medium, Fanzine and Occulum. Her story, "This Weekend" was chosen to be in *Best Microfiction 2019*. This is her first graphic novel adaptation.

Rebecca Kirby is a comic artist and illustrator based out of Philadelphia best known for her original comics, *Biopsy* and *Cramps*, which have been featured on Vice, and *Waves*, featured in Fantagraphics' *Now: The New Comics Anthology #4*.